STEP BY STEP ORGANIC
VEGETABLE GARDENING

STEP BY STEP

ORGANIC VEGETABLE GARDENING

SHEPHERD OGDEN

 HarperPerennial
A Division of HarperCollins Publishers

Excerpts and photographs at the beginning of each chapter are taken from *Step by Step to Organic Vegetable Growing* by Samuel R. Ogden.

A hardcover edition of this book was published in 1992 by HarperCollins Publishers.

First HarperPerennial edition published 1994.

Designed by Barbara DuPree Knowles

Photographs by Steve Swinburne

Illustrations by Karl Steucklen

The Library of Congress has catalogued the hardcover edition as follows:

Ogden, Shepherd.
  Step by step organic vegetable gardening / Shepherd Ogden — 1st ed.
    p.   cm.
  Includes bibliographical references and index.
  ISBN 0-06-016668-1
  1. Vegetable gardening.   2. Organic gardening.   I. Title.
SB324.3.O43 1992
635'.0484—dc20   91-55513

ISBN 0-06-092225-7 (pbk.)
   95 96 97 98 CG/RRD 10 9 8 7 6 5 4 3 2

To the women of the Ogden family
Mamie, Miss Fannie, Ellen, Ann and Molly.
Because as Big Sam knew so well:
without them, no gardens and no books.

CONTENTS

10 Vegetables for the Garden   *177*

Epilogue: Step by Step   *275*

The book in your hand represents more than fifty years of gardening experience—my grandfather's and mine—as well as tens of centuries' worth of knowledge about the commonsense culture of vegetables, which is the heritage of all gardeners willing to step back a moment from the control-crazy chemical garden practices that have become conventional in this century.

Big Sam published his first gardening book, *How to Grow Food for Your Family,* in 1942. It was a "victory garden" book, and presented the results of his (then) ten years of experience doing exactly what the title proclaimed. The emphasis was very pragmatic: it reflected the post-depression concern with home economics in the true subsistence sense of that term. Though the basics of what is now called the organic method were there, Big Sam took at face value—and presented to the reader in a series of appendices—the pest control recommendations supplied by the U.S. Department of Agriculture. These recommendations included mercury, arsenic, cyanide, and formaldehyde compounds. Some are outright poisons; all are now known to cause serious health problems ranging from brain damage to cancer.

In 1957, Countryman Press here in Vermont re-issued the book as *The New England Vegetable Garden.* But it was not a simple revision of the first edition, as Big Sam was quick to point out in the Foreword.

So it is that after fifteen years of even closer application to all aspects of vegetable gardening, I have arrived at a disagreement with the first book on one important point, and that is concerning the use of chemical fertilizers and insecticides in family gardens. When the idea first occurred to me that I should correct the record, it seemed as though the job might be accomplished by judicious editing, but once I sat down to the task it became evident that this would not be possible. It was not a question of re-writing the old book, but of writing a new one.

Added to the practicality of the earlier version was a philosophy of gardening: Big Sam sounded a warning, partly patriotic, partly prescient, that American society was moving in a direction profoundly at odds with the basic human values built up over centuries and generations. This "new" approach was called organic gardening.

He became one of a group of British and American writers who began to point out that the destructive chemical technology developed during World War II was now being used at home; that the swords of war—rather than being beaten into plowshares and put at the service of the traditional skills of agriculture—were slashing the cord that for millennia had connected farming and gardening to nature, and binding them instead to industrial economic models under which the present has value but our children's future does not.

Big Sam became a contributing editor to *Organic Gardening* magazine, and eventually Rodale Press asked him to update the book. In 1971 *Step by Step to Organic Vegetable Growing* was published. The environmental movement had been born in America, and the book became an important resource to gardeners across the country, because of its straightforward, no-nonsense approach, and for the wealth of practical knowledge drawn from nearly forty years of hands-on experience in the garden. Over the next fifteen years more than 100,000 copies were sold, and beginning gardeners all over America got their boots muddy and their hands dirty in gardens inspired by Big Sam.

By THE TIME I was old enough to notice, Big Sam grew enough vegetables for our whole village. My great aunt Fannie would make a list of the vegetables that were ready each morning of the summer, and I'd take it around to all the houses in the village. At my friends' houses I could arrange a hike to the swimming hole or a frog hunting expedition while their mother drew up her order; at other houses I might be offered a cookie while I waited. Later that afternoon I'd deliver the vegetables that Fannie had selected, washed, and wrapped, then collect my reward: a small paper bag full of treats from the penny candy department of the country store in the next town.

I took up gardening myself in 1977, at the ripe old age of twenty-eight, partly out of what I thought was necessity. After a two-year stint in the city at a high-stress job, I moved with my wife-to-be to a small cottage next to Big Sam's house in the village. The year after I came back, Big Sam had to give up gardening due to failing health; he had recently turned eighty, and lacked the strength to maintain the quarter-acre plot. I asked if we could use the space.

The first season I used what seed he had left over, along with a few packets from the local feed store. I tilled, and planted, thinned and hoed; to my amazement, all went well. By August I had to set a card table out in front of the cottage to deal with the surplus. The following year, with a winter to plan, the harvest increased, and I actually began to make money from the garden.

Few pests plagued that garden. Although summer frosts were a danger, I learned what to plant, how to read the weather, and when to run for the blankets. It all seemed so easy, so sure. Admitted: this was no ordinary garden. The soil, though wet and sour when Big Sam began, was, by the time I took over, the color and texture of chocolate cake, and smelled fresh, not moldy or pungent. From the first tender thinnings of spinach each spring until the last parsnip was dug before the ground froze, it yielded bountifully. After forty years of careful cultivation that's no surprise. But of course I was quick to give myself credit. Ellen and I decided that we'd become market gardeners.

Then the place was sold. We bought ten acres on a hillside overlooking a small intervale three miles downstream, north of the village of Londonderry, and set about making our own market garden. The land had been neglected for fifteen years or so, and had grown up to a mixed cover of woody shrubs and small trees, with occasional clearings of wetland grasses.

Our first garden on the new property, planted even before we'd built a driveway, was a disaster. All that I thought I knew from gardening at Big Sam's did me no good; I found out right away that my earlier success had been based on the rich soil of that garden, the established methods, the existing community of plants and animals that lived there.

I was devastated. The cabbages were small and stunted, a far cry from the vigorous, deep green heads I'd grown at Big Sam's; the 250 tomato plants I'd nursed through a series of May frosts in a makeshift cold frame were cut off by cutworms their first night out in the garden; the squashes were eaten right back to the ground by cucumber beetles. Then came the weeds: annuals brought in with the manure I hadn't had time to compost, perennials whose rhizomes I hadn't known to remove, even small cherry saplings that sprouted from little bits of root I'd overlooked when we cleared the trees.

My failures made me appreciate just how much time, effort, and attention was hidden in the rich soil of my grandfather's garden. I began to more fully understand that organic gardening was not just avoiding the use of chemical pesticides and fertilizers, but restoring and rebuilding the soil and the natural ecosystem of the garden to the point where both can take care of themselves, while still providing a harvest for the gardener. From that understanding my education really began; this book is a result of that education.

I was fortunate to inherit many of Big Sam's garden tools, and also a sizable portion of his library. My horticultural knowledge is based squarely on both. This book is illustrated with photographs taken in our gardens, using the actual tools and techniques discussed. This is firsthand knowledge—I have learned my gardening the same way he did: with my hands in the garden; and with my head in the study. I believe, as Big Sam did, that growing food instead of simply gathering it is the central skill, practice, technology—whatever you want to call it—that made our life as we know it possible. And I wonder, with him, how this ancient skill has come to take on the character of the industrial civilization it made possible, rather than infusing that civilization with its own perennial, cyclical—dare I say ecological?—character.

IN 1985, the year of Big Sam's death, *Step by Step to Organic Vegetable Growing* went out of print. This new edition has been completely rewritten to reflect the latest developments in organic gardening. Since its last revision in 1971, organic gardening has changed radically in America. New methods, new tools, new techniques, even new vegetables have been introduced; many simply didn't exist in 1971. It also adds to Big Sam's nearly fifty years of garden experience my own decade of work as an organic market gardener and garden center operator. I hope, however, that the straightforward, nononsense approach that made *Step by Step* so important to a whole generation of gardeners still shines through.

Though some of the methods described in this latest edition are new, there is nothing mysterious about them, no cosmic mumbo jumbo, to use Big Sam's phrase. He had no more use for woolly headed tree huggers than he did for the reductionist technocrats and chemical hucksters. Neither do I; we are both practical, hands-on, human gardeners who happen to think that the long term is important. If at least some of our parents and grandparents, and their forebears, hadn't felt the same way, we wouldn't be here today. I simply will not be the one to break that chain of humanity which I hope will stretch still many generations into the future. I'll stand with those, who, like Big Sam, have their eyes on the seventh generation.

Here is how he concluded the 1971 edition:

Without studied intent, this book has turned out to be something else than a straightforward description of gardening practice. For better or for worse, besides being a handbook, it is a treatise wherein the author philosophizes on agricultural theory and disagrees to a considerable extent with currently accepted agricultural practice. This being the case, a word of explanation in closing is appropriate.

It seems to me that the whole pattern of our mechanized and materialistic civilization is so tightly integrated that no single aspect of it can be changed or reformed. To change any part, the whole must be changed. The overall pattern is unified and tightly knit and is the expression of our cultural values and convictions. This being the case, it is futile for me to attack any single facet and with words of fearsome prophecy predict doom and destruction.

Along with automation in the factory, mechanization is inevitable on the farm. The farm worker must compete with the tenders of machines for the purchase of his necessities and his luxuries, and in order to do this he must keep in line, as nearly as he can, his production per man-hour of labor with that of the factory worker. If this be true, then, being but a single part of an unchangeable pattern, it follows that the farm factories, the large scale food producers, are forced to seek more powerful chemicals and poisons and more highly mechanized procedures, in a never ending search for higher production per man-hour, until Nature herself calls a halt to man's folly. Sir Albert Howard's Indore Process (of composting) may be feasible in an economy wherein the standard of excellence is production per unit of land, and where there is an abundance of cheap manual labor. But in a mechanized society such as we find ourselves a part of in this day and age, a completely organic procedure is impossible, and at the very best only a modified form of it can be put into practice. In the realm of gardening, those engaged in commercial production will find themselves in the same dilemma.

The home gardener, on the other hand, is a free agent. He is not confronted with the exigencies of price, production and profits. He can and should treat his soil with consideration for the laws of Nature, and to do this he must turn his back on most, if not all, of the pronouncements of the latest of scientific agricultural dogma. If this be heresy, make the most of it.

—Step by Step to Organic Vegetable Growing (1971)

As one who works in commercial organic agriculture I can vouch for the Faustian economic strength of the arguments put forth by current government and industry economists. As a market gardener I was forced to face the conflicts between modern market economics and the need, the duty, the deeply biological obligation to work within nature, rather than to greedily exploit it from a false and foolish sense of separateness.

Even though Big Sam didn't foresee the current success of commercial organic agriculture, he believed, as I do, that home gardeners can lead the way toward making economics serve the future—instead of dooming it—by not buying products that contribute to degradation of our land and the greater environment. Rather we should demand products that enhance the Earth's long term fertility. If American gardeners refuse to buy the dangerous poisons put out by the lawn and garden chemical companies—and instead demand saner, safer garden products—industry will have no choice but to meet our demands. In the process we can create gardens that will make our houses homes again.

—Shepherd Ogden

LONDONDERRY, VERMONT

ACKNOWLEDGMENTS

First things first: my grandfather Samuel R. Ogden (Big Sam to his friends and family) wrote the first *Step by Step*, and all I have done is based on the process of learning begun in his garden and his book. The mistakes are mine, but the ideas were originally his.

On the editorial side thanks are due to Susan and Larry, whose enthusiasm has carried this revival through, and to Jill, Sam and Warren who consented to serve as primary readers. The photographs are the work of Steve Swinburne, except those of Big Sam, which are taken from the 1971 edition of the book. Vermont artist (and longtime family friend) Karl Steucklen contributed the illustrations.

On the personal side, thanks also to Monica who lightened the work load at the office so I could escape to my cabin and write. Finally, without the extra efforts of my wife, Ellen, and children, Sam and Molly, to make our home an inviting place to hide from the pile of books, notes and manuscript, this project would never have been done.

STEP BY STEP ORGANIC
VEGETABLE GARDENING

CHAPTER 1

Good Reasons for a Garden

These two things are vital: to have a chance to think and perhaps gain wisdom, and to achieve a renewal and readjustment through direct contact with nature.

Samuel R. Ogden

There are many good reasons to have a garden, but one of the most important is that it gives us a chance to both control and yet be part of nature. A garden is a place where even the most powerless person can play almighty—design a small, self-contained natural world by whimsy, and change it completely at will. Yet the climatic and seasonal forces that govern it keep the gardener in touch with the pre-industrial, natural world within which our civilization exists as a momentary episode.

We Americans created the concept of untouched wilderness as nature, and now it is kept "out there." The great majority of us live within that part of the American tradition which sees nature as a dark, brutal force waiting to smash civilization. Much of the "development" of this country (a word expropriated and misused, to my way of thinking) represents a sort of preemptive first strike against nature: we strive to dominate, subdue, pave over nature, before it has a chance to rise up against us. Wilderness comprises a mere eight percent of the land in the United States, while the other ninety-two percent is, in one way or another, shaped by humanity.

Even if they want to commune with nature, most people go no farther than the crowded campground of a national park. But the more adventurous, those committed to wilderness, also often fall prey to the feeling that nature and human culture are mutually exclusive, even antagonistic. That there is so little compromise between the deep, untouched wilderness and the suburban shopping mall is a sure sign that naturalist and developer alike can see no middle ground.

Until recently farmers existed in a mixed landscape. The very existence of suburbs shows that many humans need that middle ground—a landscape that is partly wild, partly tame. After all, in practical terms, there is no frontier left in America: nature is the park, the yard, or the garden. Yet all three gardens exist *within* nature, if only we would slow down our hectic pace a little bit, open our eyes, and think about it. Open spaces are our surest connection to nature, and a well-run organic garden (or yard, or park, or even homestead, or farm), in its balance and its sustainable, cyclical interaction with the natural world, offers a good model for how we could structure our human world as a better, safer, and more pleasant place.

This feeling that we must always choose between no intervention of any kind in natural systems—total wilderness—and the complete replacement and destruction of nature—as in our high tech farms and cities—is both a symptom and result of the belief that we are separate and apart from nature; that our ordering of the world around us is inherently unnatural. As the writer Michael Pollan wrote in his recent book, *Second Nature*[1], we need "now more than ever, to learn how to use nature without damaging it. That probably can't be done as long as we continue to think of nature and culture simply as antagonists." If there is one thing that gardening teaches the observant, it is that he or she is part of nature! There is little question in my mind that the principles of good garden management, used as guidelines for other types of development, would certainly improve the quality of our neighborhoods and homes.

In addition, for those of us who are parents, having a garden helps awaken this same perspective in our kids, the next generation. We hear a lot of talk about family values these days, yet in many homes the hearth is a color console and family togetherness consists mostly of agreeing on which program to watch. The homemade music of earlier generations has been replaced by a Walkman with headphones, and the children's imaginative play by the VCR, which every child now knows how to operate by age three. A garden, however, can still capture the imagination of a child. It is the perfect combination of the wild and the tame because it is close to home, yet contains a myriad new and interesting creatures. And as the season progresses a new script of seed, sprout, flower, and fruit provides constant surprises and joy.

"But you live in the country!" I can hear. Yet it is in the cities and the suburbs where a garden provides the most reward for a child. Here in the country we are surrounded by nature: the weather, the birds, and the beasts. Just this morning I surprised a wild turkey venturing cautiously across the country road on which I live. My seven-year-old daughter knows the calls of a dozen different songbirds. But in built-up areas gardens are rare oases of nature, wonderful places, a child's wilderness. Here in the country we feel the same attraction to the village, where there is a bit of pavement and sidewalk on which our kids can learn to skateboard or ride a bike. The point is that the rural and the urban can both benefit from a bit of the other, and gardens are one of the best ways to bring a bit of nature into the hustle and bustle of urban areas.

Many urban areas have community gardens, where families can maintain a garden plot of their own, growing healthy food, enjoying a few hours together working, exploring, discovering and interacting with other families whose plots are nearby. They are just that: a source of a sense of community, a place to regain some of the old values that are missing for too many of us these days. Thus, the simple, wholesome, good sense of a garden is hard to argue with.

GARDENERS ARE, on the whole, very practical people. We take what land we have and do our best to improve it; we take the climate in which we find ourselves and learn to make the most of it. But the best of us are also wary. We don't harbor any illusions—say, that an early spring heat wave really signals the end of frost—but we also know that even the harshest winter must yield to the momentum of earth and sun as they cycle toward spring. We cultivate our gardens, not really thinking that we can absolutely control the forces that shape our success or failure. Down deep, we realize that our gardens are indeed just a part of nature, not the other way around.

The distinction between cultivation and control determines our whole approach to gardening. To control means to dominate, to subdue, to master, to dictate; but also to restrain, to curb, to hold back. To me these are precisely the forces I expect my garden to provide relief *from*.

On the other hand, to cultivate is to civilize, to improve or develop (in the proper sense of the word); to refine, to perfect; but also to promote, to foster, to encourage, even to woo or court. While control-oriented gardeners try to dictate soil fertility with chemical nutrients or eradicate pests and disease with other chemicals, organic gardeners improve their soil by fostering the existing biological life; they strive to perfect their understanding of how pest and disease problems arise so that they can encourage the natural cycles of restraint.

There is a great irony in the way control often appears in the false guise of efficiency. I had a visitor recently, a respected physician and experienced gardener. He could stay only a few minutes as he has a very busy schedule. "Really, I don't have time to fool around with cover crops and compost and all that," he said after looking over our early spring garden. "After all, what's wrong with using a little 10-10-10 (bagged synthetic fertilizer)?"

"Hey, it's no great sin," I told him, knowing that for the moment he was concerned mostly about his time, "but you're just making more work for yourself."

"How's that?" he wanted to know.

"Well, consider a plant growing in a pot. It is entirely dependent on you for its well-being. If you forget to water it, that's it; it's dead. If you forget to fertilize it, it will starve. On the other hand, a plant growing in the soil, while it may need occasional attention, draws its moisture and nutrients from a much larger stockpile; if you forget about it for a while the likelihood of problems is much smaller. Nature is doing the work for you. It's the same principle behind organics in general. Build the soil, build the community of organisms in, over, and under your garden, and if you don't have time to look after things for a couple of days they'll do it for you. Once you step in like a power-hungry general and say 'I'm taking over here!' you're stuck with all the work and all the responsibility."

That bag of soluble fertilizer is a here-today-gone-tomorrow solution, giving a quick shot of soft, susceptible growth that practically invites pest and disease problems. Stimulating biological activity in the soil, however, by incorporating compost and green manures, helps release the mineral nutrients present in the soil in an ongoing, stable, long-term way.

One of the lessons I have learned, from working both as a commercial vegetable grower and as a dispenser of garden advice (at our garden center), is that the average home gardener wants answers to very specific pest, disease, and fertility problems. In the absence of an authoritative source of sure, sane solutions to their problems, many take the advice of the pesticide peddlers. Eventually they come to worry that if they don't spray with this chemical, or dust with that powder, it will release the insects to overrun their gardens. Organic growers know that nearly the opposite is true. But if the companies that have products to sell are the only source of information, a lot of products—perhaps worthless, unnecessary, noxious, or even harmful—will get sold, and used, often for no better reason than mere worry.

Last week I was looking over the seeds at a local garden center, and an older gentleman came in. He walked straight up to the sales clerk and said, "I need something for moles." He was directed to the pesticide area, where he found a bag of "multi-purpose" granules, a combination of pesticide and fertilizer all too commonly applied to American lawns. Later, as I waited at the checkout counter, I overheard him telling another customer about his problem. It seems that the birds, which he treasures, had so scratched the lawn around their feeder that not only was the grass destroyed, but the soil was loosened sufficiently (he felt) to become attractive to moles.

Whether his analysis was right or not is beside the point. Apparently his hope was that the fertilizer would help the grass grow again, while the pesticide in the mix (Diazinon) would kill the moles, a one-shot solution. But he could not have read the label on the bag very closely, because Diazinon is extremely toxic to birds. So, while he may get his lawn back, he will likely lose that which he most hoped to save—the birds. I suggested that he just move the bird feeder occasionally; but that simple a solution wasn't convincing. Perhaps it didn't seem as powerful as a product designed by highly paid experts and sold in four-color bags.

On that same visit to the garden center I picked up a packet of seed treatment (used to protect early-planted crops from the effects of cold soil). Here is just some of what it said on the label:

Causes irreversible eye damage. Harmful if swallowed or inhaled. May cause allergic skin reactions.

Mixers, loaders & applicators, when mixing, loading & applying, must wear mid-forearm to elbow length natural or synthetic rubber, vinyl or plastic gloves impermeable to Captan, boots or overshoes; one piece overalls which have long sleeves and long pants; face shield of goggles; and a hat or other appropriate head covering.

Clothing worn while loading, mixing and applying this product must be laundered separately from other clothing before reuse. Clothing that may have been drenched or heavily contaminated must be disposed of in accordance with state and local regulations.

How many home gardeners go to the trouble to read or heed the precautions listed? I doubt the gentleman in front of me at the cash register would, and it is clear that most gardeners don't. Consider the fact that while eighty percent of pesticide use in this country is agricultural, the Poison Control Center of Los Angeles reported in 1983 that ninety-seven percent of all pesticide-related inquiries came from consumer use.[2]

Of course the manufacturer includes a disclaimer: "Buyer assumes all risks of use, storage or handling of this material not in strict accordance with directions given herewith." I think I'd rather risk that the early-planted seed wouldn't germinate, and replant if necessary (or better: just wait until the soil is ready to plant). That anyone should be allowed to sell something so dangerous to the average consumer, for such an unnecessary purpose, with so little actual likelihood of its being used properly, is unconscionable.

Given the active ingredients (not to mention the forty percent listed simply as "inert"), I don't even want to hold it in my hand while I read the label. What are the ingredients? Basically, this "protectant" is a little over thirty-five percent Captan, a fungicide that has been banned from most uses due to its carcinogenic (cancer-causing) habit, and twenty-five percent Diazinon, the active ingredient in the lawn treatment purchased by the gentleman with the mole problem. Captan and Diazinon are discussed in more detail in Chapters 7 and 9 respectively.

Home gardening in its current conventional form is a significant source of chemical pollution. The pesticide collections of the American homeowner comprise one of the largest and most dangerously diverse toxic waste problems our landfills face, and the runoff of lawn and garden treatments into storm sewers, rivers, streams, and lakes is a serious source of water pollution as well. Although pesticide contamination is widely considered to be a farm problem, suburban areas receive up to six times the rate of pesticides as farm land. Yet no public records are kept of sales to home gardeners, and the federal program to monitor pesticide poisoning incidents was discontinued in 1981.

Then there is the direct pollution of the environment at the pesticide plants where lawn and garden chemicals are formulated. That is a bill that should be presented to the manufacturer of these poisons, or to the user standing in his or her yard in goggles, gloves, and respirator. But in reality we are all subsidizing this madness with our tax dollars. If you think supermarket food is cheap, and synthetic fertilizers and pesticides economic to use, you haven't looked at the tax bill you are paying for the Superfund toxic waste cleanup. There are—and have been, all along—other ways to build the soil and control pests, without the damage being caused to the economy and the environment or the health risk to the gardener. Over the next nine chapters we'll look, step by step, at how to grow a healthy, productive garden using the time-tested techniques known as organic gardening.

CHAPTER **2**

Garden Siting and Design

In this part of the country the ideal condition would be to have a southern or southeastern slope, for such a pitch faces most directly into the sun and affords protection from our prevailing winds from the northwest. In places where the prevailing winds are strong and unrelenting and the summer season is short, these considerations are of prime importance. Country dwellers in the north can testify that snow lingers on northern and western slopes long after southern and eastern slopes are bare and warm. Samuel R. Ogden

The key to intelligent garden siting and design is to understand the geographical factors involved and then apply them to your own situation. Theory is fascinating stuff, but it doesn't grow good vegetables because it doesn't get its hands dirty; it concentrates on the general at the expense of the specific, while gardens are really communities of specifics. So let's cover a little theory, then consider a few examples drawn from the particulars of my own garden. But please, apply it to your own site and climate.

The two essentials that any garden *must* have are soil and light. From the natural abundance of the fertile, sunlit garden to the contrived cornucopia of hydroponic growing under lights, these two elements are essential. They are the two basic ingredients from which the plants create themselves as they grow, and so whether you are starting a new garden, or trying to improve one you have already, soil and light are the starting points.

Sunlight not only provides the fuel for plant growth, but as the causative factor in the creation of climate and weather, it is the backdrop for nearly every decision in siting a garden. It is the differential heating of Earth's varied surface by the sun that causes the wind; the rough topography of mountains, valleys, plains, and lakes that makes rain, sleet and snow vary from location to location; the changing daylength, and the angle of sunlight that causes the seasons to differ from north to south. Every factor important to the success of a garden except soil type and drainage (covered in Chapter 4) is related to sunlight, and how best to deal with it requires some knowledge of your climate.

WEATHER AND CLIMATE

I don't know about you, but every season in the garden, even every heat wave, drought, or rainy, cool month seems to me like the hottest, driest, or wettest time I've ever seen—an extreme, a record, the final unspringing of nature. Every storm seems to have a wind that is stronger than all that preceded it.

"It never used to rain like this when I was a kid," we think, looking out at the downpour that is drowning newly set seedlings. And at the local coffee shop during the annual brief January thaw I always overhear one patron mutter to another, "You know, we don't really have winters anymore . . . not like we used to, at least." The reason we fail to see the climate for the storms is that climate is a kind of history; our hindsight in the form of weather records shows that, on the whole, the overall American climate is remarkably constant.

The climate of growing cities is certainly changed as old farm fields are paved over for shopping malls and expressways, just as the climate of the Amazon is changing as loggers and ranchers clear-cut the trees. But the new climates that result are themselves relatively stable once established, for good or bad. (This is an excellent argument both for controlling clear-cuts and paving, as well as working to establish greenswards in urban areas.)

You can prove this to yourself—and gain a lot of knowledge about which plants and varieties grow best in your specific situation—if you keep a garden journal with daily weather notes. Each year your understanding of **your** garden will grow, and I think you'll be surprised at how constant your season is. Our garden is in the mountains of Vermont, and from our hillside we look southwest from a small intervale out over a mountain valley ringed by ski areas. We're accustomed to a lot of snow in the winter; in fact we depend on it to help the perennial plants in our vegetable and flower gardens withstand the temperatures of −30°F that we can almost always count on each winter.

The year we cleared our land, 1980, was a warm winter. There was no snow, and temperatures during February regularly hit the 50's. We planted our first peas in the new garden the second week in April. In 1983 we had a snowy winter, and more than twelve feet fell, including one storm of forty inches in late March that collapsed one of our greenhouses. I checked my garden journal and found that we planted our peas on April 15. In 1989 we had thirty-nine degrees below zero with bare ground, and it froze the soil to a depth of seven feet. During the rest of the winter, Virginia got more snow than we did. But according to our garden journal, we were able to plant our peas on April 15.

The Earth, with its thin covering of air, puny oceans, and little stubble bumps of mountains that an astronaut can barely make out from orbit is just one small part of a much larger solar system, and the sun itself is just a tiny star among all those we can see. But from our human perspective the Earth is a giant thermal engine with a seasonal momentum that one small snowstorm in the mountains of Vermont is certainly not going to affect. We may be in a ten-year or hundred-year warm spell; we humans may even alter the climate with our profligate energy use, but the new climate that results, and its constituent microclimates, will continue, predictably, at least until some new climatic trigger comes along.

While this long-term stability underlies the climate of our gardens we will continue to see only the temporal effects, the succession of cool or warm, wet or dry seasons. Thus, when siting and designing the garden, we should do what we can to fit it into both our experience of the site and the historical climatic realities of our region.

AMERICAN CLIMATES

What are those realities? The following is a broad overview of the different climatic regions of North America. Don't lose sight of the fact, though, that the best information on local climates comes from experienced local gardeners. Get to know your neighbors.

In the East the determining factors for your garden site are likely to be the latitude, the altitude, and how far you are from the ocean. The Gulf Coast states may be frost-free year-round, and northern

Georgia may have a frost-free period of eight months, while in northern Maine or Vermont you'll be lucky if you get three months of frost-free nights. Being near the ocean will *add* a week or two to a month at each end of the season. But every 300 feet or so of elevation will *cost* you a week at each end. Also, the farther you are from the ocean, the more hot weather you'll have in summer and cold weather in winter. In general, the farther south you go the more humid the air becomes. But nowhere in the East is water a serious natural problem; rainfall is sufficient for most plants, and evenly distributed throughout the year.

In the Midwest and Plains regions there is considerably less rain. Near the Great Lakes spring comes late because the winter-cooled water doesn't warm up as quickly as the surrounding land; the fall, however, is often long and mild as the Lakes have been heated by the long days full of summer sun. So proximity to the Lakes, and the orientation of the garden plot are important. Farther west, where the dampening effect of the Lakes isn't felt, the weather is more erratic, and heat and cold alternate rapidly, despite the season. But still, the farther north you are, the shorter the season, and the more pronounced the effects of daylength on your garden. Important factors to Plains gardeners are wind and water, and a garden design needs to take both into account.

The Rocky Mountain region is generally dry and sunny, but altitude is a crucial factor. Generally, if you are farther to the north and west, your climate is likely to be a bit wetter and cooler. But

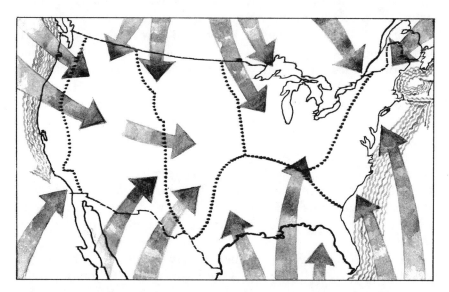

Six basic climatic regions of the USA. Arrows indicate direction from which major weather changes come. Overall, there is a west-to-east pattern.

rainfall at higher elevations can be twice, to as much as six times, the one-inch-a-month that the intermountain lowlands receive on the average each year. The length of the growing season varies considerably, too. In the southern deserts the frost-free period may be a full ten months (though the middle of summer will be too hot for many crops), while the northern Rockies will be lucky to get more than a couple of frost-free months most years. The rule-of-thumb is that each thousand feet of elevation or 3.5° (250 miles) of latitude will shorten the growing season by a week or two at each end. In addition, the terrain of the mountains favors the development of frost pockets that can further shorten the season. This, and other local effects, make experience with a particular location all the more important.

West Coast gardeners need to consider their relationship to the Pacific Ocean, which has an even greater effect on gardening than the Atlantic does on gardeners in the East. Many areas of the Pacific Coast rarely or never see a frost, yet gardeners there have a harder time growing tomatoes than we do here in Vermont. Why? Because of the cool ocean breezes, persistent fog, and long periods of cloudy, wet weather. Inland, over the first range of mountains, though, summers are hot and dry, often without a drop of rain for months on end. Even the winter rains are much less frequent.

Latitude, longitude, and altitude are all important. In general, the farther north and west you are, the cooler, wetter and cloudier the weather will be, so the more of that kind of weather you should plan for. In the winter, what is rain at lower elevations becomes snow as you move up in the mountains; in fact, the severity of a winter storm is often discussed in terms of how far down the mountains it snowed. Local variations—called microclimates—are much more pronounced in the far West, and so siting is again crucial. For example, the average maximum temperature in July at Half Moon Bay, on the central coast of California, is only 64°F, while in Tracy, just fifty miles east (but over the coastal mountains) the average July high is 95°F. In Sonoma County, California, alone there are something like twenty-four different climate zones based on the standard indicators of weather statistics. The same effect, though modified by altitude, latitude and longitude, is true all up and down the coast. Rainfall is also quite different from place to place, but in general you'll need to plan on access to water at some time during the growing season.

Here in New England we like to say "If you don't like the weather, wait five minutes." On the Pacific Coast, if you don't like the weather you can drive five miles. Here we have frost pockets, there they have fog pockets. Gardener, beware.

These broad climatic regions interact with the regional and local topography to produce a set of average (and extreme) temperature data that can be mapped. The U.S. Department of Agriculture (USDA) has taken this information and produced a set of maps of the country that show the average minimum temperature and the average spring and fall frost dates for any location in the United States. For more detailed treatment, there is an excellent two-volume, 1,185-page compilation of climatic data called *Climates of the States,* published by Gale Research[3] from National Oceanic and Atmospheric Administration (NOAA) data, that lists full information for multiple reporting stations in all fifty states. It is available at many public libraries. Combined with a knowledge of the general weather pattern, these two resources can help you determine the nature of your garden's climate.

GARDEN SITING

The climate of your whole region is the macro-climate, or big picture within which your gardening season exists. But when we talk about the effect of proximity to a lake, or the effect of increased altitude on your season, we are talking about particular smaller deviations from the norm for your region—that is, microclimates. This differentiation continues right down to the neighborhood level. My neighbor down by the stream always gets lower temperatures than I do because on winter nights the cold air flows down the surrounding hills and collects on the valley floor, creating a pool of cooler air. On the hillsides around our valley the temperature may be five to ten degrees warmer.

One of the reasons we bought the property is that we thought it would be above the average top of this cold pool of air in the summer, and thus we would miss the first few frosts of fall. Unfortunately, the "airshed" for this valley is larger than I realized. On most of those chancy spring and fall nights enough cold air filters down from above to fill halfway up the side of the valley, including most of our garden. On such a night we'll have a frost in the lower part, but not in the upper. The microclimate of our farm differs from the neighbor's, true enough, but not as much as we'd hoped. Meanwhile, other neighbors farther up on the facing side of the valley will sometimes go an extra few weeks without frost!

By taking these kinds of realities into account you can minimize their negative effects on your garden, and help out whatever good features your microclimate has to offer. Let's continue to use my own garden as an example. We are on a southwest ridge about fifty to one hundred feet above a small south-facing intervale in a larger mountain valley, at an altitude of 1,200 feet in the southern Green Mountains of Vermont, at about 43.5° north latitude.

Since we are in a cold area, the aim of our site design is to warm up the garden's microclimate. The major problems we face are cold, soggy soil, frost, and wind. First, we put our gardens on the southeast face of the ridge. At our latitude a patch of hillside that slopes to the south receives more direct sunlight (especially in the winter) than land that slopes to the north. That's because the lower the sun gets in the sky, the greater is the difference in the angle at which it strikes the two pieces of ground. In fact, every degree of slope to the south is like moving your garden south to a lower latitude. That alone adds two or three weeks to each end of the gardening season, since the soil warms up faster in the spring and stays warm longer in the fall. Because it is a southeastern slope, our garden is also protected a bit from the prevailing northwest wind, and gets sun as early as possible in the morning.

Keep in mind that, in the south, you'd want to do the opposite. In that case, you'd plant on a northern slope to decrease the power of the sun—in a sense sending your garden north during the hot months. Many experienced southern gardeners actually have two plots: one for fall and winter that is in full sun, sloping to the south; and another tucked into a shady spot on a north slope.

Second, we put our crops in raised beds, running generally east to west across the slope. Raised beds help the soil to drain better in

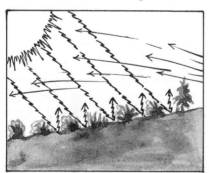 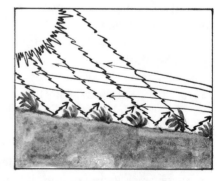

South-facing slopes *(left)* are warmer than north-facing slopes *(right)* because sunlight strikes them more directly. In most parts of the United States, south-facing slopes are also protected from the prevailing northwest wind.

spring, so it warms up faster, yet their cross-slope orientation helps check erosion. Also, the south side of each bed catches extra sun, accentuating the existing slope of the garden itself, and "moving" it farther south.

Third, since we are located down within the "frost pool" for this little valley, we have done what we can to help the cold air drain away as quickly as possible. The source of the problem is really at the south end of the intervale, where a neighbor's pasture has grown back to forest, so that the only way out for cold air that has settled in the valley is down the narrow stream bed. What we have done is to clear a gap in the trees on the downhill side of our property, and plant a windbreak—or in this case a "frostbreak"—of evergreens just above the garden, to divert the flow of cold air out into the driveway where it can escape more quickly down into the intervale. The garden also has solid six-foot stockade fencing on the uphill side, while the downhill side uses pickets; that way the air from the garden itself can filter through and escape.

Since our cold winds come from the north and west we continued the fence and windbreak around to the west, until we got to the point where the summer sun sets on the solstice, which is its northernmost reach in the sky. That way, our fence doesn't block the June sun from reaching the main part of the garden, yet it blocks the cool winds that often blow down from the Canadian tundra in early summer. This arrangement has the added benefit of channeling the midsummer breezes that come from the southwest up across the garden, bringing relief from the dog days of early August.

In order to get the most from your garden site, take all such things into account. What are the limiting factors on garden productivity in your area: temperature, humidity, available sunlight? Working from a knowledge of what the problems are and what combinations of siting, plantings, and construction can do to alter them, you should be able to increase the productivity of your garden plot by increasing the length of the growing season and reducing a lot of the stresses that cause the plants to falter.

GARDEN DESIGN

While the macro and micro climatic factors that affect garden siting are of critical importance, there are three other elements to consider before you finalize a garden design: efficiency, convenience, and—let's not forget—beauty. The design should fit the site the way a well-made shoe fits the foot. When you sketch out a garden plan at the kitchen table in the winter, it's easy to let the clean logic of graph paper lull you into thinking in squares, but unless your land is flat as a billiard table, that's unlikely to be the best, or most beautiful, shape for your garden. The frost hollows, cold, wet swales, and shady parts of the garden aren't square, yet they have a lot more to do with the success or failure of your garden than any kitchen table conception.

I once designed a garden for a garden center customer with a relatively shady site, and so had to delineate which areas were bright enough to support good growth for the various kinds of plants. Instead of getting out the compass and graph paper, then plotting our design with the limited information they gave us, we let the garden take a day to lay itself out. We went by in the early morning and, using stakes and string, ran lines along the shade-sun boundaries of the site; at noon we came back and did the same; then once more, in late afternoon, we laid out the shade boundary. By the end of the day we had a complete "shade map" of that garden for that time of year. Using it as a guide, we completed a design for the garden that made the most of the light available. This kind of geometry is based on the particulars of the site; it solves problems rather than ignoring them. Even if you don't want to let the site dictate the garden layout to that extent, at least take it into account.

The traditional layout for kitchen gardens was established many hundreds of years ago. Called the "four square" design, it is based on the intersection of two major paths within a symmetrical, enclosed area; in the days before irrigation it usually included a central well or spring. Many of the early examples of this traditional layout were monastic gardens, and while there were perhaps religious and symbolic reasons for the creation of this form, over the centuries its inherent efficiency has gained it a place in the secular world as well.

Vegetables (and fruits and flowers and herbs) were grown in raised beds marked out by the permanent paths. The four equal-sized plots that resulted (often with smaller perimeter beds around the inside of the wall, fence, or hedge that enclosed the garden) made crop rotation and planning easy. The diversity of the plantings not only made balanced demands on the soil, but preserved the natural balance of the garden's animal life—small mammals, insects, amphibians, and birds—an important factor in keeping pest problems under control.

In Europe this style became highly refined; some of the formal "potagers" of the nobility were eight acres or more, often completely surrounded by a high stone or brick wall against which tender fruits and vegetables could be grown far north of their normal range. The plantings in these gardens were quite formal, with boxwood edging the beds, and arbors at the intersection of the secondary paths trellised with espaliered fruit.

American kitchen gardens have, on the whole, been much less formal. From the beginnings of colonization there has been less emphasis on strict training of the plants, but the efficiency and utility of the classic four square layout has been largely preserved. Americans have adapted, and should continue to adapt, this traditional design to the particulars of their lives and their land. An old-fashioned garden gracing the yard of a restored Colonial-style village home in the northeast may stick to the strict four square design, but gardens on steeply sloped, irregularly shaped lots can be terraced into the slope and follow its contours to make the most of the conditions of the site. Hacienda gardens in the arid southwest, as well as those nestled next to a cottonwood stream in the midwestern prairies, can both make the most of the protection from sun and wind offered by adobe walls or tall, windbreak hedges. The basic elements, though—raised growing beds in multiple, equally sized

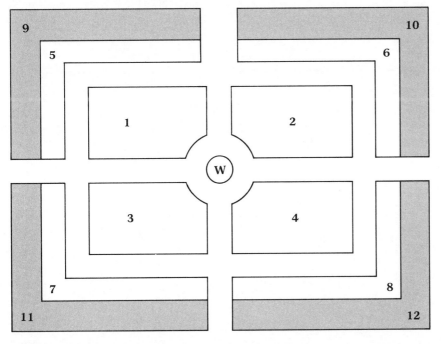

A garden laid out in four equal plots (1,2,3,4) surrounding a central well (W) makes planning easier and can be quite beautiful as well. Most traditional layouts also include perimeter beds (5,6,7,8) and some sort of enclosure (9,10,11,12), either walls or tall hedges.

plots, some form of enclosure and access to water, sun, and the house of the gardener—should remain the same. What should change is merely the details that reflect regional, personal, and site-specific realities: the shape and size of the beds, and the specific vegetables and varieties grown in them. Ideally each design should reflect the sensibilities and opinions of the gardener who created it, as adapted to that site.

Big Sam's garden followed these principles, and I include below the layout from the 1971 edition of *Step by Step*.

Within these plots he planted in rows, and many gardeners prefer that approach. To me, though, it's a demonstrable fact that planting in beds—whether raised or not—is the most efficient way to plan a home garden. Big Sam made an effective argument for planting in closely spaced rows, leaving just enough room to walk gingerly between them when the plants were young, and then letting the plants grow over the row at maturity to exclude weeds. But to my mind, he didn't take his reasoning to its logical conclusion: that there is little need for every row to have a path next to it.

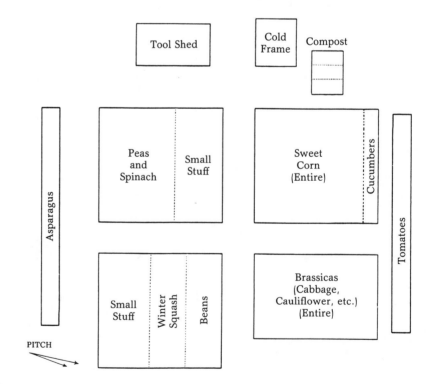

By planting in beds, you eliminate two-thirds to three-quarters of the paths, lessening not only the amount of open space that will need regular cultivation, but also the soil compaction and concomitant constraint on root development that accompanies every path. The amount of wasted space is apparent if you examine closely any row-based plant-spacing chart. It gives one distance for in-row spacing and another, much larger spacing, for how far apart the rows should be in order to accommodate the paths. Much of that path space can be saved, meaning both higher yields and less maintenance for the same sized garden. And the efficiencies of bed planting extend to ease of cultivation, too, as we'll see in Chapter 9.

Raised beds save space by eliminating unnecessary paths; they also reduce harmful soil compaction caused by walking between rows.

When planting in beds, you space the plants equidistant from one another over the whole surface of the bed. The net increase in efficiency from this change alone—forgeting for a moment the reduced soil compaction, and that compost and other soil amendments can be concentrated on the growing areas rather than scattered randomly, over path and row alike—will likely be at least 15 percent. It can be as high as 50 percent, when considered in terms of yield instead of just the number of plants per square foot.

The large plot layout seen in Big Sam's garden is not incompatible with a seasonal bed system, where beds are formed in the spring and left in place for a single season. Let me use the example of a garden I once put in just for fun, a small demonstration garden here at our trial fields, designed solely to prove that a vegetable garden could be beautiful. Though it was designed "on the fly" with little thought to efficiency, it still produced a much higher yield than a row garden of the same size, and it looked a lot nicer, too.

First I marked out a rectangle in the open garden area next to our upper greenhouse that measured twenty by fifty feet, and roto-tilled it, which took a couple of hours. Since the greenhouses were rect-angular, and I felt a geometric pattern would look best in that spot, I then took stakes and twine and made a large X connecting the opposite corners. The spot where the lines crossed was the center of the plot, and I drove a stake to mark it. Then I went to work on building up the growing beds.

I lightly shoveled a path under the lines, using a flat-bottomed shovel, then I took down the lines. Next, I stood in the center and gave the other end of an eight-foot piece of twine to my seven-year-old daughter, and had her pull it taut. Then she walked around me, making a circular path four feet in from the sides of the plot. After that I took in four feet of the twine so it was only four feet long, and had her walk the circle again, which she thought both mysterious and exciting. That gave me a second path four feet in from the first. I then shoveled out those paths, and within a few hours had a funky, formal vegetable garden with a whimsical touch—and it took no more work or trouble than a standard, square bed design!

After these basics were set, I neatly raked up the edges of the beds and added a few extra small paths to round out the design; then I erected a large post in the center, on which I mounted a sprinkler so I could water the entire garden from that one spot. From the top of the post I ran twine out to the edges of the eight-foot circle and planted pole beans beside each line. Inside the bean teepee, I planted cool weather greens that would benefit from the shade and made a small sitting area for the kids to have their tea parties. The varied sizes and shapes of beds in this garden provided a real wealth of design and cropping possibilities, along with visual and horticultural diversity.

How big a garden should you have? Pacing is a good way to keep things in human terms. You might want to make a family garden twenty to twenty-five paces across and fifty paces long if you have the room, but that's pretty ambitious for a beginner. Ten by twenty paces is probably more realistic for most families these days. Once you've got the size and the rough layout—again, remember that there is no reason why your garden has to be some regular geometric shape, though within some larger landscape designs that might be best—walk through the plot as you might once it is planted, and you'll almost instantly know where the paths should be.

If you're breaking new ground, it will take a significant amount of work to get the ground cleared and ready for gardening; there is no way around this one-time investment, though the long-term benefits will repay it amply. The procedure for establishing a new garden can be found in Chapter 4. But the time required to convert an existing row-cropped garden of this size to a system of seasonal beds—that is to roto-till, mark, and shovel the paths of a garden the size we've been discussing here—is slightly less than a day.

As I've said, a beginning gardener might want to start with a smaller space, and in fact I recommend it because a small garden, well tended, is much more satisfying than a large, neglected one. That doesn't mean you'll miss out on the fun, the challenges, and the diversity that a large garden contains. You can have a great garden—without too much work but with plenty of time to sit and enjoy it—in just fifty or one hundred square feet. If you start too big, things may get out of hand; let the size grow along with your experience. Vegetable gardening shouldn't be a chore; weeding and cultivating can be just as pleasurable as harvesting if you keep things manageable. There can be wonderful, quiet moments of observation, of close interaction with the whole community of plants and animals in your garden, a respite from the hurry and worry of the work day. Remember: you're not just commuting from planting to harvest; in a properly sized garden the means and ends are equally enjoyable.

Just as you should determine the size of the garden by your own needs and wants, you should size the beds precisely for yourself and your family, not by some book's theoretical measure. You'll be taking care of them, not me! The shape can be just about anything you want or that fits the space you have; just remember the four-square concept we discussed above. What matters is the width, and determining the maximum width for your beds is easy: stoop down, reach forward, and touch the ground with your outstretched hand. Don't make any bed more than twice that distance and you'll be able to reach the center from the paths without straining. That's all there is to it. I'd also recommend, though, that no bed be more than ten or twelve paces long, so you never have to walk farther than that to get around to the other side. Otherwise you'll be tempted to step across.

Whatever its size and shape, your garden site should be as close to the house—particularly the kitchen—as possible. If you're in a densely populated area you're not likely to have much choice, but even if you've got forty acres out front and another forty back of the house, you should still keep the garden close by. It discourages creatures from making midnight raids at the same time it encourages you and your family to spend more time there, to step out quickly for that little extra something for the kitchen, whether it be a snippet of fresh rosemary for the lamb chops or handful of zinnias for the vase. If getting to the garden is a chore, your gardening will be a chore as well.

The inherent planting efficiency of a bed garden can be enhanced even further if you plan for low maintenance right from the beginning. Consider permanent sides to the beds, using whatever local materials are available. Do not use treated lumber, though, since you will be eating the plants grown in these beds. The manufacture of treated lumber creates pollution problems you may not see but nonetheless cause when you purchase it. (The different types of treated wood and their characteristics are discussed in more detail in Chapter 3.) Stone is one of the best materials if you have it available, but brick, concrete, and some naturally rot-resistant woods native to your area also make good choices.

Mulch the main access paths with a thick layer of bark, sand, or cinders—whatever is suitable, local, cheap, and responsible. Some gardeners, like my grandfather, simply plant grass and maintain sod paths. Be forewarned, though, that sod paths will be constantly migrating into the garden and will require yearly attention.

Make the beds modular. That is, even if they are not exactly the same size, try to have at least one dimension the same; if you want to extend the growing season with movable tunnels that protect the plants from heat or cold, you'll be able to use them on more than one bed without having to reconstruct them each time they're moved.

Whatever kind of land and climate you have to work with, remember that the kind of garden that will put you in touch with the quiet rhythms of growth is by definition a garden of human, not industrial, scale. I feel a family garden should be small enough so that any of the major garden tasks can be accomplished in a day or less. Spring soil preparation, seeding and setting of transplants, fall cleanup, none of these should take more than a single Saturday of pleasant work for the family.

Our own garden, made permanent after eight years of being shunted around among the leftover corners of our larger trial gardens, is 60 feet by 120 feet. This is much larger than the average, but we have the room and, as long-time homesteaders, we are trying to provide for a larger proportion of our food needs. Using the labor-saving techniques outlined above, we are able to keep the labor requirement to a minimum.

GARDEN STRUCTURES

It is the dream of many gardeners, especially those in northern climates, to have a greenhouse. Unfortunately, for a home gardener, it is almost impossible to justify economically. There is no way it's going to pay for itself, unless you build the frame from salvaged materials and never heat it. Under those conditions, of course, it is simply a large, above-ground cold frame, or a walk-in cloche.

The only true greenhouse that is really justifiable on ecological grounds is a solar greenhouse, because it practically heats itself. The production cycle of fossil fuels and electricity is inherently detrimental to the environment; to use them for heating a personal greenhouse is irresponsible when simple design features that capture and store the sun's heat can make it an ecologically positive structure, a way to lessen your dependence on food grown far away and shipped long distances at great energy cost. Though freestanding greenhouses are technically better, because they get more light, I would nonetheless opt for one that is attached to the south side of the house or garage. By building a solar greenhouse attached to your own house, you'll not only enjoy the benefits of growing plants and crops, you'll actually help heat your house. On this basis a greenhouse becomes a great investment both for yourself and for the world.

The details of greenhouse design and management are beyond the scope of this book. Suffice it to say that you could easily grow enough seedlings for an average sized home garden in a little six-by-eight-foot greenhouse attached to the house, say, outside a set of patio doors. For a larger garden, or if you want to grow food in it, an eight-by-twenty-four-foot greenhouse is a very good size; it is an efficient shape, and fits in well architecturally with most houses. You'll find references in the Bibliography to some excellent books on the subject.

A cold frame, however, is within the reach of almost every gardener's budget. In fact, you can often build a respectable one for nothing more than the cost of your time. Old storm windows, some leftover lumber and a course (layer) or two of cinder blocks will make a really first rate, permanent frame. For temporary use, even simpler materials will suffice, like a rectangle of hay bales with an old window laid on top.

Big Sam's cold frame was an important part of his garden, and I include here his plans and instructions for construction of one, from six-by-six to twelve-by-six:

I have had several cold frames and have finally developed a design which is not only easy and economical to build but is permanent as well. Cold frame sash can be purchased at any building supply depot. They come three feet wide by six feet long, so the size of your cold frame, depending on your needs, will be in multiples of these dimensions; that is either three by six, six by six, nine by six, or like mine, twelve by six. The frame itself is to be built of cement or cinder blocks, the dimensions of which are eight by sixteen inches, and for our purpose can be laid up dry; that is, without the use of mortar. Their weight will hold them in place, the laying of them will present no problem, nor will the services of a professional be required. The front wall will be two courses high and the back wall will be four courses high, so that the pitch of the sash from back to front will be sixteen inches, which is ample to provide for runoff. The length of the front and back walls will depend on the number of sash used. The two end walls will be the same length in any case and will require five cement blocks for each of the three bottom courses and three for the top course, making a

A cold frame allows many vegetables to be started even before outdoor conditions permit, but siting and construction are both important to its success.

total of eighteen blocks for each wall. Now, depending upon the length of the bed (I do not recommend anything less than two sash), the number of blocks needed will be as follows: For a four sash bed, two courses in front of ten blocks each, and four courses in back of ten blocks each, making a total of sixty blocks. A two sash bed will take half of this, or thirty blocks, so we can figure a total of ninety-six blocks for the four sash bed and sixty-six for the two sash. Additional material in the form of two by four scantlings will be required as shown on the diagram. Having the materials now on hand, it is time to begin construction.

First, excavate a hole sixteen inches deep, the size depending on the number of sash used, making sure that it is large enough to allow for the eight inch thick cement block wall all the way around. Now lay up the walls, checking to be sure that the first course is level, that each block sits firm and true, and, most important, that the inside dimensions all around compare exactly with the dimensions of the sash to be used. Now fill all the holes in the blocks with earth and tamp firmly before starting the next course. At each corner one will lap over the other butt, breaking the joints on the second course, so that the second laps where the first butted, etc. A study of the accompanying drawing will clarify this procedure. Continue in this manner until the walls are laid. With the earth from the excavation, bank up around the back and side walls until the banking is flush with the top of the walls. The front wall, of course, will be flush with the ground, or, better, an inch or two above the surface. Fill the bottom of the pit with six inches of well-rotted manure on top of which will be placed good, rich topsoil which has been mixed with compost or composted manure. Now we are ready for the frame which will support the sash; it is simple in construction and is made of two by fours, consisting of front, back and side sills with cross supports depending upon the size of the bed. Again, details of this construction can be obtained from the drawing. The sash, which should be hinged to the back sill, can be raised and lowered at will, with notched props to hold the sash open as needed.

This type of coldframe, a permanent and valuable addition to any home garden, can be built at a minimum of expense by using your own labor, and within a few years it should pay for itself. As a substitute for sash, use rigid sheets of Fiberglas.

While the materials have changed since Big Sam's time—cold frame sash as such is no longer generally available, though rigid insulating acrylic panels are an improvement as well as a replacement—the principles of construction are still good. Placement of the cold frame should take into account not only the orientation of the garden—since obviously it should face south, or at least nearly so in the North—but it should also be in a convenient location. If your cold frame is close to the house you're more likely to keep an eye on it and be able to better regulate its ventilation.

Also, today we have new and better materials for construction. The sash, as mentioned above, can be replaced with modern acrylic greenhouse panels, which have a much stronger insulating effect than glass, come in wider sheets, and are almost impossible to break; the outside of the block walls can be lined with landscape fabric to keep weed roots from the rear wall berm from working their way in; and foam insulation in the same location will turn the cement blocks into an effective solar heat storage mass. For even more thermal mass, drums of water could be placed inside the cold frame. With these additions, the gardener will have nearly a year-round gardening frame, even where winter temperatures regularly drop below zero.

The last major structure you'll need in your garden is a shed for storage of tools, and to work in when the weather is uncooperative. Traditionally, the potting shed is to the gardener almost what the workshop is to the woodworker, and while the gardener generally works at his or her craft outdoors, there is a need for an indoor workspace.

The requirements of a potting shed are few, and in many situations may be met by existing buildings; but where construction of a building for the purpose is necessary or desirable, either on its own or in combination with a greenhouse and/or cold frames, a few basic considerations should be taken into account.

First, since the potting shed is a place to store tools, there should be sufficient space to hang all your hand tools well up off the ground. Simple nails in the wall will suffice, but the more organized you are the more enjoyable your time in the garden will be and the less of it will be spent cursing a lost tool. In addition to the hand tools, there should be room for any power equipment you own, the tool cleaning tub of oily sand described in Chapter 3, and any consumable supplies like potting soil, pots, and such. Fertilizers and pest controls, even organic ones, should be kept in a latched cupboard or room to protect curious kids and animals.

Second, the potting shed should provide enough space for the gardener to sit comfortably at a workbench to do the tasks that can be done indoors. This includes, but is obviously not limited to, the sharpening and oiling of tools, plus the sowing, pricking out, and potting on of seedlings. A well-designed shed need be no larger than, say, six feet by eight feet. It could adjoin another building, whose exterior wall might suffice for hanging tools; then even less space will do. Whatever its size, though, a tool or potting shed does not need to be fancy; we are simply trying to get in out of the weather, not build an edifice that will stand with the pyramids.

One last aspect of basic garden design is compost piles. While many gardeners—Big Sam and I included—start out building their piles on any piece of open ground, you should at least consider making a permanent composting area part of the overall garden plan. If you do, take mind of the fact that compost piles need a lot of air. Any combination of materials and methods that expose the pile to the air, while holding it in place, will work well. Well designed aerobic compost bins can be bought ready-made from several different companies, but the capacity of most of these is only a cubic yard or so. For larger gardens, you'll be better off constructing a series of bins, so that multiple piles can be created and matured in succession. (This process is described in detail in Chapter 5.)

Suitable materials include metal fencing; wood, including salvaged trucking pallets (portable platforms for moving materials); and concrete blocks. The metal fence should be the inexpensive type that comes in 25-foot rolls "woven" into a grid of rectangles. It is formed into one or more upright circles and held erect by a couple of metal posts. Or a mesh bin could be made from sections of heavy duty concrete reinforcing steel mesh welded to rectangles of channel iron, which could be fastened vertically at the corners. A bin made from salvaged pallets works the same way, though, and is certainly cheaper. The problem with all of these is that the sides are of a fixed height, and the materials to be composted will have to be lifted over it; with a bit of creative siting this problem might be overcome, but in most cases a simpler solution is to make the bin so its walls can be built up as the pile itself grows.

One way is to make the retaining walls from cinder blocks laid so the holes are horizontal. They are stacked in the same fashion as for building the coldframe walls, that is, butted at the corners for stability, yet the horizontal orientation of the holes allows air into the pile along the whole wall. Don't build this wall much higher than three courses, or the outward pressure of the pile might cause it to fall over and you'll have a mess on your hands. The pile can be heaped considerably higher, though.

The composting area should be central to the garden, so the dis-

ENCLOSED COMPOST PILES Made of:

Woven wire fencing

Concrete form wire

Concrete blocks

Recycled warehouse pallets

tance that materials will need to be transported is minimized. Ideally, the center of the four square garden design could be a small potting shed/greenhouse/cold frame with compost piles arrayed around it under the eaves of a large overhang. This would be the most efficient possible setup.

Our own garden can serve as an example again. We put the composting area at the uphill end of the garden, and cut into the hill a bit so that the retaining wall used to form the driveway turnaround could serve as the rear wall of the bins. This makes movement of manure and other composting materials from around the property simple; to unload onto the piles we just back the truck into the turnaround and pull the materials from the back of the truck right onto the piles.

CHAPTER 3

Tools and Equipment

*For the preparation of the soil and the cultivation of the gar-
den it is necessary to have certain tools and implements. To
start, the garden soil must be turned over, and this must be
done by hand or by the use of a plow. Small gardens can be
handled well enough by hand, and the decision on this point
will have to be made by the gardener himself. If it is to be
done by hand I recommend the use of a short handled spading fork, with heavy tines of well-tempered tool steel. Cheap,
flimsy forks will soon be prized out of shape so that the tines
are not in line, and the usefulness of the tool is ended.*

Samuel R. Ogden

The subject of tools and equipment is a tricky one. There is a
tendency to want a tool for every purpose, almost to the point where
the tools use the gardener instead of the other way around. It helps
to remember that with technology of any kind, the best solution is
usually the least solution. You'll almost certainly enjoy gardening
more using a small range of well made, functional tools than by
filling the garden shed with a wall full of useless gadgets that end
up frustrating more than they satisfy. On a practical level it comes
down to whether you'd rather spend your time in the garden with
the plants or in the garage with the machines.

HAND TOOLS

I agree with Big Sam that the most important tool an organic gardener can own is a garden or spading fork. Whether preparing a
bed for planting, dividing established perennials, mixing compost,

or aerating a lawn, it is the most versatile tool I have (except the hand that holds it). With just a garden fork and a little legwork you can maintain almost any sized garden once it is established.

A good garden fork is indeed a heavy duty implement, usually mounted with a "D" type handle, although occasionally you'll see one with a long, straight handle. I have both. The "D" handle is best for spring soil preparation, because it gives your hand a lateral grip that helps keep an off-center forkload of soil from tipping. But the long-handled fork provides more leverage for loosening subsoil when double digging, and allows you to work standing straighter. If you can have only one, though, choose the "D" handled fork because of its versatility.

The four tines of an American style fork measure ½ to ¾ of an inch wide and eight to twelve inches long, somewhat pointed on the end so they enter the ground easily, but broad and flattened in cross section so that they disturb rather than cut. This is the same kind of tine used on a potato fork, which has to extract potatoes from the ground without harming them. English style forks have tines with a square cross section.

Garden forks are made from a stiff, tempered steel that can stand up to the same kind of digging and prying action as a shovel. The best have solid forged heads and a closed socket, or a long strap of steel joining the blade to the handle, to prevent breakage. I have broken a few myself and now wouldn't buy another with a cheap, riveted handle. The advantage of a fork over a spade is that it breaks up the soil instead of just moving it around. For digging, certainly a spade is the tool of choice, but for loosening and aerating the soil, as well as incorporating amendments, nothing works so well as a good quality garden fork.

Companion to the garden fork is the spade itself. While most American gardeners are familiar with the conventional long-handled shovel, the European spade is more useful for general garden work. It has a flat-sectioned, square, or slightly rounded blade, and a "D" type handle like that of the fork. The straight blade makes the garden spade good for edging beds, or for peeling back the sod where a new bed is to be. Heavy duty spades have treads formed or welded atop the blade to cushion the foot for that kind of heavy digging. The square design of the blade is also well suited for light trenching, chopping, and tamping.

The shovel is really a construction tool, suited for moving heavy, loose material like sand, small gravel, and cinders. For lighter, less dense materials like grain, sawdust, or snow, there are shovels or

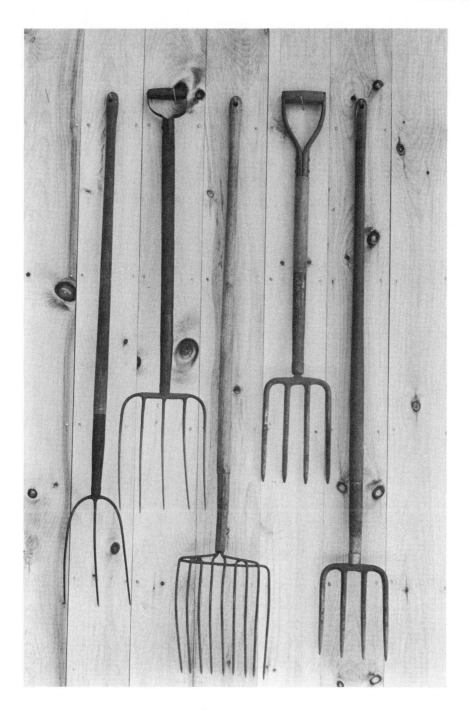

VARIOUS KINDS OF FORKS *Left to right:* Hay fork; manure fork; stable fork; "D" handle garden fork; and straight-handle garden fork.

VARIOUS KINDS OF SHOVELS AND SPADES *Left to right:* Grain or snow shovel; flat blade garden spade; long-handle trenching spade; long-handle digging shovel; and "D"-handle digging shovel.

scoops with large, high-sided aluminum or plastic blades. A shovel can also be used for digging round holes, as the back of the blade is curved. The slope of the blade will taper the hole inward from the edge, which is ideal for preparing a transplanting hole. A nursery spade, with its pointed, round-backed blade, resembles a miniature shovel, except that the angle of the blade to the handle is reversed. This is so that, when digging up established plants, the handle will be back out of the way of the plant, allowing more freedom to work. A trenching spade has a round-backed blade about eight inches across at the tread, sixteen to eighteen inches long, and five to six inches across at the bottom. With it you can cut narrow trenches for drainage (or for blanching) quickly and efficiently.

You can not only make a garden, but maintain it with a garden fork and spade alone, but a few more tools will make the process more efficient and enjoyable. The first of these is a cultivator. Where vegetables will grow, so will weeds; to stop the weeds we need to uproot them, and this can be done either by hand—once they have gotten big enough to grab onto—or as soon as they germinate, by simply disturbing the soil with a cultivator. Cultivators come in an incredible range of sizes and forms; it seems that there is one for every situation, whether it be widely spaced transplants or broadcast greens, and every gardener seems not only to have a favorite, but also to have dreamed about inventing one. I have three or four that I'd hate to be without: my stirrup hoes, a hook, a hand harrow, and my grandfather's own home-fabricated "Ogden hoe."

This last, named for Big Sam's uncle who taught him how to make it, is essentially the complement to the old-fashioned "Warren hoe," still widely available, which has a triangular blade that comes to a single point, and is used for furrowing. You can easily make one by cutting off the lower corners of a standard broad hoe. The Ogden hoe is also triangular, but the reverse of the former: the blade descends from a single point at the handle mount to sharp points at the lower corners. These form a flat-bottomed triangle the width of a standard broad hoe. One can be made by cutting off the upper corners of a standard broad hoe. In my opinion it is superior to both the standard hoe and the Warren hoe because if held in the normal fashion, neck up, it can be used for hilling, yet if the handle is rotated so that one of the corner points is down, it can be used for furrowing as well.

I inherited my cultivating hook from my grandfather. It is smaller than a potato hook, with quarter-inch-thick, round-sectioned tines, sharpened at the end, which penetrate the soil only a half-inch or

VARIOUS KINDS OF HOES *Left to right:* "Warren" hoe; "Ogden" hoe; standard broad hoe; and standard narrow hoe.

so at rest. As you pull it toward you it digs in, but it's a lot easier on the back than a full-sized potato hook. Cultivating hooks are widely available, but if you buy one, I'd suggest bending the two outside tines inward just a bit, so you can use it to cultivate really close in to plants in the row. A hook of this type can be used like a conventional broad hoe to chop the soil surface, though that may disturb the shallow roots of vegetables almost as much as the hoe. I use it to sweep across the surface of the soil, back and forth, even crossways, lightly disturbing the surface without bothering anything but newly sprouting weed seedlings. Until I discovered the stirrup hoe, the hook was my favorite cultivator.

I also have a full range of other cultivators that I've inherited or picked up over the years from one place or another: a "Warren" hoe, two Dutch scuffle hoes (plus various poorly crafted imitations of each that I've received as samples over the years because of our mail order business), and an assortment of the conventional square-bladed broad hoes. The only one of the broad hoes I use much is the narrowest, which is only an inch or two wide, and thus ideal for cultivating closely planted root crops as they near maturity. Used as a skimmer, it is almost as quick as a stirrup hoe (see below); its tenure in the garden shed is pretty well guaranteed by the fact that stirrup hoes narrower than three inches jam easily on the sticks and stones that pepper the surface of our garden. These obstructions can't pass through the hoe so easily as they do with the larger-size stirrups.

I also have a "hand harrow," a long-handled tool used for preparing a fine seedbed and for breaking up lightly crusted soil after a rain. It consists of three stubby arms mounted into the head, each of which is tipped with a pair of offset spike-toothed rollers. As you push the hand harrow, the meshing of the spike rollers not only breaks the crusty surface of the soil, but uproots small weeds. It is a great tool for established gardens, but if there is a lot of "trash"— that is, small rocks and bits of root or clumps of partially decomposed straw mulch, say—on the surface, the tines will quickly pick them up and jam.

I don't know who invented the stirrup hoe, but I sure am glad they thought of it. Because of its built-in depth-regulating design, you can work more quickly with a stirrup hoe than with a cultivating hook, and there is much less disturbance of neighboring plants' roots. This is because you don't have to chop to get the weeds; instead, the blade skims along just below the surface of the soil, slicing off the weeds at their most vulnerable point, which is the stem connection between leaf and root. The head of a stirrup hoe

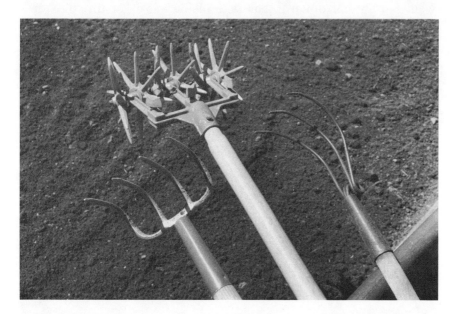

USEFUL CULTIVATORS *Left to right:* Cultivating hook; rolling "hand harrow"; and lightweight spring tooth cultivator.

has a pair of holes threaded by a small pin. On that axle is mounted a sharpened, stainless steel "stirrup" which, because of the pin mounting, is able to pivot fifteen degrees or so back and forth in line with the handle. So when you pull a stirrup hoe it skims along at an angle to the ground, scooping up just the top quarter-inch or so of the soil and vaulting it half an inch. Small rocks, twigs, and other trash pass right through, but weeds are dislodged, and unless it rains right away their severed stems quickly wither in the sun.

I have become so partial to stirrup hoes that I have three different sizes, but you can certainly get by with one. The best all-around size is five inches across the base of the stirrup; when you buy, check the oscillating motion of the stirrup carefully.

You probably own a rake, and might think to use it for cultivation, but most are not up to the task. I sometimes use a rake to clear the surface of a seedbed that was prepared and then not promptly planted, but the angle of the tines causes them to dig in rather than simply skim along the surface. You can keep the work shallow with a little arm power, though it is barely worth the trouble to do so; better to re-prepare the bed, or use a hook or hand harrow to get it in shape.

There are two uses for which a rake is invaluable, though. The first is for removal of weeds, and for this a modified leaf rake works well. Simply cut down a leaf rake (using a pair of tin snips or a

STIRRUP HOES *Left to right:* Five-inch, seven-inch, and three-inch widths.

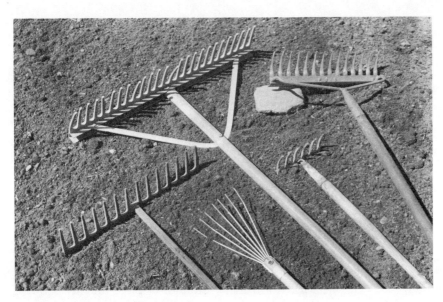

RAKES *Clockwise from left:* Heavy iron rake; lightweight leveling rake; copper bed-forming rake with scraper edge; narrow iron rake; and narrow leaf rake.

hacksaw) so that it is just as wide as the row spacing you use most commonly in your garden. Then, if after the weeds are skimmed the weather is not dry enough to wither them, they can be easily raked up and taken to the compost pile. We actually have both a leaf and a stiff-tined steel rake cut down for this purpose, but you should certainly be able to get by with just one or the other.

The second use I have for a rake is in forming beds. The proper kind of rake to do this job must be stoutly built so that you can really move soil with it. This does not mean it must be heavy, though. Our rake collection includes everything from a six-foot iron rake with straight-forged tines, which weighs a good six pounds, to a two-foot-wide aluminum-magnesium alloy landscaper's rake, that weighs less than half that. My favorite, though, is a lightweight one with the tines and the scraping blade on the back made entirely of copper. It was sold to me as a "bio-dynamic bed finishing rake," and the designer's intent was that the copper, in working the soil, would leave behind a trace element residue to assist in the control of soil-borne diseases, as copper is naturally fungicidal. Regardless of its disease control abilities, though, this lightweight rake is a joy to work with once the primary bed-forming has been accomplished with heavier tools. The scraper edge on the back of the rake makes mounding and smoothing much easier.

The final tool of this type—handle tools—that I consider necessary is a pitchfork, much lighter than a garden fork, with round, pointed tines like the cultivating hook. Its name expresses its function, which is to pick up piles of garden refuse that are awkward or messy to grab with your arms, and pitch them into a wheelbarrow or onto the compost pile. If you buy wisely, this lightweight fork will also serve to turn the compost piles. There are several forms, not all of which are appropriate: a hay fork has two to four rolled steel, round-section tines; a manure fork has four to six square or flattened, forged tines; there is also a thing I call a stable fork, which has a dozen or more rolled, round tines (see illustration on page 31). You want the manure fork. The hay fork lets too much slip between its widely spaced tines, and on the stable fork the tines are so close together—to make shoveling horse and sheep manure easier—that the vines and stalks of garden plants get skewered and then stuck on the fork. I am lucky enough to have all three, but if you can have only one, choose the manure fork.

Along with my grandfather, I recommend that you have not just one, but two stout garden lines available for marking rows and paths. Quite often it will save considerable time to be able to use both at the same time. They should be long enough to run the full width or length of your garden, and the stakes should be strong enough so that the line can be brought taut without danger of breaking them. In addition, we use a mechanical planter to speed sowing of row crops. There are a number of models on the market, from simple to elaborate; keep in mind that they are largely unnecessary for gardens of less than 500 square feet.

One other piece of equipment that will help maintain your hand tools is a scraper tub. This is a tub or half wine barrel, filled with sand, into which you dump the waste oil generated by oil changes on any equipment you may own. The resulting oily, sand-filled tub should be kept right near where the tools are hung. That way each time you return a spade or fork or hoe to its nail you can jam it down into the sand a few times to rub off any newly acquired corrosion (and oil the metal at the same time).

GARDEN CART

If your garden is larger than a few hundred square feet you'll probably want a cart of some sort for hauling materials between the garden and compost pile. There are two basic kinds: conventional wheelbarrows and two-wheeled carts.

Two-wheeled garden cart. Adaptable design is good for raised bed gardens because it can straddle properly sized beds. Handles bulky materials well.

Standard wheelbarrow (with rustproof composite plastic barrow). Best for mixing, hauling, and dumping heavy, dense materials like soil and compost.

The former is best for heavy, dense materials, and works well for hauling and dumping operations like spreading compost, but it doesn't fit well in tightly spaced gardens. Carts have the advantage of being able to straddle properly sized beds, which makes them very convenient at planting time. With a piece of plywood laid on top across its sides you have a work surface good enough to write on, and any seeds or seedlings can wait in the cool shade underneath, along with a few necessary tools and supplies. A few years back some manufacturers designed very intricate systems for these carts: removable sides, racks to hold rolls of plastic mulch so you could unroll it by pulling the cart along the bed, other square racks for holding transplants, even runners to replace the wheels in winter time so firewood could be carried across the snow. But on uneven ground they pitch wildly from side to side, making them hard to control, and their overall lighter construction makes two-wheel carts less long-lasting.

While I use both, I find it hard to choose. Both can be useful, both can be frustrating. Whichever you decide on, get the biggest and best you can afford—a cheap cart or barrow isn't worth the manure you haul in it.

PESTICIDES

Throughout this book you will see recommendations for particular pest controls, very few of which involve spraying or dusting of pesticides. Nonetheless, a basic understanding of what pesticides are and how they work is invaluable. Pesticides run the gamut from homemade remedies to high-tech and toxic chemicals, and in one form or another they have been in use since humans first began cultivating plants. The ancient Sumerians and Chinese used mineral and botanical compounds to control various pests.

There are four main categories of pesticides: insecticides, bactericides, fungicides, and herbicides, but we will concern ourselves only with insecticides because, except for fungicides like Captan or Thiram, most vegetable garden use of pesticides is for the control of insects. There are four basic types using three general methods of action. Pesticides can be biological, botanical, mineral, or synthetic, and they generally kill either by infection or poisoning, though some pesticides act mechanically. We will discuss them in terms of their origin, stating the method of action for each class.

Biological pesticides are those that kill by infection, and they essentially involve the destruction of one organism by another. The best example is the microbial insecticide *Bacillus thuringiensis,* or Bt, which is a naturally occurring bacterium that infects the gut of soft-bodied caterpillars. By applying a solution of this bacteria to the edible parts of affected plants, we guarantee that the pest caterpillar becomes infected with the bacterium, then sickens and dies. The old, homemade remedy of "bug juice," described in detail under Broccoli in Chapter 10, is also a bacterial spray. Other bacterial pesticides have been developed; in most cases they are quite specific to the pests for which they are applied, and thus safe for humans. A problem may arise with widespread use of bacterial sprays, however, if the pest species develop genetic resistance to the diseases they cause.

Botanical pesticides are those derived from plants. Pyrethrum and rotenone are two well-known and widely used botanical dusts. Both are contact poisons and, as such, are relatively toxic to a wide range of organisms, including humans. They are, however, short-lived in the environment, and not known for the kinds of long-term health and pollution problems associated with synthetics. Sprays made from pepper or garlic juice have also been used since time immemorial as pest and disease controls, respectively. Garlic juice depends on its sulfur content for effectiveness, as sulfur is toxic to all kinds of bacteria and fungi.

Mineral pesticides are those composed of mined materials. The sulfur naturally present in garlic is also available in pure form for use as a fungicide, as is elemental copper. Both can be toxic at high levels, but are rarely used extensively enough to cause immediate problems. Arsenic and mercury are far more toxic, and were once widely used, though rarely now. Diatomaceous earth is mined from ancient marine crustacean deposits and forms a gritty dust that gets into the joints of the exoskeleton, or shell, of hard-bodied insects, wears holes in it, and thus causes them to die of dehydration.

Synthetic pesticides are those that are man-made. Soap is a relatively benign example; like diatomaceous earth, liquid soap sprays, properly formulated, can break the skin of many insect species and so kill them by dehydration.

Most of the modern chemical pesticides are synthetic materials, and among them are different kinds, with different levels of toxicity and effectiveness. The first generation of synthetics, developed primarily as a result of Allied chemical warfare research during World War II, were the organochlorines, or chlorinated hydrocarbons. The most famous (or infamous) of these is DDT; but others, some even more toxic, include Chlordane, Aldrin, Endrin, and Dieldrin. These are all nerve poisons. In addition to their effectiveness at killing not only insect pests but other wildlife, they are responsible for numerous human deaths and illnesses. They persist both in the environment and in the tissues of plants and animals (including humans), so that exposure to these extremely toxic chemicals is cumulative over time.

A second group, developed by the Germans for their own nerve gases during World War II are the organophosphates. As problems began to develop with DDT and the others, these new compounds found wide use both on farms and in the garden. Look on the hardware store shelf: you'll see two widely used organophosphate pesticides: Diazinon and Malathion. Diazinon was mentioned briefly in Chapter 1, and is dealt with in more detail in Chapter 9. While they seem not to be as toxic to humans as the organochlorine pesticides, organophosphates are very toxic to bees and other beneficial insects, so their use interferes with the natural balance of the garden.

The third category of synthetic pesticides that interests us here is the carbamates, developed in the late 1940's. Their method of action and toxicity are similar to organophosphates. The major carbamate insecticide used in home gardens is carbaryl, sold under the trade name Sevin. Aldicarb, or Temik, a farm insecticide, was responsible for a highly publicized mass poisoning some years ago after it was illegally applied to a crop of watermelons sold to a supermarket chain.

Prevention of problems is, of course, the hallmark of a good gardener, organic or otherwise. But for most of us, there will be outbreaks of pests and diseases. The most basic form of control is to physically remove pests or diseased parts from the plant, where possible, and destroy them. This is easy with the occasional infected leaf and slow-moving grubs or caterpillars; no disease or pest species has ever developed a resistance to being burned or crushed underfoot. But with tiny, fast-moving flies and beetles, or widespread disease, sprays and dusts are often the only practical method of control.

Under no conditions would I use any of the synthetic insecticides (or fungicides). I use the botanical and mineral controls only if absolutely necessary, as their effect on other species in the garden (including me!) disrupts the balance I seek to maintain. Only the microbial insecticides like *Bacillus thuringiensis* are truly selective—that is, hurt only the pest—and thus fit into an organic program of pest control. As a matter of principle, though, even they should be used only as a last resort, not as a crutch.

PEST CONTROL EQUIPMENT

If you will be using dusts and sprays you will need the equipment to apply them, and safety equipment for yourself. As noted above, many of the pest controls that are considered organic, because of their natural origin, are nonetheless as toxic to humans as they are to the pests they are meant to attack—so you should wear protective clothing while using them. They are preferable to synthetics primarily because they break down quickly into benign materials, and thus have no long-term, unintended side effects on the environment. A paper mask is sufficient, but I wear an actual respirator to be certain; gloves and goggles are not necessary, but still . . . we organic gardeners are a cautious lot. For a discussion of pest control methods, see Chapter 9 and individual vegetable entries in Chapter 10.

The best kind of duster to get is the kind that has a rotating blower to power the dust, some sort of hopper to hold the powder, and a relatively long, adjustable nozzle to direct the dust. If your garden is large, get one that has a shoulder strap, as holding the unit while rotating the crank will quickly tire your hands. The adjustable nozzle is important because you need to get the dust up under the plants where the pests hide; unless you plan to get down on your hands and knees each time you dust, the extension tube on the nozzle comes in handy. For small gardens a trombone type plunger duster will work, but you'll wear out your arms trying to cover any substantial amount of space with one.

The same concerns apply to spray equipment. The little pump-up cans you see at the hardware store may be fine for a small garden, but if yours is bigger than about 500 square feet, go for a backpack sprayer and save yourself a lot of aggravation. There are a number of good models on the market that allow you to pump with one arm and spray with the other. These sprayers work very well for foliar feeding (applying dilute liquid fertilizer to plant leaves) as well as pest control.

MULCHES AND ROW COVERS

One of the most important changes in the materials and methods of gardening over the twenty years since Big Sam last revised *Step by Step* is the development of agricultural plastics. Non-chemical methods of controlling weeds and pests, inexpensive ways to lengthen the growing season, and water-stingy drip irrigation—all have been made possible by plastics technology.

Mulch is an essential part of many gardens, particularly organic gardens; the range of materials used rivals that used for building a compost pile. I have seen just about everything from flat stones and boards, to straw, hay, seaweed, old pieces of carpet, and even thick layers of newspaper used as a mulch. Think about the nature of what you use. Newspaper, for example: black and white newsprint is generally considered safe, though for aesthetic reasons I wouldn't use it in my garden; but if it has colored inks, it may contain significant amounts of toxic compounds. In fact, I use very little mulch at all, as most materials that work well as a mulch are also attractive to slugs, one of the most obnoxious pests of humid climate gardens.

Plastic mulches made from very thin polyethylene (only a few thousandths of an inch thick) provide many of the benefits of an organic mulch without giving slugs a place to hide. Over the course of the season polyethylene will prevent weed growth, preserve soil moisture, and depending on the color of the plastic, raise or lower the temperature of the top few inches of soil. The only benefit of an organic mulch it doesn't offer is the addition of organic matter to the soil. In fact, while polyethylene becomes brittle and shreds easily after only a few months in the sun, the resulting scraps of plastic are nearly indestructible and present a real disposal problem. Newer formulas for making the plastic include additives to make the mulch degrade further, but its essential nature is unchanged. As with other industrial materials, I recommend using this only when absolutely necessary, and with full knowledge of the true costs. Plastic mulches are inexpensive to buy and come in three- or four-foot widths, just right for raised beds, but season-end disposal of the used plastic brings home its environmental cost.

There are film mulches made from recycled fiber, treated with just enough preservative to retard their breakdown until late in the season, when the plants have grown over the row and need no help to shade out sprouting weeds. Unfortunately, they are relatively expensive to use, and the preservatives themselves are not beyond suspicion as contaminants of the soil. If you do use a film mulch—either kind—be sure to put irrigation lines beneath it, or lay it down only when the soil is at optimum moisture levels. Mulch laid on wet soil will keep it soggy throughout the season, but if laid on dry soil, these largely waterproof films will nearly starve the plants for water.

Another recent use for plastic is in covers that can be used to rig "mini-greenhouses" or cloches (plant covers) over growing plants. There are two basic types—conventional clear films and textured, milky white "spunbonded" fabrics—and within each a number of variations in material.

Clear plastics, because of their tendency to overheat in sunny weather, must be somehow supported above the plants, and vented. Irrigation also needs to be considered since most clear covers shed rain. The most common arrangement is a very thin clear cover about a foot or two tall and two feet wide, with parallel longitudinal slits cut in the plastic for ventilation, supported by hoops made from 9-gauge fence wire stuck six to eight inches into the ground on each side of the row. A plastic soil mulch is almost required when using this kind of cover, because the environment under the cover favors weeds as much as it does the plants. All in all, the labor involved in erecting these cover and mulch combinations is barely worth the few weeks' use they get. In milder climates, however, their useful life might be much longer.

Fabric covers don't overheat as easily, and have a number of other advantages over clear covers. First off, they are so lightweight (the lightest weigh in at only a third of an ounce per square yard) that they don't need any support. These "floating" row covers are simply laid over the row, and the edges buried, leaving all the slack fabric loose over the plants. As the crops grow, they pick up the row cover like the foil top on one of those pre-pack pans of popping corn. Since they are porous instead of solid, they allow the passage of both air and water, eliminating the need to provide ventilation and irrigation. But because they accelerate the growth of weeds as well as crop plants, you'll want to put down a film mulch, or periodically remove the cover to cultivate the bed beneath.

Perhaps best of all, floating row covers, if thoroughly sealed with soil around the edges, will keep out all kinds of flying insects. This function (as a pest barrier) alone more than offsets the fact that their manufacture is just as energy-intensive as that of plastic film mulches and row covers.

Pest problems for which most gardeners would spray—with either a synthetic or an organic pesticide—can now be controlled with row covers. For example, a floating row cover placed over broccoli transplants, immediately after setting, is more effective in preventing cabbage root maggot infestations than the insecticide Diazinon; the same row cover will protect all kinds of plants from flea beetles, as well as keeping cucumber beetles from attacking squash family plants until they are large and vigorous enough to outgrow the attack.

Not only can row covers protect from pests and cold, they can provide protection from heat, too. Lath and metal screening, as well as cheesecloth, have long been used to provide shade for cool weather crops when the temperature rises, but new woven plastic meshes are lighter, easier to install, and can be designed for just about any degree of shade. They are made of much more substantial thicknesses of material, and so will last for many seasons, though it still makes sense to store them in the dark during the off season to decrease the rate at which sunlight makes them brittle.

IRRIGATION EQUIPMENT

While all of these plastic-based films are useful to gardeners, even organic gardeners, the same raw materials have also been fabricated into a myriad other forms, including new kinds of irrigation equipment virtually impossible to make out of other materials. Since gardens in most parts of America will require watering to keep the plants in good condition and growing vigorously, this may well be plastic's most important horticultural use.

There are three basic ways of watering, and each uses particular kinds of equipment. First, though, a note on hoses: as with most of a gardener's basic equipment, this is no place to skimp. Cheap, plastic hoses quickly become brittle and stiff, which makes moving them around the garden not only a hassle, but frequently a real danger to the plants. After a few seasons of Christmastime hints, I now have plenty of reinforced rubber hose, ¾ inch in diameter, in a range of different lengths, so that I can use the minimum length for each job. Not only is this neater, but it preserves water pressure for the job at hand: running sprinklers. The performance of any kind of irrigation system is highly pressure-dependent, and there's no sense losing pressure before the water even gets to the business end of the hose.

Water will be supplied to the garden either in the form of overhead sprinklers, or by a system of pipes, tubes, and hoses that drip or ooze water at the base of the plants. Each method has its benefits and its problems. Overhead watering is what most people in the East think of when you mentioning watering. That used to be true in the water-hungry West as well, but with the development of the plastics industry over the past twenty years, on- or under-ground irrigation has become very common, especially in mild areas where the ground doesn't freeze solid in the winter. Drip-and-ooze systems are very efficient in terms of water use; but unless you bury the pipes eight to twelve inches deep, you'll need to remove them each time you prepare or cultivate the garden. They are also hard to clean if they become clogged.

There are two basic kinds of drip-ooze systems, and each is suited for different plants. What I call "discrete interval emitter," or drip irrigation lines, have small metered outlets at regular spacings (usually every foot or foot and a half, though you can make up your own lines from scratch at any spacing you like). This kind works quite well for plants that are spaced fairly far apart from one another, like tomatoes or squash. Each plant has its own emitter and stays well watered, while the weeds and open ground between them stay dry, which saves weeding as well as watering. On the other hand, ooze tubes work better for closely spaced crops, like carrots or spinach. An ooze tube is a porous walled hose, and uniformly oozes water over its entire surface. This moistens the whole area for a foot or two on each side of the hose (depending on soil type).

Purely as a practical matter, it makes sense to have some of each type, but the emitter types are usually made of virgin polyethylene or a related formula, while the ooze tube can be made from recycled auto tires. Since discarded tires are an enormous American landfill problem, and water shortages an increasingly frequent occurrence, using ooze tube irrigation is a satisfying way for a home gardener to solve two problems at once.

The equipment for overhead watering is much more diverse, most of the difference being at the end of the hose. For really large gardens, professional impact sprinkler heads are the way to go. There are some new Israeli-designed, plastic impeller types that perform better, but they are difficult to find. Either kind should be mounted on six-foot-tall supply pipes if you want to get even coverage. That way the water spray is above all but the tallest crops.

Oscillating wand type sprinklers can water square or rectangular spaces. But in my experience the coverage is not really even, and the motion of the spray head on wet ground makes a bit of a mess in open soil. Diffusion-type sprayers may make a lot of sense for small, rectangular, raised bed gardens. Diffusion sprayers don't move, but instead direct a spray of water against a specially shaped

INSTALLING DRIP IRRIGATION

Below: Typical drip emitter.

Above: Lay the irrigation line with an emitter where each plant will be.

Above, left: Put a shovelful of compost on top of each emitter.
Above, right: Anchor end of plastic mulch, roll it out over the row, and *(left)* anchor edges with soil.

Top, left: when ready to plant, cut a two-inch cross at each emitter (visible because of the compost), and *(left)* set a plant in each spot, pruning *(above)* if necessary.

part that causes the stream to splatter in a particular pattern. They, too, are sloppy, but, both of these put water out faster than impact sprinklers.

Some people prefer to water by hand; for a small garden that may be all that's necessary. But you should still choose your spray head with care. The trigger grip types are useful for washing (and for transplanting; see Chapter 8), but are too hard to control for irrigation. The same is true of nozzle types, but even more so. What you should get is a fan spray, which breaks the stream into a wide, relatively narrow band. This slows down the process enough so that the soil has time to soak up the water, and the shape makes it efficient, too. Dedicated hand-waterers like to put a gooseneck extension handle on the end of the hose leading to the spray head, not only to make holding it for extended periods more comfortable, but also so they can get the head down low and spray upward in an arching stream. By doing this they mimic the force of natural rainfall more closely. For details see the irrigation section of Chapter 9.

One last piece of irrigation equipment we find useful is a siphon proportioner. This is a small device that screws into the hose line. By suction it pulls liquid fertilizer from a pail at a constant rate (depending on the water pressure and flow). It makes care of early spring seedlings much easier and allows convenient side dressing of crops later in the season as well. Whatever kind of fertilizer you use, even if not organic, this is an invaluable device for fertilizing seedlings. An anti-backflow device is built in to keep fertilizer or water from traveling back into the sill cock.

The amount of water your garden gets, whether from rain or irrigation, is vitally important to its success. A small, inexpensive rain gauge is all you need to track this successfully; just empty it after each rain (or watering) and keep a running tally. After a few seasons you'll have a good feeling for just how wet or dry your garden is.

TRELLISES

Trellises are an integral part of garden equipment. Many crops are not only more productive but more resistant to disease when grown on supports, whether it's something as simple as a stake in the ground, or expensive store-bought pipe and mesh trellises for trailing and climbing plants. While many garden centers sell inexpensive conical wire tomato cages, most are way too small for an indeterminate tomato, and any tomato plant that is small enough for them probably doesn't need the support. You can make better wire cages from concrete reinforcing wire (available from most building supply stores). The conventional way is to cut a 6-foot section of the 4-foot-wide wire, and bend it around to make a column that surrounds the plant. This should be anchored with a stout stake against wind.

Even so, they don't have much lateral strength, and in a windy location may blow right over once the plants are grown. A better solution, using the same materials, was taught me by a French seed salesman who visited our garden one summer to see the vegetable trial plantings (for which he had supplied the seed). Instead of taking the concrete wire and making a column, you cut the wire to any manageable length and then bend it lengthwise, over the rows, in an arch. This way, as the plants grow they will pass up through the mesh and rest on it, safely off the ground, but absolutely certain not to blow over. An added benefit is that you can drape plastic over these makeshift "quonset" trellises for the first few weeks to encourage early plant growth. Whatever kind of wire you use, and however you use it, though, make sure that the mesh is a minimum of five inches square so you can reach through to harvest any fruit growing inside.

Over the years we've tried a large number of different trellising systems, more or less high-tech, some store-bought and some homemade, and have become convinced that the cheapest all around, most adaptable, least trouble to store and easiest to maintain is made from vertical wooden posts with lengths of electrical conduit running horizontally between them. All that is required for this kind of trellis is a collection of electrical conduit sections and solid, sharpened 2-inch-by-2-inch wooden stakes—two, four, and eight feet long—that can be strung up with untreated twine in various configurations. We use untreated twine so that once the crop is harvested we can simply cut down the lines—with the plants still attached, roll up the whole affair, and throw it on the compost pile. Treated twine will not rot as fast, and puts bio-cides into the compost.

The biggest problem is making the posts last. An organic garden thrives by enhancing what Bill Wolf, of Necessary Trading, an organic garden supply company in Virginia, calls the "decay cycle"— his name for what a scientist would call the nitrogen cycle. Unless we prevent it, the posts themselves are going to be "cycled," which is to say that they're going to rot. Basically, you either have to let them rot and replace them frequently, or treat them in some fashion. Made from a resistant wood like redwood, cypress, cedar, or locust, the posts will last a good number of years. If these woods are native to your area and abundant, that is probably the best choice. Unfortunately, most are much less abundant than they once were, due to overuse, and adding to that overuse will only make matters worse. Redwood and cypress are so rot-resistant they have been widely used for greenhouses and may last a decade or more when used as stakes. Our rot-resistant native wood here in the northeast mountains is cedar, and in the lowlands there is locust. Cedar will last at least three to five years, and locust eight to ten years. You can make all of these last considerably longer by keeping them high, dry, and dirt-free when they aren't being used.

The other strategy is to treat the wood, traditionally by painting it. Keep in mind, though, that the ability of the paint to retard rotting is going to be in direct relation to its toxicity to soil organisms. The moisture-sealing effect of paint helps but is not the major effect; most paints that are really effective for uses of this type contain fungicidal and bactericidal ingredients. Covering the surface of the wood is not nearly as effective as dipping or soaking it, though. Standing the butt end of prepared stakes overnight in a pail of a preservative like Cuprinol (active ingredient: copper naphthenate) allows the preservative to be drawn up inside the wood where the worst damage occurs.

Better yet (from the perspective of rot resistance) is pressure-treated wood. The green stained wood you see at a lumber yard is treated with CCA, and will usually say so right on it, though it may have only the trade name of the process used. The initials stand for chromated copper arsenate, a combination of three heavy metals with fungicidal properties. Freshly treated wood should be handled with gloves to avoid absorbing any of the CCA through your skin. If you cut treated wood, wear a dust mask to avoid breathing the dust, and don't—I repeat do not—burn the scraps. Buy only the kind that has the specification .40 stamped on it; it costs the most, but will last thirty-five to forty years even in constant direct contact with wet ground. Though long-term studies show that the CCA stays in the wood and does not leach into the ground, I will not use treated lumber to make raised beds, particularly for growing food crops.

Avoid the natural-colored treated wood that has been painted, dipped, or pressure-treated with pentachlorophenol (PCP). This is a very dangerous, persistent pesticide and almost invariably contains trace amounts of dioxin, the key contaminant of the Vietnam herbicide Agent Orange. It is unlikely to be available by the time you read this, but even if you do see it, don't buy it, or any preservative that contains it.

If you choose to use treated wood, or even to treat it yourself, keep it to a minimum. When you buy treated wood, or treat it yourself—even by painting—you not only expose yourself to the chemicals involved, but you create demand for them, which means pollution somewhere else: where they are manufactured. Use treated wood only where absolutely necessary, use as little as possible, and make sure it lasts as long as possible.

Electrical conduit is available in 10-foot lengths at hardware and building supply stores and is a relatively inexpensive material for trellises. For shorter runs it can be cut down with a tube cutter or hacksaw. We buy the ¾-inch-diameter size, flatten three inches or so at each end with a hammer, and then drill a ¼-inch hole an inch in from the end.

To erect this kind of trellis is simple. Set the first stake and gently pound it in the ground to a depth of 18 inches or so. Lay the conduit next to it, running along the row; its length will determine the spot to erect the second post. Set the second post so that the top is generally level with the first, then lay up the conduit so that the flattened ends are on top of the stakes and screw down through the holes into the top of the stakes. We use black sheetrock screws, which go in easily and hold well. Once the solid members are fastened together, the trellis is rigged with untreated twine. The first step is to tie a taut line from stake to stake only an inch or so off the ground (make sure it doesn't touch or it will rot prematurely).

From this point the method of rigging will differ according to the crop being grown. For tomatoes and large vining crops like cucumbers or beans, run a single line down from the top bar, cinch it to the bottom cross line, then tie it around the base of the plant with an oversized non-slip knot (a slip knot will tighten up over the course of the season and eventually strangle the plant). Tomatoes need slack left in the line but for the others the vertical lines can be reasonably taut, and horizontal lines can be run every foot or so up the trellis to provide support for lateral branches. In sum, plants that grow by twining, or can be manually twined (like tomatoes) need mostly vertical lines, while those like peas and cucumbers which climb by gripping with tendrils need more horizontal members. Details of how we rig these trellises for each crop are in the respective sections of Chapter 10. In our own garden we construct these trellises in two lengths: five and ten feet. This makes the most efficient use of the conduit given the size of our beds, but there are innumerable other possibilities that might be more applicable to your own garden.

POWER TOOLS

To my mind, power tools are the least important equipment for any garden under 500 square feet. During my ten years as a market gardener I was absolutely dependent on machines to get enough work done to make a living—even a meager one. I started out with 2,500 square feet, double-dug by hand, and kept expanding until I had three acres of raised beds maintained with a tractor-mounted

Clockwise from above: Erecting a string trellis (this one is for tall peas). Set the posts and install top bar; tie bottom string an inch off the ground; add vertical and horizontal cross lines suited to the needs of the crop.

tiller. Along the way I tried many different types of garden machinery. Statistically, one of the most dangerous occupations in the country is agriculture, and the reason (if you forget the pesticide exposure many farmers must endure) is the machinery. Accidents do happen, and to work safely with power machinery requires that one's attention be on safety—on the machine, that is—as much as on the garden.

It is the same basic, humane argument I have against pesticides: when your thoughts have to dwell on protecting yourself and others (including the plants) from accidental injury rather than the task at hand—on that task's meaning and context, and on new ways that it could be done better—you have sold your birthright and become an extension of the technology. For me, that is a cosmic line in the sandy loam over which I do not wish to step; it is one fence which doesn't have greener grass beyond. Even if home-scale tillers, cultivators, mowers, trimmers, shredders, and chippers are not quite as dangerous as their farm-scale relatives, they are every bit as noisy, smelly, and unpleasant to work with. So while we still use the tractor to maintain our test gardens, I've gone back to working by hand in our own family garden, which I want to be a place of quiet contemplation and discovery, a place where I—and my kids—can enjoy the pleasures of the garden itself, not just one more situation where the needs of a machine will determine the pace of my activities.

Thus my favorite tools are hand tools. I like, both conceptually and practically, for a tool to be an extension of me, not the other way around. (More detail in Chapter 9.) I believe that there is a connection between the quality of work, the quality of life, and the way in which each is pursued. The more intimately involved you become with a task, the more carefully it will be done and the richer will be your experience of it and its result. Machines allow us to do more, but let us experience less.

Realistically, as gardeners in a modern industrialized society, we can't avoid some use of power machinery, but I think we ought to be more aware of appropriate use. A small garden can easily be prepared by hand with nothing more than a spade and garden fork; given time, all garden material will compost, without shredding; and given the human energy (which comes, after all, from the food you grow in the garden) the lawn can be cut with a hand mower. That said, let's consider what power tools may be appropriate both to the job at hand and to the planet.

The three machines that we use most frequently are a lawn mower, a line trimmer, and a roto-tiller, in that order. Grass is a good cover for garden paths, and not hard to maintain with a mower. Experts agree that you should use a mulching mower, which shreds the cut grass instead of bagging it, so that it mulches and fertilizes the sod as it cuts. If you do rake up or bag your clippings, use them for compost or mulch in the garden; do not send them to the landfill. Guidelines for using grass clippings are in the composting section of Chapter 5. The size, features, and quality of the machine you buy should be determined by the particulars of your situation.

Light duty line trimmers are ideal for cutting tall growth and for places that a mower can't reach. They can be particularly helpful in harvesting cover crops and battling weeds in waste places too small, rough, or irregular for mowing, like drainage swales, fence lines, and storage areas. The best kinds have a shoulder harness and a pair of handlebars rising out of a straight power shaft; these two features go a long way toward lessening the fatigue that comes with long bouts of trimming. Again, balance your budget against the features that you need.

When Big Sam last revised *Step by Step to Organic Vegetable Growing* in 1971, he discussed the differences between a walk-behind plow and a roto-tiller. The walking plow is now nearly extinct; though there are many kinds of tillers we will limit ourselves to three: lightweight, no-wheel tillers; front-end tillers; and rear-tine tillers.

The newest of the these are the no-wheel tillers. Their design was made possible by the development of truly lightweight two-stroke engines which made it feasible for the machine to be picked up and carried to the garden for use. These differ from conventional tillers in that the tines are one-piece star-shaped wheels made of lightweight steel, which are sharper and rotate much faster. Whether these characteristics are of real value, or are simply requirements of the high-revving two-stroke engines they use I can't say. However, because of their light weight and lack of wheels, they do make more sense for the raised bed gardener—especially one whose beds are timber-framed—because, if the bed is not too wide, they will turn the soil from the edge of the bed without stepping in it, which is one of the major problems of the larger tillers. These units cost about $200 to $400.

The next step up in size is the front-end tiller. They are generally powered by a lawn-mower-sized engine mounted above the tines, which are of the standard alternating left and right "L" shaped configuration. A front-end tiller will usually have a set of wheels behind the tines, so you can tilt the whole machine back and roll it to the garden. Once there, it effectively "walks" on the rotating tines. This kind of tiller is not really effective at breaking sod or turning under heavy cover crops for initial garden preparation, as it tends to walk over anything it can't immediately cut into with its tines. Thus, to make it chop sod you have to hold it back with brute force, which is quite tiring. In an established garden it works well enough; but I have to wonder what the point is then, as cultivation of the average garden is quicker by hand, with a good hoe, and you can work backwards, covering your tracks as you go, which isn't possible with any kind of walk-behind machinery. The last time I checked, prices were in the $400 to $600 range.

The top rung in roto-tillers (short of buying a tractor with a tiller attachment) is the self-propelled rear-tine tiller. With a good, heavy-duty model you can break sod, turn under cover crops, do spring garden preparation—even hill potatoes if your garden is absolutely level and the soil in great condition. I have one and I do use it occasionally, though for the average gardener I think it would make more sense to rent one in the spring for initial preparation, and perhaps again in the fall to turn under the remains of your crops. The $1,000 to $2,000 cost of large roto-tillers is, in my analysis, rarely justified by the amount of work that needs to be done.

Some of the largest components of yard and garden waste—leaves and prunings, as well as spent corn, sunflower and brassica plants—do not rot quickly. My grandfather had an extra compost pile for these kinds of garden waste and so do I. But if you are short of space, leaves and shrub trimmings can be sent through a small chipper-shredder first, and then added to the compost pile. (See the procedures described in Chapter 5.)

If you buy a chipper-shredder, buy it for the job it must do: many of the inexpensive electric models can handle only brush and twigs—the throat of the machine is not large enough to take a broccoli, corn, or sunflower stalk, nor can leaves be efficiently fed into them; other models are designed almost exclusively to shred leaves and have large throats, but will clog immediately if fed solid material; the larger (and more expensive) gas-powered models will handle both, but only if the material is fairly dry and stiff.

Don't be misled by advertisements that show them consuming branches big enough for firewood (that's not what most of your waste is, anyway) into thinking they will handle everything else, too. I have tried both gas and electric models, and none of them effectively chops up spoiled hay, still-green tomato stalks, or pea vines. If you hope to speed up the composting process by first shredding the materials, you'll be disappointed. You'll also spend a lot of time cleaning out the machine. Small electric shredders cost about $200–$500, while gas-powered models will run you $500 to $1,000. Make sure the garden generates enough refuse to justify such an investment. Enough said.

As I implied earlier, my favorite tools are the two I was born with—my hands. One of the great things about hand work is that you don't have to restrict yourself to a single task, as you are almost forced to with a manufactured tool. Your hand is adaptable. Consider weeding: you can pull your fingers through the top inch or so of soil, breaking up the rain-compacted surface, and then, with the same movement of the wrist, but a slight re-alignment of the fingers, smooth it out again. If, in your haste, you bump a newly set transplant, your hand, unlike that fast-moving, sharp-edged hoe—which would shear off a tomato or pepper seedling as if it were merely another weed—recognizes it as a plant to be saved and passes it by. Only your hand, when it meets a rock, can instantly transform itself from a cultivator into a grabber and toss the offender off into the puckerbrush; only your hand, if it uncovers a grub, can quickly perform the best and only completely effective form of pest control—crushing it; only your hand if it accidently disturbs a young seedling, can immediately replace it and firm the soil around its roots. The tool-bound gardener must put down his tool, the farmer must dismount (assuming he even notices the damage) before switching tasks.

Just about the harshest criticism one market gardener can aim at another is that he "farms from the seat of a tractor." What this means is that he doesn't really know what is happening at the plant level—and that is where the garden is alive, at the plant level, at the soil level. Many commercial growers are forced into this position by economic necessity; but as home gardeners we don't face the same pressures.

If you want to really know and enjoy your garden, don't neglect the intimacy that comes with hand work. Get down on your hands and knees, run your hands through the soil, smell it; there are as many living things in one double handful of soil as there are people on earth! Check the undersides of plant leaves for insect eggs instead of just walking by and dousing them with spray, even organic spray. You might find that the time you spend taking care of your garden is a whole lot more satisfying, and a lot less like work.

Another small piece of equipment, which like the rain gauge mentioned earlier, will put you in closer touch with what is actually happening in your garden is a soil and compost thermometer. This is a small, weather-and-break-proof thermometer mounted on a spike that you can stick into the ground (or the compost pile). Soil temperature is critical to germination of seeds, and planting at the proper time removes the need for seed treatment, so for an organic gardener this is nearly an essential piece of equipment. The same thermometer can be used to monitor the temperature swings in your compost pile, which is an excellent gauge of its progress at turning garden refuse into nature's best soil-conditioning fertilizer. As with the rain gauge, after a few years you will gain a practical insight into the actual progress of the seasons in your own garden.

BOOKS

The last type of tool I want to discuss is one of the most important: reference books. I was lucky when I began gardening to have a very knowledgeable gardener in the family. But, even so, I found myself looking beyond the immediate experience Big Sam had accumulated, to the storehouse of horticultural knowledge in the many fine garden books written over the years. Both on general matters and when I need to know something very specific, like the identity of a particular weed or insect, the nutritive content of some available material for the compost pile, or just the recommended spacing for a given vegetable, I consult my library. Even now that I have fourteen years' experience of my own, and have written books on the subject myself, I still find bits and pieces of useful information from reading—raw material for the mental compost pile. In the Bibliography I have included the most valuable books a gardener can own. Some are classics of the organic tradition, some are identification guides, and some help to understand natural cycles like weather. Others bear the mark of a particular intelligence and are valuable for the assortment of tips, tricks, and techniques that the author developed during his or her seasons in the garden. I own them all and wouldn't part with one.

The most important book you can own, though, is your own, and it will, by necessity, start out blank. A garden journal—that records the weather, your garden activities for the day, the names of plants and the conditions under which they were seeded, planted, cultivated, or harvested, and the results of those activities—will, over time, give you the kind of site-specific information that no other source can provide. Within a very few seasons you will know, with as much certainty as is possible, which plants do well in your garden, and when you should seed or set them out for best results. You will know how many plants you want or need to get a given yield, and which spots in your garden are warmer or colder, wetter or drier. And in doing so you will be adding to the accumulated human knowledge of horticulture.

CHAPTER 4

Soil and Stability

> *When we choose the site for our garden we more or less have to take the soil as we find it, whether it be glacial or alluvial, podzolized or lateralized, whether it be Stony Berkshire or Hagerstown Frederick; in all but exceptional cases it will not be perfect, either in plant food content or physical structure. We must take that which is available and make it over into what we want it to be. The good gardener can take the most unprepossessing bit of land and change it from fallow waste into a lush and productive garden.*
>
> *Samuel R. Ogden*

By volume, a productive garden soil is 25 percent air, 25 percent water, 40 to 45 percent minerals, and about 5 percent organic matter, including a whole Noah's Ark of plants and animals ranging from microscopic fungi and bacteria to worms, insects, and burrowing mammals. A double handful of this soil contains more organisms, mostly microscopic, than there are people on earth. Fueled by the heat and light of the sun, this community of soil life has, over eons, evolved complex strategies for extracting from the inanimate 95 percent of the soil all the nutrients life needs to prosper. The inherent fertility of virgin soils, quickly depleted by careless cultivation, was built up by this multitude and is the basis on which human life depends. In this context, our 10,000-year agricultural history is but a recent development, and the hundred-year-old invention of man-made fertilizers hardly a proven practice.

One of the basic principles of organic gardening is to feed the soil and let the soil feed the plants; then the plants can feed you. Man must take his place in the community of organisms drawing its sustenance from, and adding to, the soil. We must leave the soil better, richer, than we found it. From a practical standpoint, there are two parts to the process of creating a continuing healthy, productive garden: first, we must find (or rebuild) a fertile, friable soil; and second, we must maintain that fertility despite the drain of year-in, year-out harvest. Input must equal or exceed output; violate this equation and eventually your garden will decline.

A simplistic understanding of this process often leads clean-handed theoreticians to skip the soil and concentrate on the plant. They assume that to grow a plant you need only apply inputs to some sort of medium that can hold the roots and support the plant, then inoculate it with a seed and stand back while the plant unfolds like one of those little smoke snakes we played with as children. Unfortunately, this reductionist vision assumes that the chemist knows and supplies everything the plant needs; it assumes that if the plant is green and grows, all is well.

The technical basis on which this belief is founded was developed by a German chemist, Justis von Liebig, in the last half of the nineteenth century. He analyzed the chemical constituents of harvested plant tissue, and determined that it was largely composed of three elements: nitrogen, phosphorus, and potassium—the NPK listed today on every bag of purchased fertilizer. That there were hundreds, or maybe even thousands of other constituents, became of little concern; he found that plants responded to applications of simple compounds of these chemicals, particularly nitrogen.

Some seventy years later, another German chemist named Fritz Bosch developed a method of synthesizing ammonia (which is one part nitrogen and four parts hydrogen). He was awarded the Nobel prize in chemistry for this discovery, which made the manufacture of nitrogen economically feasible. Bosch's method was used by the Germans not to feed the world, however, but to try to dominate it— to manufacture the explosives that led Kaiser Wilhelm into World War I. Bosch became deeply involved in warfare chemistry and directed the first use of chemical weapons in 1915. By the end of World War II a whole class of chemical killers had been developed by both sides.

Once hostilities ceased, all this technology was turned toward agricultural use. Ammonia is now injected directly into the soil from tank trucks to provide nutrients that the dead land can't provide, and chemicals that were created to kill our enemies are sprayed on the crops that we ourselves will eat. On the surface, gardening and farming have become a simple matter of inputs and outputs; but beneath the surface is a legacy of death, destruction, and pollution that continues to this day.

The multi-billion dollar yearly agricultural chemical business is a direct result of this profound simplification. The Achilles heel of man's manipulation of nature is the substitution of an economically efficient and profitable simplicity for the (seemingly) inefficient yet stable complexity of natural systems and methods. Today immense amounts of ammonia are synthesized from methane (natural gas) and used to produce synthetic fertilizers. But less than half of that applied to the soil is actually used by the plants; the rest evaporates or leaches into streams, ponds, and groundwater, where it causes nitrate pollution so diffuse and widespread it may be impossible to clean up. Yet someday we will have to pay to correct the damage wreaked on the Earth by the widespread, ill-advised acceptance of this Faustian bargain.

Of course it's possible to produce vegetable crops with chemicals alone, under artificial conditions—in fact it's routinely done in hydroponic greenhouses. But while these vegetables may look normal, they lack some of the complex constituents of vegetables grown in a healthy, fertile soil. A recent report in the *New York Times* told of new research which revealed that the plant pigment beta-carotene (responsible for the orange color of carrots), could help prevent cancer and heart disease. Beta-carotene, which is a precursor of vitamin A, is an ingredient in some over-the-counter vitamin pills; but the researcher who reported the findings recommended eating foods rich in beta-carotene rather than taking the vitamin pills. Why? Because beta-carotene is only one of about five hundred "carotenoids," the larger group of related compounds to which it belongs. Other research had convinced him that combinations of different carotenoids are much more effective than beta-carotene alone. Carrots (and other foods like melons, kale, collards, winter squash, and pumpkins) contain a whole range of these carotenoids; the vitamin supplements, while they can be profitably manufactured, do not.[4]

The richer and more complex the soil in which plants are grown, the better they are able to find what they need to create a more complex and therefore more nutritious root, shoot, or fruit. The outputs cannot be any better than the inputs once the natural fertility of virgin soil, on which the plants draw, is exhausted, and the hidden but essential quality of the crops can only drop when they must rely solely on the NPK supplements they're fed from a bag. To believe otherwise is horticultural hubris.

So let's take a look at N, P and K, what each does both in the plant and in the environment, and then at some of the other essential nutrients that are left out of the convenient modern "fast food" fertilizers, along with the non-nutrient elements necessary for plant growth.

Nitrogen—the N of N-P-K—is the most important plant nutrient, because it is an essential building block of chlorophyll (the green pigment in leaves without which photosynthesis, and therefore plant growth, cannot occur) as well as a number of other enzymes and hormones central to a plant's growth processes. It is also the most likely nutrient to be deficient. Its source is the air we breathe, and it exists in the soil only as a byproduct of the soil's teeming microbial life, rather than as part of the earth's mineral store of nutrients. When nitrogen is deficient, plants concentrate it in their youngest leaves, so the older, large leaves turn pale, and in severe cases may wither and fall. Ninety-nine percent of total soil nitrogen is in the organic matter, both living and dead, that the organic gardener is primarily concerned with, and only about one percent in the soluble inorganic forms found in most quick-fix fertilizers.

Because nitrogen is so essential to plant health, and its supply so fleeting, most plants will consume it far beyond their needs in an orgy of greed, throwing off their own metabolism in the process. Delayed maturity, uneven ripening, and overly succulent growth are all signs of a nitrogen excess. An excess of nitrogen will lead to harvest problems as well. The harvest taken from plants grown with too much nitrogen will not store well, and is likely to be low in vitamins A and C, as well as high in accumulated nitrates, which are toxic.

In the garden environment, nitrogen is in a constant state of change and movement, cycling perpetually through the air, soil, water, and the bodies of plants and animals. It enters the soil in rainwater, or through bacterial extraction from the air (discussed in more detail later in this chapter), and in the form of applied fertilizers, either organic or chemical; it can be lost back to the air through volatilization, or washed away by rain and irrigation water; otherwise it is available for use by soil bacteria, plants, and the animals that eat them, and then recycled upon their death and decomposition.

Phosphorus, represented by the letter P in discussions of chemistry, is also critical to plant growth. While nitrogen fuels the plant, phosphorus is essential to the distribution and storage of that energy in the form of sugars and starches. Without sufficient phosphorus, plants again will be stunted, though the leaves instead of being pale will be purplish from the accumulated sugars created by photosynthesis that cannot be utilized in the absence of sufficient phosphorus. It differs from nitrogen, however, in that phosphorus is a soil mineral, and also in that it stays put. Phosphorus moves through the garden environment primarily by being used by plants and animals and then recycled in the form of compost or manure, though most manures are relatively low in phosphorus.

Phosphorus is usually added in the form of mined phosphate rock, bone meal, or phosphate fertilizers made from them by treatment with sulfuric acid. Excessive phosphorus is rarely a problem, since nitrogen is more easily absorbed by plants. Where uptake is excessive, though, it can affect a plant's ability to take up other necessary elements that the plant needs in trace amounts. Once applied, phosphorus will stay put, as it bonds easily with many other soil minerals like aluminum (in acid soils) or calcium (in alkaline soils). Because it becomes "tied" up at high or low pH levels (which we will discuss shortly), phosphorus is much more easily available to plants if the soil pH is kept close to neutral. Organic gardeners prefer to use phosphate rock for building this important soil component, since the nutrients are released slowly over time, by the action of soil microbes breaking down its compound forms.

Third of the big-three nutrients is potassium, listed as K (for the Latin name *Kalium*). It regulates the processes of plant food creation, transportation, and storage that is fueled by nitrogen and facilitated by phosphorus. Unlike nitrogen and phosphorus, it is not a constituent of plant cells themselves; rather, it is part of the fluid that fills plant tissue, contributing to the ability of stems and leaves to hold themselves upright. Biennial root crops like carrots and beets are also dependent on potassium to complete the conversion of sugar to starch that makes overwintering of the root and subsequent seed production the following season possible.

Its cycle in the environment is similar to that of phosphorus, though it is not long held in soil organic matter; it is, however, more available in most manures and in compost made from fresh green materials. While it is mobile within the plant, potassium does not leach, or wash out of the soil, readily; when applied in the form of mined rock powder (such as greensand or granite dust) it is available for long-term use by plants. Other good organic sources are green manure crops such as ryegrass and buckwheat (discussed below) and wood ash, which also contributes a small amount of phosphorus. It is possible to apply too much potassium—especially in small gardens—if you use large quantities of wood ash; this may then lead to a phosphorus or magnesium deficiency.

Three so-called secondary nutrients are now given more credit for the health of growing plants than at first thought: calcium, magnesium, and sulfur. Sulfur never used to be a problem, and still isn't for organic gardeners. Even old-time synthetic fertilizers contained sufficient sulfur (as an impurity) for most plant needs. But newer, more refined fertilizers are "purer," and so sulfur deficiencies have become more of a problem. Deficiency symptoms are similar to those of nitrogen, with which it works in the synthesis of amino acids and proteins that the plant needs. In most manures, composts, and cover crops, sulfur is present in the proper proportion to nitrogen. (More on this shortly.)

Magnesium is the central element in chlorophyll, to which the nitrogen is chemically bound. It performs a function similar to that of hemoglobin in human blood; without it the plant will be anemic. It also relates to phosphorus the way sulfur does to nitrogen. It is sufficiently important to humans that even when a deficiency causes no appreciable damage to plants, their value as food will be lower due to its lack. Unfortunately, potassium, magnesium, and calcium all compete for uptake by plants, and unless care is paid to keep them in balance, deficiencies can result. Fortunately, most composts supply ample magnesium. The simplest solution when starting a new garden in areas with acid soils is to use a high magnesium, or dolomitic, limestone, thus adding both magnesium and calcium at the same time.

Finally, calcium is important because of the critical role it plays in the structure of cell walls, especially at the growing tips of both roots and tops. But calcium deficiency problems with maturing plants, such as tipburn in lettuce and cabbage, or blossom-end rot in tomatoes, can exist despite relatively abundant calcium in the soil, due to problems with its extraction from the soil by the plant. Specific solutions to these problems are discussed in the individual plant entries of Chapter 10.

A number of other nutrients are needed by the plants in your garden in very small amounts, and are thus called micro-nutrients. A balanced program of soil enrichment and maintenance (as outlined over the next few chapters) pretty much guarantees that none will be seriously deficient, but if in doubt, kelp meal can be used as a micro-nutrient fertilizer to establish starter amounts of a wide range of different elements. Made from dried seaweed, which has drawn its substance from the diverse ingredients of the world's oceans, kelp meal is rich in minor nutrients. Just a partial list of the makeup of dry seaweed includes, beyond nitrogen, phosphorus, and potassium: boron, copper, iron, manganese, molybdenum, zinc, calcium, iodine, a range of sulfates, and perhaps most important of all, up to 25 percent of alginic acid, which stimulates biological activity in the soil and improves soil structure.

That is the key to avoiding nutrient deficiencies in an organic program of soil building: balance. As we've seen, the excessive buildup of one essential nutrient often leads to the displacement of another; blind feeding of the plants in the garden often leads to impoverishment of the garden itself, and in the long run, poorer plants.

GARDEN MAKING

The first step in starting any new garden is to get the soil into an easily workable condition. Most vegetable species grow best in a soil that is near neutral in acidity, loose in texture, able to hold significant moisture without becoming soggy, and free of competition from the roots of established trees. Even small rocks and roots should be removed if possible; they are great protectors of weed seedlings: every place the hoe hits a rock and skips during cultivation, a weed is sure to appear.

Immediately after breaking ground for a new garden you should test the soil. You can buy kits to do this, or buy a soil sample pouch at a garden center and send a sample of your soil to a state laboratory for testing. Within a few weeks the lab will send back a detailed report on the soil's current nutrient levels, with a recommendation for fertilizers. Unfortunately, most soil labs ignore organic materials and offer their advice solely in terms of chemical fertilizers. If you will be using bagged organic fertilizers, you will find their NPK levels printed on the bag. If you will be using "raw materials," however, you'll need to know the nutrient content of various organic materials like manure, leaves, blood meal, seaweed, and rock powders.

The accompanying chart lists NPK levels of these materials based on their weight. Ideally, they should be composted first, and the compost used for enriching the soil. (Composting is covered in the next chapter.) But this is not always convenient, or even possible. Very bulky materials like hay, straw, seaweed, or leaves can be used as a mulch first, and allowed to break down partly before being turned under to complete their decomposition. Fresh animal manures can be spread and turned under immediately so their nutrients are caught in the soil rather than being lost to the air while the pile waits for other materials to arrive; just don't plant crops for

NUTRIENT COMPOSITION OF COMMON MATERIALS

Material	% Nitrogen	% Phosphorus	% Potassium	Comments
Alfalfa Hay	2.5	0.5	2.1	Use as mulch first
Apples (pomace)	0.2	0.2	0.2	
Blood Meal	15.0	1.3	0.7	Good for side dressing.
Bone Meal	4.0	21.0	0.2	
Chicken Manure (fresh)	1.6	1.5	0.9	Compost, or delay planting at least 3 wks.
Colloidal Phosphate	0.0	2.0	2.0	Supplies calcium, too.
Cow Manure (fresh)	0.3	0.2	0.1	Compost, or delay planting at least 3 wks.
Cornstalks (fresh)	0.3	0.1	0.3	
Cottonseed Meal	7.0	2.5	1.5	Acidic
Grass Clippings (fresh)	1.2	0.3	2.0	Mix with dry material when composting to avoid nutrient loss.
Granite Dust	0.0	0.0	4.0	
Greensand	0.0	0.0	5.0	High in trace minerals.
Horse Manure (fresh)	0.7	0.3	0.6	Compost, or delay planting at least 3 wks.
Dried Kelp	1.5	0.5	2.5	High in trace minerals.
Beech Leaves	0.7	0.1	0.7	Mix w/ other materials.
Maple Leaves	0.7	0.1	0.8	Mix w/ other materials.
Oak Leaves	0.7	0.1	0.5	Very acidic.
Pig Manure (fresh)	0.5	0.3	0.5	Compost, or delay planting at least 3 wks.
Pine Needles	0.5	0.1	0.0	Very acidic.
Rabbit Manure (fresh)	2.4	1.4	0.6	Compost, or delay planting at least 3 wks.
Rock Phosphate	0.0	3.0	0.0	
Salt Marsh Hay	1.1	0.3	0.8	Use as mulch first.
Sawdust	0.2	0.0	0.2	Compost first.
Seaweed (varies)	1.7	0.8	4.9	High in trace minerals.
Sheep Manure (fresh)	0.7	0.3	0.9	Compost, or delay planting at least 3 wks.
Straw	0.7	0.2	1.2	Use as mulch first.
Wood Ash	0.0	1.5	7.0	Do not over-apply.
Worm Castings	0.5	0.5	0.3	High in organic matter.

at least a month so the manure has a chance to break down. Materials like rock phosphate, greensand, wood ash, or blood and bone meals can be added at any time and mixed into the top few inches of the soil. They can also be used to fortify a compost pile.

To make sure that your test sample represents actual conditions at the plants' root level, take three or four samples from around the whole plot. Don't take a sample from any place that was recently fertilized or limed; it will distort the results. To get a clean sample from root level, take a shovelful of soil out of the ground and set it aside, then slice another section, only an inch or so thick, from the side of the hole. With a pen knife or scrap of wood, scrape away the top inch or so, and take your sample from an inch or two wide vertical section of what remains. Mix that small bit with the other samples from around the area to be tested; all roots, leaves, rocks, and other material should be removed, and the test sample should be dry and fully pulverized before mailing.

One of the most critical aspects of a soil test is the pH report, which tells you if your soil is overly acid or alkaline. This is important, because all nutrients are more or less available depending on the pH balance. On a scale of 0–14, each whole number of the scale represents a tenfold difference from the next number. Thus, taking the number 7 as neutral (which it is on the pH scale), a pH of 6 indicates that the soil is ten times as acidic, while a pH of 8 indicates it is ten times as alkaline. The soil report will usually include a recommendation of how much lime (to raise the pH) or sulfur (to lower the pH) should be added, and in what form. Keep in mind: if the pH of your soil is more than two points away from neutral, you should break the application of lime or sulfur into two or more applications to avoid shocking the resident soil life with too radical a change.

Big Sam felt that once an ideal pH of 6.0–6.8 (at which the widest range of nutrients is optimally available) had been established, an ongoing program of manure and compost applications would remove the need for any further attention to soil pH. Except for special conditions, the latest research backs up this belief. Only if your soil is of the most extreme acid or alkaline nature, or your garden is subject to serious acid rain and snowfall, should an ongoing program of pH balancing be necessary.

Soil Building   Ideally, you should start preparing a new garden a year ahead and cover-crop the area for a season before making it into a garden. Cover-cropping means growing a vigorous, thickly sown crop of soil-improving plants to choke out existing (usually undesirable) plants. The principle can be adapted to any region by changing the crops used. Just make sure to keep the ground covered continuously with fast-growing crops so the weeds don't have a chance to grow. We cover-cropped our garden one plot at a time until, after four years, the entire garden had been cleansed of weeds and the soil greatly improved. During the first season after cover-cropping we've found weeding almost entirely unnecessary until mid-summer and—if we are diligent about maintenance—minimal thereafter. As an example, here is the plan we used:

Start by roto-tilling or digging the ground as early in spring as possible and immediately sow annual ryegrass; you don't need to worry right away about smooth soil, or removing the rocks and

BASIC SOIL BUILDING Cover crops enhance the natural soil community and build the organic matter that is the heart of organic gardening.

roots, though you might as well grab the ones you see. Once the last frost date arrives, turn under the annual ryegrass and immediately plant buckwheat. When the buckwheat starts to flower (in about a month) turn it under, and plant buckwheat again to make sure that the ground is kept covered and weed species don't have a chance to reestablish themselves. At some point during this first summer do a soil test to determine any gross deficiencies or imbalances in the soil.

If the first planting is very weak because the soil is totally depleted, you may want to manure the plot early on. If so, do the test first, and keep track (in your garden journal) of how much manure you added. Keep replanting buckwheat until Labor Day, then switch back to annual ryegrass. Before tilling and planting this time, though, remove all the roots and rocks that have come to the surface, and add any soil amendments found to be necessary by the soil test; they work best if they have the winter to break down. In cold areas like ours, the annual ryegrass will grow quickly in the cool fall weather to prevent any of the original cover from returning, then it will winterkill, leaving a thick mulch of dead foliage on the ground for the winter, protecting it from erosion but preventing regrowth of weeds.

In the spring, roto-till, and the garden is ready to plant. In warmer areas, where the annual ryegrass doesn't die off, you'll need to wait up to three weeks after spring tilling to let it decompose before planting your crops.

This method works for any size of garden, and can be accomplished with hand tools as well as with a roto-tiller; just mow the cover-crop with a string trimmer or scythe before turning it under. Start in one corner of the plot and work across, taking small slices with the full depth of a spading fork. Lift the soil just a bit above the ground, give a quick twist while dropping the fork out from under its load, then raise the tines quickly again, slapping the bottom of the falling soil with the tines. That will break it up nicely. Any clods that remain can be swiped sideways with the slightly offset edge of the fork and pulverized in place. If you come across any rocks in the process (in Vermont we always do!) toss them to the side of the garden or into a wheelbarrow.

Some cover crops—called green manures—are used to add nutrients to the soil as well as to choke out undesirable plants. This can happen in two ways. One is to turn under young, vigorous growth, instead of waiting until the tissues harden as the crop begins to flower; this young growth breaks down quickly and stimulates the biological activity of organisms in the soil; these then break out and release nutrients contained in the mineral portion of the soil. This is feeding the soil by feeding the community of decomposers—plants and animals that live on decaying organic matter—whose activities increase the fertility of the soil in a qualitative way that no chemical brew can match.

Earthworms alone can number up to half a million an acre (in healthy soils, rich in organic matter), and the total mass of their bodies is equal to the weight of all the power tools in the average gardener's garage combined, including the roto-tiller, lawn mower, chainsaw, snowblower, even a garden tractor. But the earthworm is much more powerful for its size than any of these—able to move stones up to fifty times its own weight as it burrows through the soil, sometimes to a depth of twelve feet or more. And earthworms move more earth: the amount of soil displaced by their activity is up to five tons per acre per year, according to one USDA researcher.[5]

Such soil is not merely moved from one place to another, either, but digested by the worms as they "eat" their way through the earth. This is of consequence because most soils in this country contain far more mineral nutrients than are accounted for in a soil test. The soil test reports only *available* nutrients, while most of the resident soil nutrients are bound up (until released) in stable chemical compounds. The "castings" left behind by earthworms are more than five times as rich in nitrogen, phosphorus, and potassium than the surrounding soil, and their tunnels represent a significant source of drainage and aeration for the soil in which they live.

How much locked up fertility are we talking about? Let's use nitrogen as an example since it is the single most frequently added nutrient. In the two million pounds of soil covering the top six inches of an acre of healthy, fertile ground, there will be up to 100,000 pounds of organic matter, of which, say, 5 percent will be mineral nitrogen, or 5,000 pounds. If only five percent of this can be made available, that amounts to 250 pounds of nitrogen per acre, well above the requirements of even the hungriest vegetable crops. So by turning under succulent growth, which raises the organic matter level and makes food available for the soil organisms (that are actually the majority inhabitants of planet Earth), we help them take the stored fertility of the soil and pay it out in a form readily available to the roots of the crops we wish to grow. Caustic chemical fertilizers and toxic pesticides upset this soil community. In diminishing its capacity for releasing the inherent mineral fertility of the soil, we partially create the need for quick-acting soluble nitrogen fertilizers in a self-fulfilling prophecy of dependence and depletion.

Then there is the quarter of soil volume which is air, itself more than three-quarters nitrogen. The second way that green manures can add nutrients to the soil is by capturing this soil-bound atmospheric nitrogen. Legumes are plants that have the ability to form a symbiotic relationship with a group of soil bacteria known as *rhizobia*. Beans and peas are legumes, as are clover, alfalfa, and vetch. The *rhizobia* bacteria, of which there are many species specific to particular legumes, live on the roots of the host legume and form small colonies called nodules. They are able to draw nitrogen from the air for their own nourishment and store it in nitrate form, which is just how plants like their nitrogen. By planting a legume crop that has been "inoculated" with the proper strain of *rhizobia* and then by turning it under after the nodules have had time to form, the gardener can convert atmospheric nitrogen into nitrates, and do so essentially for free, beyond the cost of seed and inoculant.

With creative planning you can accomplish both aims of green manuring at once. Here in the Northeast, a mixture of winter rye and hairy vetch will provide both succulent green matter to stimulate biological activity and fix atmospheric nitrogen. Whatever the condition of the land when you begin, cover crops and green manures will help you get a new garden off to a good start. For their use as part of an ongoing fertility and weed control program, see Chapter 6.

If it's already fall when you are ready to establish your new garden, you can get a head start on the following spring by manuring, liming, and then turning over the proposed garden area and covering it with a single large sheet of black plastic; that keeps the soil in total darkness so the weeds can't come back. Weight down the plastic with rocks and boards, to keep the wind from blowing it away. If possible, do a soil test beforehand. If that isn't possible, five pounds of lime and a few bushels of manure per hundred square feet is a good rule-of-thumb for new gardens here in the East. (If you can't get manure, use bagged organic fertilizer at the labeled rate.) Try to do the preparation early enough in the fall so that the existing plant cover will try to re-grow and thereby wear itself out; by spring you'll have bare ground to start with.

If it's springtime and you can't wait a year—and the spot you've chosen is currently in lawn or pasture—you can clear a spot and make a garden right away. Here's how: cut out a strip of sod the

GARDEN MAKING, STARTING THE PREVIOUS FALL

Turn over the existing ground.

Above left: Add any amendments, based on soil test. *Above right:* Once soil is prepared, lay a continuous sheet of black plastic to prevent growth of weeds. *Right:* Anchor the edges well with stones or boards.

GARDEN MAKING, RIGHT AWAY *Clockwise from above:* Use a straight back garden spade to cut out a strip of sod; pry up an edge of the strip with the spade; and then roll up the sod, cutting loose the roots as you go with a utility knife.

length of your proposed garden with a sharp-edged, flat-bladed spade, then work the spade under the edge and roll it back like carpet, taking the thinnest layer possible. I like to do this on my hands and knees, using a dull, broad-bladed field knife to cut loose the roots as I go. That allows me to roll the sod up neatly without it pulling apart. It's a bit dirtier this way, but it's less work.

Once the sod has been removed, you can use it somewhere else around the place to patch a spot of lawn or pasture that isn't doing well; or use it instead of cinder blocks to make the sides of your first compost pile. Just be sure to stack the sods with their roots face-up so they won't take root and start growing again.

The biggest problem I've seen with new gardens cut out of existing sod is that insect pupae in the soil will attack the newly sown plants when they awake; this is not surprising since you've taken away the food source that was there when they went into hibernation, and they wake up hungry. The second big problem is re-sprouting of perennial plants from their roots. In one early garden of ours we lost 180 out of 200 tomato transplants to cutworms. Then we had to abandon the rest when they were swamped with witch-

grass that sprouted from rhizomes we left behind when we prepared the ground.

So if the spot you've chosen for your garden is an old pasture overgrown with perennial grasses, or brush and saplings, be sure to clear out not only the roots and rocks, but every single rhizome, grub, cocoon, and cutworm you see, or the grass and shrubbery will begin sprouting right in the middle of your garden and once the cutworms get to work, that's all that will be left. Don't worry, but do be thorough; you'll be glad you were.

Especially if the area is infested with perennial grasses like quack grass or witchgrass—and you don't want to lose a season choking them out with cover crops—you really should sift the top six inches of soil through a piece of ½-inch hardware screening to be sure you've gotten all the grass rhizomes; the tiniest shred is a near guarantee of eventual problems. If you put these weeds on your new compost pile, be sure to bury them deep enough with manure or other material so that their shoots can't make it to the surface. I would recommend—no matter how much of a hurry you are in—that you grow a choke-out cover crop on at least a quarter of your garden-to-be; that way you've got a start on a good rotation, and if you keep at it you'll beat your weed problem once and for all within the course of four seasons (to cover all four quarters).

Just about the worst soil condition for establishing a new garden is the compacted spoil left over from the construction of a new house. If you are present when the excavation is done, make sure that the machine operator puts the topsoil aside and then replaces it after all the other work is done; otherwise you may be left with a surface layer that is actually mineral subsoil, which on its own is entirely unable to support a decent garden. If that happens, you can still establish a fertile, thriving garden, but it will be a lot more work.

The classic method of soil improvement for small gardens—which can make virtually any soil productive within a season—is called double digging, or "bastard trenching." It's your best hope if you are starting with any hard, solid soil. Though a lot of work, it's worth the effort for a small garden. Wait until the soil is moist, but neither very wet, nor very dry, and you'll have the least work and do the most good. This is especially true of clay or "adobe" soils; when dry they are nearly impossible to penetrate, and if you work them while wet, they are goopy, but then dry into brick-hard clods.

First remove the plant cover, if any. Then start at one edge of the proposed plot and, with a spade, dig a trench along one side, about eight inches to a foot deep, and set the soil aside, either on a tarp or in a wheelbarrow. You'll need it at the end of the process to fill in the final trench you dig. Then loosen the soil in the bottom of the trench with a spading fork by jamming it down into the subsoil and working the handle back and forth in every direction. If you can, physically lift the soil and drop it back into the bottom of the trench to break it apart. With poor soils, especially construction spoil, it helps to add some compost, manure, or other organic matter to the loosened material in the bottom of the trench. Next, remove another strip of soil to widen the trench, break it up, and place it on top of the loosened soil and manure in the bottom of the first strip you've dug, without inverting the layers. Then loosen the bottom of the second strip in the same way, and continue the process until you reach the other side of the bed. Take the soil you removed from the very first strip to fill in the last area of the trench.

The results of the soil test will tell you whether to add various amendments to the soil to carry your garden through the first year (while you establish your compost piles). When adding a number of different organic amendments, alternate light and dark colored materials so you don't lose track of where you've spread what. Almost all soils, regardless of their condition, will benefit from the addition of organic matter. Whether in the form of compost (often called the black gold of organic gardeners) grass clippings, spoiled hay, rotted leaves, even shredded yard waste or manure, organic matter helps

DOUBLE DIGGING *From left:* Dig a trench one spade wide along the edge of the plot to be prepared and put the soil on a tarp or in a barrow. Loosen the soil in the bottom of the trench, and add any compost, manure or other amendments. Dig a second, parallel trench, placing the soil from it into the first. Repeat this process for the entire width of the plot, and fill in the final trench with the soil from the barrow or tarp.

lighten heavy soils and provides precious water-holding capacity for light ones. If you didn't have a chance to build up this important constituent of healthy garden soil by cover-cropping and green manuring, you can add it now. Just don't use fresh manure on ground where you'll be planting immediately; it needs a minimum of three weeks to break down, and a month or two is better. Ideally, you should compost manure before spreading it on the garden—or apply it in the fall before planting your winter cover crop, turn it under, and let it mellow.

Improving Drainage   The one kind of soil organic matter can't help directly is a cold, sour (that is acidic), and poorly drained soil. Organic matter will only help once the drainage has been improved. Like double digging, or removing large roots and rocks, this can be a significant amount of work, but it only has to be done once, and it pays permanent dividends; for a small garden none of these tasks need take more than a weekend, and the benefits will be felt for years after.

There are really only two ways to dry a soggy soil: raise the garden or lower the water table. Building raised beds, as discussed in Chapter 2, may be the simplest solution for a small garden, say up to a thousand square feet. Use whatever materials you have at hand to build retaining walls for the growing beds, then shovel the topsoil from path areas into them, adding whatever amendments are necessary along the way. Put down a weed barrier and thick mulch in the pathway. Try to get the mulch level deep enough so that even in wet weather the surface of the path is dry; if possible design the paths so that they act as drainage channels to let surface water run off, away from the garden. The retaining walls will probably need to be eight to twelve inches tall at least, with the soil mounded above that another few inches. Less than that may not solve a serious soggy soil problem.

We have a plot in our outer garden that is in a slough on the saddle of the hill with a hardpan layer about eighteen inches below the surface. After a heavy rain, the whole slough fills up like a subterranean lake, and though you won't see standing water on the surface, the soil in that whole section is like soup for weeks afterward. Our first attempt to put a garden in that spot involved waiting three years for a drought that dried it out enough to get in with a tractor-mounted roto-tiller, chop up the sod, and then form the whole section into a series of high beds. Unfortunately, the amount of water we found we had in that spot was enough to fill the paths

To beat drainage problems, build raised beds *(left)* or lower the water table by installing drainage tile *(below)*.

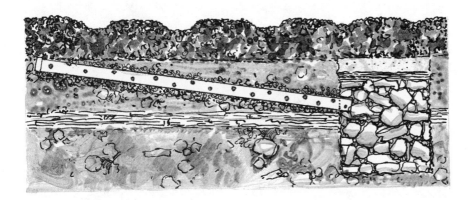

up to the surface of the beds, at which point it cut gullies across them and made a bee line for the next saddle down the hill.

To solve the problem we bulldozed a small pond on that lower level, and dug a two-feet-deep drainage ditch the length of the saddle, passing right through the center of the low spot and then spilling over the uphill bank of the pond. After a rain the outlet pipe runs like someone had turned on a faucet.

The first step in drainage work is to figure out where the water is coming from, and at what level. Both surface runoff from rain or snowmelt, and sub-surface runoff, where water travels horizontally on top of an impenetrable layer of subsoil, can cause problems for your garden.

Surface water that runs across the garden during rainy weather may look awful but is relatively easy to prevent. Simply put in a diversion ditch on the uphill side of the garden, sloping downhill and off to the side, around the edge of the garden. Make sure the water has someplace good to go; not just off your property and onto someone else's, but into a water course, drain, or sewer. A simple diversion ditch can be made with a standard round-bladed shovel. Skim back the sod (if any) along the course to which you want to divert the runoff, and flip it temporarily on to the uphill side. Then deepen the ditch from top to bottom so that it drops at least an inch

Surface water can be diverted by digging a shallow swale *(above)*, but underground drainage problems may require more significant trenching *(below)*. Drainage tile should be covered with soil barrier to prevent clogging.

for every ten feet of length. Mound the soil you remove along the downhill side in a low berm, and when you're done, take the sod you removed at the beginning and put it upright on the top. Soon it will root itself in the berm on the downhill side, firming the berm against erosion and giving you a simple, long-term solution to surface water diversion.

For really serious subsoil drainage problems you should call in a professional. But if you just want to protect a relatively small area, and you're willing to do a little heavy work, here's how. You can rent a trenching machine if you need to dig a long trench, but short trenches can be easily dug with a special Dutch spade that has a long narrow blade—only about six inches wide and eighteen inches long. When digging with a trenching spade you should take very small slices with each spadeful, working your way backwards up from the outlet at the bottom, so that any water present in the ditch can escape instead of interfering with your digging. Just rough in the trench on the first pass, then get the precise slope as you work your way back down to the outlet; it should have a slope of roughly half an inch for every ten linear feet, so that the water can flow freely within the pipe you'll install. Dig down to the full depth you can reach with the spade.

Once the trench is finished it should be five or six inches wide at the bottom and at least 18 inches deep. If the total length of all your trenches combined is less than forty feet you might as well use the standard white drain tile from the lumber yard. It comes in ten-foot sections and four inches in diameter and is fairly rigid, with one end flared so that the pieces fit together. When laying rigid drain tile (as it is known) put the flared end downhill so it doesn't collect soil. Be sure to buy a cap for the top of each run to keep soil out, and a grate for the outlet to keep animals from entering. For runs longer than about fifty feet, so called "elephant tile" is better. It is much thinner and less expensive than the rigid and easier to work with, though it doesn't withstand crushing as well and thus can't be used where the pipe must run under a driveway or road.

You'll also need some drain fabric, which is a synthetic soil barrier very similar to landscape fabric or weed barrier cloth. For drainage get the eighteen-inch-wide size; you'll need enough to wrap up the whole length of drain. Lay the soil barrier loosely across the top of the trench and either assemble the rigid pipe or unroll the elephant tile along the trench, on top of the cloth. Then wrap the cloth over the pipe or tile, overlapping the excess, and carefully drop the whole assembly into the bottom of the trench where it should fit snugly. Fill the trench back in and you're done. At its shallowest point under the garden the drainage tile should be at least a foot beneath the surface so that you won't hit it during spring preparation of the garden.

You can improve the performance of this kind of drain by adding crushed gravel (half-inch is a good size) around the pipe. You'll need wider drain fabric to completely surround the gravel and the pipe, at least three feet across. Line the trench with the fabric, shovel in about six inches of gravel, lay the pipe, then cover it with another six inches of gravel and cover it by folding the excess fabric carefully over the top. When replacing the soil make sure that no gaps are left in the fabric for soil to work its way down into the gravel and clog it.

CHAPTER **5**

Food for the Garden

In my experience, well-rotted manure will need nothing added to make it suitable for garden use. If you can get sufficient quantities of this . . . you are all set for your garden. If you cannot, then you will have to resort to a compost pile. In any event, a compost pile is a sensible and even necessary adjunct to a garden, for it means the conservation of waste and a reduction in the expense of operation.

The difference between manure and compost is simple: in the first instance, an animal feeds on vegetation and passes the material through its body, extracting nourishment in the process. Thus the waste consists of organic material which has been fragmented and treated with body juices, then subjected to further decomposition due to the complicated action of oxygen and bacteria while the manure is stacked in piles. Compost is, in general, made in the same way, with the exception that one step in the process is omitted, that of passing through the body of some animal. The end products are highly similar and, for our purposes, nearly identical.

Samuel R. Ogden

In its essence, all soil improvement involves the concentration of nutrients. Manure represents, in concentrated form, all the plants eaten by the animal that produced it; compost and leaf mold concentrate the nutrients from a variety of plants growing over a large area into a soil-like material. Cover crops, which grow by scavenging the depths of the soil for nutrients, concentrate all that goodness in the top few inches of the soil when we turn them under. In the last chapter we discussed this in terms of initial garden making; in this chapter we will cover the ongoing maintenance of fertility in the garden.

MANURE

A quick review of the table of nutrients in the previous chapter will show that there are significant differences in the nutrient level (and balance) of fresh animal manure. Rotted manure—that which has been allowed to sit, out of the rain yet moist and sufficiently packed down to exclude air—is usually richer by weight (as it loses much of its weight during the rotting process) and more stable in terms of its nutrients, since micro-organisms have already had a chance to do some of their work. While the balance of nutrients in manure is relatively good, improper use or storage can cause a significant loss of nitrogen.

However, it isn't necessary to store manure or wait for it to rot. Fresh manure can be spread directly on a new garden; if turned under immediately, there will be only minor losses of nitrogen and other nutrients. Planting should be delayed three weeks to a month to allow it to break down and stabilize. But once the garden has been established, direct application may only be feasible in the early spring and late fall as fresh manure is too strong for most plants.

Fresh cow or horse manure applied in the fall, at the rate of two to three bushels (about 100–150 pounds) per hundred square feet, will supply enough nutrients for general vegetable cropping. If stronger manures are used, decrease this volume a bit; if there is a lot of bedding mixed in, increase it. One important point: fresh manure should be turned under immediately, or significant amounts of nitrogen will be lost.

Country gardeners may want to keep a few chickens or rabbits, or even a horse; from then on manure will be available whenever they like. Others, without the room to keep animals, can often locate a livestock or poultry keeper with manure to spare. In fact, they may be glad you asked. For most gardeners, though, occasional use of purchased organic fertilizers—either dry bagged manure or in granular form—plus composting, may be the most reasonable plan of action. At the end of the chapter we will discuss purchased organic fertilizers in a bit more detail.

COMPOST

There is no doubt that composting is the heart of modern organic gardening. Though I value the books and other tools I inherited from my grandfather, the most important thing I got from him when he retired was his compost pile. For while you can buy books or tools, compost must be made. The new gardeners among you may not yet fully appreciate this truth; the old hands certainly will.

Compost can be rightly called a culture, because what it contains is not merely a store of nutrients and a mass of the raw materials from which a friable soil can be made, but also a whole community of organisms whose activities and interactions are responsible for the fertility and productivity of a long-established garden. A handful of compost is like a seed, or time capsule, in that it stores a microcosm of the garden from whose plants and soil it was made.

The effects of maintaining this "culture" can be quite significant. Scientists working to reestablish forests on eroded, clear-cut slopes of Oregon's southern Klamath Mountains found that "adding less than half a cup of soil from the root zone of a healthy conifer plantation to each planting hole doubled growth and increased survival of conifer seedlings by 50 percent in the first year" after transplanting. By the third year only those seedlings receiving the "soil culture" were still living.[6] The researchers concluded that it was the wide range of micro-organisms in the healthy soil, specially and specifically adapted to living with the roots of conifers, that made the difference. Just as we saw last chapter in the cases of beta-carotene and dried seaweed, natural products and materials are superior to manufactured ones because they contain a whole range of complexes of related substances; this complexity is what confers a stability that the purer, more "efficient" manufactured products simply can't match.

On the one hand, building a compost pile is like building a fire; on the other hand, it is like baking bread. A fire needs dry fuel, air, and a source of ignition heat to start, and depends for its success on placing the fuel and air in the right relation to each other—compactly enough so that the fire feeds on itself to build its heat, but loosely enough so that it can get enough air. A compost pile needs moist fuel, air, and a source of bacteria to start, and it, too, depends on the proper placement of the ingredients. Yet like making bread it depends on both bacteria and a warm protected place for them to do their work.

By starting my own compost piles with the last few bushels from my grandfather's, I was able to bring forward the essence of his garden and connect my own to its tradition and development, to reestablish its culture. His books and tools were valuable, and full of family tradition for me, but the compost was a living link to the garden where I began, and in one sense—since it contained all the living soil organisms from a long-established, productive garden—a recipe for success.

The more diverse the ingredients that go into a compost pile, the more nutritionally balanced the finished product will be. One of the great advantages of compost over purchased fertilizers is that it's loaded with concentrated micro-nutrients. When you shred and then compost the leaves of a shade tree, you are bringing to your garden nutrients collected by that tree from a much greater depth than the vegetables you grow can ever reach. When you compost the household food waste produced in your kitchen you are collecting nutrients that are, literally, from all over the world. And once you've brought those nutrients into your garden, composting keeps them there. Keep in mind that this means you should never put anything on your compost pile that has been treated with pesticides. Store-bought produce may not represent much of a threat to the community of micro-organisms that devour it, but grass clippings from a golf course or park recently treated with pesticides can wreak havoc with your composting operation. It's best to avoid such materials entirely.

Composting is a form of recycling. The harvest from many plants is only a small bit of its bulk. We eat the whole lettuce plant, but with corn, for example, the ear that we eat represents only about ten percent of the plant; by composting its stalk we keep the remaining ninety percent of the nutrients in the garden. Seen this way it is not so surprising that composting will build long-term fertility into any soil, since its nutrient "savings account" is being constantly added to.

This is aside from the cash and resource savings that a compost pile represents. Last chapter we alluded to the energy cost of synthetic fertilizers. Almost 2 percent of the natural gas consumed in this country is used to manufacture nitrogen fertilizers; there is the equivalent of 1/3 to 1/2 gallon of gasoline in every pound of nitrogen fertilizer in terms of the energy consumed. That energy is non-renewable; once burned, it is gone, and not only unavailable for our further use, but a pollutant that fouls the atmosphere.

The energy of a compost pile—the bacterial energy of decomposition which takes refuse that would otherwise end up clogging the community landfill, and turns it into free fertilizer—is not just renewable, but constantly going on all around us in a never-ending cycle of decay and rebirth. The essence of the organic method is to tap into these natural cycles and let them do the work. Because of this, as well as the obvious material benefits, composting is central to organic gardening.

What is most wasteful about manufactured fertilizers, though, is that 30 to 50 percent of the nitrogen and 20 percent of the potassium and phosphorus in them is washed away into our streams, ponds, and groundwater aquifers before plants can use it. There, these nutrients are no longer an asset, but another pollutant that someday must be removed. In fact, nitrate pollution of water supplies is already becoming a serious problem nationwide. Before blaming this entirely on the farmers, consider the aggregate impact of 50,000 suburban homeowners—each dosing his parcel of lawn with a combination fertilizer and herbicide—on the underground water supply of even a small city. When you think of a gentle spring rain percolating down through the soils of that average community, it is no surprise that bottled water sells so well!

Compost, on the other hand, with its low apparent "analysis"— that is the official N-P-K listing which indicates the *immediately available* nutrients—is a stable, slow-release fertilizer whose nutrients will not easily wash out. In laboratory experiments, a highly composted soil sample can be drenched with up to seven times its weight in water spread over a dozen washings that mimic ample summer rains, without losing a significant amount of its mineral nutrients. The nutrients in a fertile, friable soil are so tightly bound to the complex soil particle structure that they are released primarily through the chemical transfers initiated by plant roots, not simply dissolved in water and washed away. The standard analysis does not pick them up because they aren't there in the form that the tests are looking for; they don't become "available" until the acids and enzymes secreted by plant roots and the multitude of soil microorganisms *make* them available, on an as-needed basis.

So while the advocates of quick-acting soluble fertilizers may be technically correct (in the narrowest sense) when they say that plants can't tell where a given amount of nutrient came from, they miss the point. The efficiency of slow-release, recycled nutrients is simply better, more varied and balanced, and less prone to causing problems than the packaged product. The nutrients are available over a longer period, to be taken up at the plant's will, without the danger or possibility of overdoses, or creation of pollution problems elsewhere. Over time this balanced storehouse of both macro- and micro-nutrients increases. Of course, organic materials can create problems if used improperly: the runoff from fresh manure, unwisely spread on fields that will not be promptly plowed, can wash into ponds and rivers, polluting them just as quickly and surely as a synthetic fertilizer. Proper materials are only part of the organic method; proper handling of those materials needs equal attention.

Not even the most devoted adherent of bagged fertilizer will claim that it improves soil structure. Compost helps make cold, soggy soils like ours warmer and drier, and yet will help make sandy and gravel soils more drought-resistant as well, bringing each toward that middle ground that most plants favor: a loose, loamy soil with a neutral pH.

It does this by improving what is called the "crumb structure" of the soil. A fertile, friable soil somewhat resembles moist gingerbread. The addition of compost builds this kind of soil, not only by its own physical properties, but by the soil life it includes. Tiny, colorless fungi, responsible for the initial stages of decomposition in a compost pile, not only bind soils with their far-reaching, threadlike bodies, but produce elements that bacteria then turn into a kind of glue that causes loose soil particles to clump together into "aggregates." Many species of soil fungi in this community also directly help plant roots gather food, in exchange for plant foods they are unable to produce for themselves.

Earthworms are one of the most indispensable inhabitants of both the compost pile and the garden. The mucus coating that makes them feel slimy is what allows them easy passage even through tough soils. This lubricant remains on the walls of their tunnels, binding the soil particles there in the same process of aggregation that is so crucial to good soil structure. As the earthworm eats its way through the material in the compost pile, it mixes the raw materials with its own pH-balancing digestive secretions and the diverse bacterial population of its gut. As a result, earthworm castings are one of the best manures available, and an active earthworm may well produce its own weight in castings daily.

Not only are manufactured fertilizers unable to equal this improvement program, this soil-building function (despite their higher long-term cost), but they are caustic chemicals and actually degrade the soil, because they kill or drive off the fungi, the bacteria, and the earthworms—all of these beneficial inhabitants of a fertile soil. These valuable residents will return in time; but by using manufactured fertilizer, the bag gardener not only pays out hard-earned cash, but creates a potential pollution problem and sets back the development of a truly fertile garden soil, all for a quick shot of growth. This is even more of a folly during dry periods, because organically fortified soils hold water better in droughty weather and are thus able to continue providing nutrients, while soils with poorer structure, even if fortified with soluble nutrients, cannot pass them on to the plants if there is not sufficient water to dissolve them. After a rain there will be a quick flush of growth as the nutrients are picked up by the water, made temporarily available to the plants, and then just as quickly washed away. The companies that make these products know this. Look at the ads they use to sell them; you'll notice they emphasize rapid growth and the size of the crop, but not its flavor and nutritional content.

There are relatively fast methods of making compost which require **Making** a fair, but not unreasonable, amount of effort and attention, and **Compost** then there are slower but less arduous methods. In both cases the process by which garden refuse, kitchen garbage, manure, yard trimmings, and decomposable trash are transmuted into the black gold of compost is similar. Whether a free-standing compost pile is built, or the materials are kept in a bin or other enclosure during the composting process, is immaterial; only the appearance is different.

    The fast method is like building a fire, and it differs from the slow method solely in that air is actively incorporated into the pile. The fuel is carbon: dry plant matter like leaves, straw, hay, or dry weeds and yard trimmings. The heat comes from nitrogen. The surest form of nitrogen to fuel the compost pile is manure. Where it is available it should be used (with the exception of manure from pets or people which, unless specially treated, may contain pathogens). Where manure is not available the readiest sources of nitrogen are freshly cut grass clippings, freshly pulled weeds, and kitchen garbage, that is, vegetable and fruit trimmings, coffee grounds, spoiled leftovers, and the like. If none of these is available, purchase supplements like blood meal, available at garden centers. It also makes sense to include a bit of soil or compost from an earlier pile, to serve as a "starter" by providing a population of decomposing organisms early-on (though they would eventually find the pile anyway). Such compost starters can also be bought ready-made if a starter source isn't available.

Two last elements that are important are moisture and the size and shape of the pile. The micro-organisms that drive the composting process forward require moisture. If the materials used are not succulent, the pile should be watered as it is built, and periodically afterward to keep it uniformly moist. If the materials are just glistening and damp to the touch, but not soaking wet, conditions are likely to be ideal. Size and shape of the pile become important as it heats up—which increases the biological activity within and speeds along the composting—because there must be enough bulk in relation to its surface area so that it generates more heat than it loses. Many experienced composters actually insulate their piles with a layer of straw or manure to conserve its natural heat. An effective minimum size for free-standing piles seems to be about 4 feet on a side (or longer if you need more compost) and about 4 feet tall. Some commercially manufactured compost bins are insulated, and so make it possible for a smaller volume of material to attain the critical heat levels needed for fast composting.

CARBON/NITROGEN RATIO OF COMMON COMPOST MATERIALS

Material	C/N Ratio
Grass Clippings	20 to 1
Weeds (green)	19 to 1
Leaves	60 to 1
Paper	170 to 1
Kitchen Scraps	15 to 1
Sawdust	450 to 1
Hen Manure (no litter)	7 to 1
Hen Manure (w/litter)	10 to 1
Straw	100 to 1
Seaweed	25 to 1
Pine Needles	70 to 1
Corn Stalks	60 to 1
Alfalfa Hay	13 to 1

The ingredients should be kept in proper proportion when assembling a compost pile. A common rule-of-thumb is that you'll want, by volume, four to five times as much carbon-rich material as there is nitrogen-rich refuse. They are kept well mixed by layering them on the pile as they are collected. Two of the most common products of the American yard, however, require special attention. Autumn leaves, unless shredded before piling, tend to pack down and exclude air, and lawn clippings are so rich and succulent that unless dried first or mixed thoroughly with drier material, they will rot into a slimy mess instead of composting. Both are excellent sources of nutrients, though, and composting them saves money and landfill space at the same time it provides nutrients for your garden.

One of the more difficult tasks is to make sure that air can get to all parts of the pile throughout the composting process. The first layer should be of shrub prunings, twigs, or other light materials. As the pile increases in size, larger branches or even poles can be laid horizontally on top, and then later, during its decomposition, withdrawn to allow air to enter. Some other methods of getting air into a compost pile to speed its decomposition are to stick vertical lengths of drainage tile into the first layers of the pile and then build it right up around them; poke holes with a bar or piece of iron pipe once the pile is finished; or, as many gardeners do, turn the pile with a manure fork each time it starts to cool down, placing the materials from the outside of the pile on the inside and vice versa. For gardeners with limited space and fairly formal yards, there are manufactured compost tumblers that will accomplish this process of re-aeration without the heavy lifting.

The basic proportion between the dry, fuel-type materials in the pile and the moister, heat-supplying materials should be four or five to one. The soil or compost fraction usually covers lightly each layer of the nitrogenous material to hold its moisture and discourage scavenging animals (not a problem if a bin is used for the pile). In our hot piles we alternate six-to-eight-inch layers of dry matter with one-to-two-inch layers of manure and half-to-one-inch layers of compost from the previous pile. Many composters, including us, like to add a bit of phosphorus to the pile, as it is proportionately low in both compost and manure. We use rock phosphate, and sprinkle three or four handfuls over the compost layer before starting again with the dry layer. Piles that use no manure tend to be a bit more acidic, and wood ash or bone meal would make a good addition, as they would more effectively raise the pH a bit.

This layering process should continue until the pile is 4 feet tall. Water it if necessary to assure that there is sufficient moisture for decomposition to proceed. Within a few days the pile should begin to heat noticeably. During cool weather it may actually steam; but during the spring and summer months (when composting proceeds

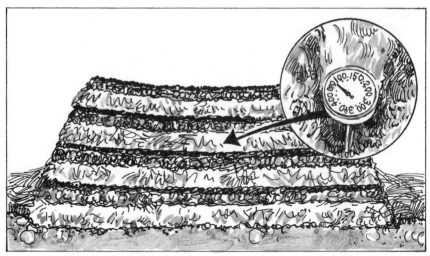

Compost piles work best if built in layers, and are a minimum of 3–4 feet wide on all sides. When the pile begins to cool, supply more air to restart the composting process. Compost is ready when it becomes dark, crumbly and cool.

most quickly, anyway) you can check it simply by thrusting your fist into the pile. In the center it may well be too hot to touch, between 120° and 140° Fahrenheit. Once it begins to cool down—if you want to keep the process moving as quickly as possible—consider supplying more air, either by turning the pile, or by the other methods mentioned above. If you are of a precise mind, you can check its progress with a thermometer. We use a small, inexpensive meat thermometer; after thrusting my fist into the pile, I stick the thermometer into the end of the passage so that it is within the heart of the pile. As soon as it drops below 100°F, I consider the pile ready for turning.

A properly proportioned pile, made with the right ingredients and closely managed, can be ready for use in as little as two weeks, having been turned twice or three times over that period. This is particularly true if the materials from which the pile is built are shredded before composting; the smaller particle size makes the work of decomposition easier for the micro-organisms in the pile. If you have a garden spot that you want to improve as quickly as possible, simply scour the neighborhood for leaves, hay, stable cleanings, sawdust, and manure, rent a shredder, and make a whole series of piles. Even without turning—if you build the piles properly, with provision for getting air to the center—you should be able to produce large amounts of ripe compost in a month.

Big Sam's garden was well established by the time I was born, and he had his methods so well worked out that this kind of hurry-up composting was unnecessary, and he had adopted a method of slow composting that, while it took quite a while to produce finished compost, yielded him a steady supply with very little labor. He called it the "lazy man's method", and here's how he went about it:

I start in the spring by laying out on a level piece of well-drained ground a rectangle about five feet by twelve feet, marking the corners with stakes. Then I lay up an outside wall of one or two thicknesses of sod or cement blocks. My system requires the maintenance of two compost piles, one of which ages for a year while the other is being built, so in preparing for current use the pile which has stood a year, I strip it of all outside material, much of which is only partly decomposed, and place it within the borders of my sod strips as the first layer in my new compost pile. From now on all decomposable garbage from our house, and from our neighbor's as well, if I can get them to sort their waste, is spread on the pile and covered with a thin layer of topsoil before it has a chance to become nasty.

Early in the spring there will not be much but garbage to place on the pile, but as summer comes on there will be garden weeds, pea vines, etc. As the pile grows, I keep building up the sides with sod or other material that will stay in place, and keep covering the succeeding layers with topsoil, or, if available, with thin layers of manure.

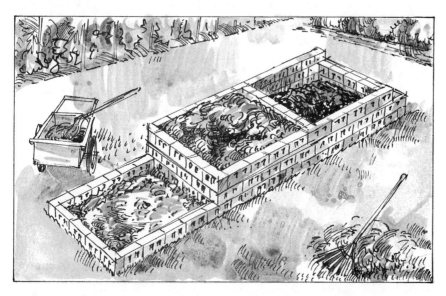

For a continuous supply of fertile compost, build three piles in succession so that one is always ready to use.

In the fall all the cleanup of the garden goes on to the pile, squash, tomato and bean vines, the remains of the cabbages, cauliflowers, broccoli, and so forth. Then I cover the pile with sods, root side up, or manure, and leave it for nature to take its course, not touching it again until a year from the following spring. By that time the pile is two years old, having taken six months to build and eighteen months to cure.

This kind of composting is also called anaerobic composting because it proceeds without worrying about getting air into the pile. It is essentially controlled rotting, and as Big Sam was fond of pointing out, the only real difference between well rotted manure and compost is that the manure went through the gut of a domestic animal first. Both began as vegetation, but the manure was pre-digested by the animal before being deposited and allowed to rot. The process of both rotting and composting is also digestion, and either rotted manure or plant compost can be used to fertilize and improve the soil structure of your garden. Which you will use depends largely—as does the method of composting you choose—on the particulars of your situation.

If you have access to good rotted manure, or a place to compost it, it is the simplest product to use; if not, then composting will provide you with just as many of the benefits, but with a bit more effort. If you have plenty of space and abundant raw materials (or just don't need that much compost), but are short of time to manage a quick compost pile, by all means follow Big Sam's long-term, low-work method.

Using Compost Gardeners with access to manure will most likely use their compost as special fertilizer for favored plants, and guidelines for this kind of treatment are in the vegetable section under the individual entries. It is applied as a side dressing during times of peak nutrient demand, or used to replace the soil at the spot where transplanted crops will be set.

Those who depend on compost and soil-building cover crops should spread it more generally on the beds, just before planting, at a rate of two to three bushels per hundred square feet. That is 100–150 pounds of compost, or about a pound to a pound and a half per square foot. A well made compost pile measuring 4 feet square at the base and 4 feet high will contain 64 cubic feet and weigh about a ton, which should be enough compost to fertilize a garden of up to 2,000 square feet. The same sized pile could help make a smaller garden into a super productive plot virtually overnight.

Unfortunately, not all organic gardeners have access to manure or the room for a compost pile or tumbler. Perhaps your garden is just a few window boxes on a balcony. It could be that backyard space is precious, and there is only room for a couple of half barrels and a small growing bed between the sidewalk and the front porch; but you can still treat properly what soil you have by using purchased organic fertilizers and soil builders instead of synthetics. You may even be able to buy fully prepared compost from the county or town in which you live, as many local governments now sponsor composting projects at local landfills. **Organic Fertilizers**

With the growing interest in organic gardening, though, many companies have brought what they call "organic" or "natural" fertilizers to market, and you are likely to find one or more of them available at your local hardware store or garden center. Just be sure to read the label of what you buy, since the dream of profits has led more than one businessperson down the road to subtle deception. A few products are little more than standard synthetic fertilizers with a bit of some organic material such as fish meal added (and then blazoned in large type on the bag). These kinds of products will not build the soil.

Here's what to look for when you buy organic fertilizer. First, check the NPK listing; if any of the numbers is above eight, look for a list of ingredients; most organic materials are lower than that in *immediately available* nutrients, which is what the number must legally mean. Remember, that is the advantage of organic materials: that their nutrients are not immediately available, but rather are released slowly, over time, at a rate the plants can use without waste.

Second, scan the list of ingredients for words like ammonium, muriate, urea, nitrate, phosphoric, or superphosphate; if these words or their variants are part of the ingredients, don't buy. The words phosphate and sulfate themselves are not necessarily indicators of processed or synthesized materials; but if combined with any of the key words above, they are. Other ingredients to watch out for are cottonseed meal and leather tankage, not because they aren't organic, but because they are frequently contaminated with harmful residues. The same points apply to liquid fertilizers.

When using commercial organic fertilizers, follow the instructions and the recommended application rates listed on the package. Don't double up because the listed NPK is lower than what you might be used to using. And be careful to keep track of your soil's organic matter level; these purchased fertilizers, unless they are made from composted manures (many are), do not add organic matter to the soil—and organic matter is at the heart of organic gardening.

CHAPTER 6

Garden Planning

The general principle (of crop rotation and garden planning) is not dependent upon the number of plots . . . and beneficent effects will result if only two plots are used. There is no inviolable rule for the alternation of crops that I know of. . . . In general, crops differing widely in their food requirements should follow one another. Leaf crops remove nitrogen from the soil, the legumes replace it. Root crops require abundant potash and seed crops demand ample supplies of phosphorus. From these general principles, and from the depths of one's experience, each will work out the plan of rotation which best suits the type and size of his undertaking.

Samuel R. Ogden

Organic garden planning on a yearly basis involves three basic concepts: crop rotation, successions, and interplanting. Each spring you should draw up a garden plan that lays out the location of the crops you'll grow for that season, both those that will occupy a spot for the whole season, and those that may just occupy a spot as a quick crop, a green manure, or part of a short crop succession. Each of these seasonal plans should be kept with your garden journal, so that year to year you can keep track of what has grown where, and balance the demands that each crop makes on the soil. Over time you'll be able to use these records to develop a system of planting that will give the best possible results in your garden.

CROP ROTATION

The most basic form of crop rotation is also the simplest: never plant the same thing in the same place twice. Thus, if you planted carrots or some other root crop in a spot last year, plant something else there that yields aboveground this year. Big Sam's two-year, two-plot plan was a bit more detailed than that: "... peas, small seeds, and, if there is room, cucumbers and squash in one plot, with the cabbage family, corn, beans, and onion plants in the other. Thus peas, radishes, looseleaf lettuce, and spinach will be early plantings in one plot, while early cabbage and onion plants will be early plantings in the other."

Figuring out rotations, and finding an elegant solution to the puzzle of planning, can be fascinating. A good plan, one that satisfies all three of the aims of rotation—balancing nutrient demands, foiling insect and disease attacks, and making the most of the garden's sun and soil while deterring weeds—becomes a sort of seasonal dance in which the crops move from spot to spot, and helps create a garden that is constantly new and intriguing. Let's look at these three basic aims of rotation one by one to see what kinds of common needs they may have, and then work up a sample plan that meets them.

Nutrient Rotation   The challenge here is trying to balance the nutrient demands each crop makes on the soil. For high yields and high quality, all your crops will require a range of nutrients, available in proper proportion, and at the proper times during the growth of the plants. It is a basic tenet of organic gardening, in fact, that they need a wider range than the simple N-P-K formulae offered by most bagged synthetic fertilizers if they are to be healthy enough to resist disease and insect attack without the crutch of pesticides. It is also basic that the slow, continual release of nutrients from compost, manure, and the ongoing biological processes of a living soil is superior to an occasional shot of concentrated fertilizer. Still, certain groups of plants like more or less of various nutrients, especially the big three—nitrogen, phosphorus, and potassium—and we can work out a system that arranges the crops according to their relative need for each.

Let's divide our crops into four types: leaves, fruits, roots, and cleaners/builders. Plants grown and harvested for their leaves thrive on nitrogen. Phosphorus is especially important to the flowering and fruiting of plants, so, if we are looking to harvest them for their fruits we need to make sure there is ample phosphorus available. Root crops are potassium lovers, but make relatively light demands on the soil for nitrogen or phosphorus. Legumes, through a symbiotic relationship with certain soil bacteria, are able to draw nitrogen from the air and store it in their roots. Because of this they are known as soil builders; after harvest this stored nitrogen is released for use by following crops.

This descending hierarchy of nutrient demands suggests one way to arrange crops in rotation. After initial fertilization, the first season is devoted to leafy salad crops like lettuce, chicory, mustards, and others, plus the nitrogen-loving members of the cabbage family: cabbage, broccoli, cauliflower, Brussels sprouts, and kale. In the next season, this same section of the garden would be planted to fruiting crops like tomatoes, peppers, eggplants, squashes, melons, cucumbers, and pumpkins, that can do well with the slightly reduced levels of nitrogen and will thrive on the phosphorus levels remaining. The third season our plan would put root crops like car-

PLANTS GROUPED BY NUTRIENT DEMANDS

Leaves (High N)	Fruits (High P)	Roots (High K)	Cleaners and Builders
RELATIVE DEMAND	RELATIVE DEMAND	RELATIVE DEMAND	
Heavy	*Heavy*	*Heavy*	*Cleaners*
Lettuce	Squashes	Onions	Corn
Salad Greens	Cucumbers	Shallots	Potatoes
Chicory	Melons	Garlic	
Spinach	Pumpkins	Scallions	
		Leeks	
Light	*Light*	*Light*	*Builders*
Broccoli	Tomatoes	Carrots	Beans
Brussels Sprouts	Peppers	Beets	Peas
	Eggplants	Turnips	
Cabbage		Radishes	
Cauliflower			
Kale			
Kohlrabi			

rots, beets, turnips, radishes, and the whole range of crops in the onion family, including leeks, garlic, and shallots in the plot, since their relatively low fertility requirements (with a preference for potassium) are ideally suited to the state of the soil at that point. In the fourth season of this rotation, legumes such as beans and peas are planted to help rebuild nitrogen levels in anticipation of another round of the rotation cycle.

Within each of these four groups, half of the crops are somewhat greedier than the others. The greens can use more nitrogen than the broccoli (and its relatives), the squashes and cucumbers like a richer soil than the tomato family, and onions, leeks, shallots, and garlic benefit from more nitrogen than do the other root crops. Thus we might subdivide the plots further and feed the hungry half a bit extra before spring planting, to make sure they get all the nutrients they need to reach their productive potential. This supplemental feeding can take the form of additional compost or, if compost is short, an application of organic fertilizer. While the fourth group, peas and beans, have similar nutrient requirements, they grow at different seasons. That makes it possible to take half of that plot, give it the additional compost, and plant corn and/or potatoes, which are often left out of kitchen gardens because of their large space requirement.

This four-square, two-part plot rotation is easy to understand if you draw yourself a plan. In a classic four-square garden like ours or Big Sam's, each season would find one group in each plot, with the space allocated to the crops within the group according to the desired harvest. The contents of the plots are then switched in an orderly musical chairs kind of fashion, keeping the hungry crops in one half and the less demanding crops in the other. At the end of each rotation, the two halves can be switched.

One additional element we will consider later is the use of off-season cover crops which, properly chosen, can themselves add significantly to the fertility of the soil.

Prevention
Rotation

Rotations can also break the cycles of pest and disease problems that build up in soils planted repeatedly to the same crop. The key is to plan your rotation so that no two crops subject to similar diseases follow one another within the disease's incubation period. For example, try not to plant cabbage or its relatives in the same plot more than once every four years, as the various fungal and bacterial diseases that plague that botanical family are able to overwinter in the soil. Without a host the following season, though—because you moved the cabbage family out, to a different plot—these diseases are not able to survive. By the time the plot is in cabbages again the pathogen is long since dead. The same is true for the squash family, carrot family, onion family, and the rest. If you can avoid planting the same family of plants in the same place in successive years you'll go a long way toward preventing the buildup of disease organisms in your garden's soil.

The same principle holds for insect pests. Crop rotation makes it harder for emerging insects to find their preferred food each spring. By the time the larvae of the cucumber beetle locate the new spot where the cucumbers have been moved to, the plants have gotten a good head start and are better able to resist their attack. A related tactic—called trap cropping—works for a number of different insect pests and plant families; it involves setting a few plants of an affected species in the old spot as a trap for the emerging pests. You can try this with eggplants and potatoes, and see for yourself how well it works. Take a few extra early eggplants and set them out a week or so ahead of your normal schedule, right where you had potatoes the year before (not normally a good idea). Colorado potato beetles love eggplants above all else. As soon as they appear, they'll find the eggplants you set there and chow down. All you have to do is stop by once a day and pick them off the plants. Plant your main crop of potatoes and eggplants elsewhere, after you've had a week or two to trap the beetles, and the pest problem will be greatly reduced.

PLANTS GROUPED BY PLANT FAMILY
(and thus subject to similar problems)

Squash	Mustard	Tomato	Beet	Legumes	Onion	Carrot
Melons	Broccoli	Tomatoes	Beets	Beans	Onions	Carrots
Squash	Br. Sprouts	Eggplants	Spinach	Peas	Leeks	Dill
Cucumber	Cabbage	Peppers	Chard		Scallions	Parsnips
Pumpkins	Cauliflower	Potatoes			Garlic	Parsley
	Kohlrabi				Shallots	
	Kale					
	Mustard					
	Radishes					
	Turnips					

Weed-Reducing Rotation A final benefit of rotations is in combating weeds and soil compaction. Because different plants have different root characteristics and require more or less weeding and cultivation through the season, where you grow them affects the weed population in that spot. Thus a crop that doesn't compete well against weeds, like corn or carrots or onions, might be planted in the plot where potatoes or squashes were the year before. Because the squashes and potatoes were likely subject to frequent, shallow cultivation (and in the case of potatoes, hilling), annual weeds will be less vigorous in that area of the garden. Also, by alternating shallow-rooted plants like cabbages or lettuce with deep-rooted plants like tomatoes or squash, we allow the plants' roots to do much of the soil loosening that would otherwise have to be done by hand.

One last effect of this type is the traditional "allelopathic" relations between succeeding and preceding crops. That's a fancy way of saying that some plants leave behind residues that will help or hinder other particular plant families. The classic example is the standard corn–soybean rotation of the American Midwest; both help the other beyond the level of just their different nutrient needs. Some gardeners feel that beets and carrots hinder any following crop and are themselves hindered by following a legume. There is an enormous amount of such information around, some of it merely hearsay, some of it well documented. Gathering information on these "companion" crops and testing it yourself is fascinating.

Green Manures and Cover Crops As mentioned earlier, the off-season cover on a vegetable garden can also contribute to an effective crop rotation scheme. While crop rotation evens out nutrient demands on the soil, it will still be necessary to bring nutrients into the system because you will be removing nutrients in the form of crops. In Chapter 4 we saw that crop residues stimulate biological activity in the soil and so release its inherent fertility. Here we'll just discuss the different types of cover crops and green manures, and their uses within an overall crop rotation scheme.

Big Sam didn't have much use for cover crops and green manures, though the cropping plan and layout of his garden were suitable for them; in fact, because of the early date that he retired his garden for the fall, crops like annual ryegrass would have been almost ideal for him. Here is what he had to say on the subject:

One other source of organic material for the garden is so-called green manure. Green manure consists of a cover crop planted on the plot for the express purpose of plowing the green material under. These crops are generally forage or grain crops, such as rye or clover, or legumes, such as cow peas, soy beans, etc. This procedure I do not recommend for small gardens; the soil is out of use for a season, it requires the services of a big plow, and, unless the conditions are just right, the required decomposition may not take place.

There are some problems with using green manures in the home garden, particularly one with raised beds, but they can be overcome easily with a little attention to detail. One of the first things that makes a difference with cover crops and green manures is proper selection. You should choose the cover crop based on the results you want. Are you trying to choke out weeds, or build nitrogen reserves, or both? Are you trying to unlock an impenetrable subsoil, or protect the topsoil from winter erosion, or discourage a particular pest or disease that has become established in your garden? It helps to analyze which of these things is of primary importance, and sow accordingly. Second, make sure you've selected a species and variety of cover crop appropriate to your region's climate, your garden's soil type, and the season. My feeling is that if Big Sam hadn't limited himself to the few crops he mentions above, he could have found ones appropriate to his garden as well.

There are basically four ways that these crops can be of use: as soil protectors, soil builders, soil conditioners, and soil cleansers. One of the simplest and best uses of a green manure is as a winter cover crop to protect the soil from erosion. The standard here in New England is winter rye, which is the grain rye. It is sown immediately after harvest, but always by October 15 in our locale. Rye grows quickly in the cool fall weather and covers the soil; in the spring it re-grows, but if mowed at eight to twelve inches tall it will die off and can be turned under (though not without some effort). After allowing three weeks to a month for it to decompose, the plot can be planted. My guess is that Big Sam's objection to rye was this three-week waiting period in the spring, as the season in his garden was very short and every week mattered. It is becoming common now to mix hairy vetch, a hardy legume, with the rye to provide extra nitrogen for the crop that is to follow, while decreasing the density of the rye, which makes turning under easier. Vetch will add up to eighty pounds per acre of nitrogen to the soil over the course of its life. In experiments at the Rodale Research Center in

Pennsylvania, researchers have been able to sow some spring crops directly into growing hairy vetch, without tilling. They then mow the vetch and leave the cuttings in place as a mulch for the spring crop.

I have a favorite winter cover crop to solve the spring timing problem. Annual ryegrass has a great advantage over winter rye in a short season area like ours: sown on clear ground, anytime from early August till late October, ryegrass grows quickly enough to choke out any emergent weeds and forms a very dense, fine-leaved cover. By midwinter it dies off from the cold and mats down to form a protective mulch that decomposes quickly in the spring after turning under. This saves the three-week waiting period.

Consider your own climate and soil, then look at the possibilities for winter cover crops in your own garden. Once you've created a rich, friable soil, it's a waste to let it sit exposed to nutrient-leaching rains and erosion. Keep some kind of crop growing year round, and you'll lock in the nutrients that your vegetables will need when their growing time comes.

If you leave garden crops in the ground late into the fall you can actually broadcast the cover crop seed into the plot immediately after your last cultivation—once the crop is nearly mature, and before harvest. Irrigate if the weather is dry; the cover crop will grow right up among the maturing vegetables, and by harvest time will already be well established. As a "living mulch" it will help control fall weeds, too. Don't worry about competition—the crop's roots are well established and its growth already slowing as it nears maturity; just pay attention to the timing.

Legumes are the great soil builders. Their ability to work with rhizobia soil bacteria to extract the abundant nitrogen in the atmosphere can be a primary source of fertility for gardens with enough organic matter to support a high level of biological activity. They can also be used as a fall cover crop, if you get them in early enough to become established by the onset of freezing weather (check with your local USDA extension agent for the proper sowing time in your area). To really build up the nitrogen reserves of the soil, however, a plot should be turned over to alfalfa or clover for a full season. The usual method here in northern New England is to sow the legume (we use alsike clover) in early spring, in combination with oats—which grow quickly and provide protection for the young legume plants. You can harvest the oats once they mature, or simply mow them once the young clover or alfalfa is fully established, and leave the clippings on the ground as a mulch for the legume. It isn't necessary to give up one whole section of the garden for this purpose. Just a portion of each bed could be sown to cover crops each year; eventually the whole bed will have been improved.

While alfalfa is considered the king of the legumes, it requires a neutral, well drained soil to thrive. Clovers are a bit more forgiving, and there are many different strains, adapted for different conditions. You can even sow leftover bean or pea seed. Whatever legume you use, be sure to get *rhizobia* inoculant at the same time you buy the seed, and treat the seed with it—by dusting the inoculant powder on moistened seed—before planting. Even if the plot has had the same legume growing in it before, the inoculant more than pays for itself by guaranteeing optimal nitrogen fixation. (See Chapter 4, as well as the entries in Chapter 10 under beans and peas, for a discussion of legumes and their relationship with *rhizobia*.)

Legumes like alfalfa and clover also function as soil conditioners because they have strong, deep roots that can penetrate the subsoil, and over time break up a hard pan that is interfering with proper drainage of the topsoil. Culture is the same as for nitrogen fixation (discussed above), but leaving the crop in place for at least a whole season is even more fundamental. Any deep-rooted crop can perform the same function. Chicory has been used for this purpose, as has comfrey. You should stay away from comfrey, though, as it is hard to get rid of once established. When my grandfather's place was sold some years ago, the new owners didn't plan to have a garden, so I dug out his compost to help get me through the first year on my own land. I wondered what the large rough-leaved plant growing on the side of the pile was, but didn't think too much about all the small root pieces that my shovel took along with the rich black humus in the pile. I found out when I planted the garden, though. It took me two years of cover cropping and clean cultivation to get rid of the comfrey. Now I keep one clump over by the goose yard, as it is their favorite food, but I don't let it anywhere near the garden.

The other use of cover crops and green manures as soil conditioners is simply to stimulate the overall biological activity of the soil. This process was discussed in Chapter 4. All we need to say here is that you can get a cover crop grown, turned under, and fully decomposed in as little as six weeks, but the benefits will last for much longer than that. We often use leftover mustard or cress seed, both of which are inexpensive and grow quickly. The crop used is not as important as keeping the soil covered with growing plants. When you enhance the natural nutrient cycling of the soil by this green manuring, you ensure available nutrients for your next vegetable crop. It is like putting money into a Christmas club account.

The last use of cover crops and green manures I want to mention is as a cleansing crop. A thickly planted crop of ryegrass (in cool weather) or buckwheat (in warm weather) will grow so dense, so quickly, that it will choke out just about any weed known. In Chapter 4 we described how these crops could be used to eradicate established weeds, but they can be used in an ongoing weed control program as well. Other cover crops help cleanse the soil of pests and diseases by the allelopathic excretions of their roots: the Mexican marigold has been shown by university research to drive out harmful soil nematodes; and rye has been shown to kill certain disease spores. All these crops and cropping systems represent ways that the gardener can finesse a desired effect from the community of his or her garden, what the English writer Edward Hyams called "the soil community."

Putting It All Together

In the final analysis, all of the rotational factors we've mentioned—nutrients, pests, diseases, cultivation, allelopathy, and stimulating the soil community—are interrelated. The connections between different plant communities in nature are complex and stable; the good gardener will do well—and have fun—figuring out a combination of plants and planting schemes that meets as many of the different goals of rotational planning as possible. In general, the more units, or steps, you have in your rotation, the more subtle you can be with the combinations and the more options for planning you'll have. Something as simple as dividing each plot into sub-sections can make a big difference. Thus, treating half of each of four plots separately, as we did above, effectively creates eight plots and makes it possible to give more subtle treatment to each group of plants. If you have a hard time keeping records, just take pictures of the beds each season, and mark on the back which plot and what year each photo is. You'll end up with a nice scrapbook as well as a rotation reference. Sketch a quick schematic plan—that, too, can be very helpful later on.

Taking what we've discussed above—and the tentative plan we established in the beginning—let's set up a full-figured sample rotation for a four-square garden. In this case we will include cover crops. We'll divide each of the four plots in half so that those crops within each group that require a little more pampering can be given the best prepared area, and receive a bit of special attention. Remember that this is just one of many possibilities; it is figured for my garden, in my climate. Your own plan should take the particulars of your own situation into account.

In this discussion, each plot has two parts, which we'll call A and B. The plants in part B get a little extra attention, usually in the form of extra compost. (Though when available we spread an inch or so of mellow compost every spring.) This is a record of one plot over four years. To visualize the full rotation just keep in mind that each of these crop sequences is happening in one of the four plots each season. Also, keep in mind that since crop rotation is an ongoing process, it can be entered (for purposes of our analysis) at any point.

We will start the fall before the year of leaf crops (Fall o for the sake of discussion). Make an application of manure at three bushels per hundred square feet, turn it under, lime if necessary, then sow annual ryegrass. If manure (or an equivalent amount of compost) isn't available, use bagged organic fertilizer at full label application rates.

Spring 1: If the ryegrass survives the winter (it doesn't here) it should be mowed, then turned under a month before spring planting. Otherwise it can be left until planting time to act as a mulch. Compost is applied if available, with B getting the lion's share; then A is planted to cabbage family plants, called brassicas, while lettuce and salad greens are grown in B.

Fall 1: After harvest of the last succession of salad greens (see later for a discussion of succession planting), and while the brassicas are still growing, sow the appropriate clover for the particular soil and climatic conditions (we use alsike clover because of our soil type). This should be done by the beginning of September at the latest in our garden.

Spring 2: Turn under the clover a month before planting, then set the tomato family plants in A and squash family plants in B. A handful of bone meal or rock phosphate (which is much cheaper) mixed into the bottom of the planting hole when these plants are set out will guarantee plenty of phosphorus for a bountiful fruit set and prompt maturity. A shovelful of compost can be mixed into all the planting holes, but the squashes should get preference.

Fall 2: After harvest, sow annual ryegrass to the whole plot, and lime if necessary; if you have wood ash, use it instead, as ashes are high in the potassium that root crops love.

Spring 3: Turn under the dead ryegrass and spread an inch or so of compost on B. Plant the true root crops in A; they can get by on the remaining fertility. Onions, leeks, shallots, garlic, and celeriac are not true root crops and need more nitrogen to yield well; they should be put in part B.

Fall 3: Follow the early plantings of root crops in A with buckwheat (during the frost-free period) and then annual ryegrass; later plantings can be followed directly by the ryegrass. Lime, if necessary to keep the pH around 6.5 to 7.0. In B plant clover as soon as the onions are harvested; do not lime.

Spring 4: Turn under the dead ryegrass in A and plant peas, then beans once the frost is gone. Turn under the clover in B a month before planting potatoes and corn. Put a shovelful of compost into each hill at planting time.

Fall 4 (same as Fall o): Keep A in peas and beans (or other legumes) until fall, then plant annual ryegrass. After harvest of potatoes sow ryegrass on open ground and among the maturing corn plants. Lime, if necessary.

In our garden a number of minor crops are interspersed with these major vegetables: dill and other herbs are grown in with the brassicas; parsley and basil go among the tomatoes, eggplants, and peppers; fast growing greens like arugula and cress are grown in concert with the early climbing peas. As long as they are kept with their companions throughout the rotation, any number of these small space crops can be worked in without disturbing the plan. To show how this sample rotation would look in my own garden here is a plan:

Our sample rotation for all four plots and all four years (showing just the vegetable crops): during the first year, leaf crops are in Plot 1, soil builders and cleaners in Plot 2, root crops in Plot 3, and fruiting crops in Plot 4. In the second year, each group moves clockwise one notch so that the leafy crops are grown where the builders and cleaners were the previous year, the fruiting crops grow where the leafy crops were, and so on. Thus, no crop grows in the same plot more than once in four years. By reversing the A and B portions of each plot at the end of every cycle, the rotation is effectively doubled to eight years, which will greatly lessen the likelihood of pest and disease problems as well as balancing nutrient demands placed on the soil.

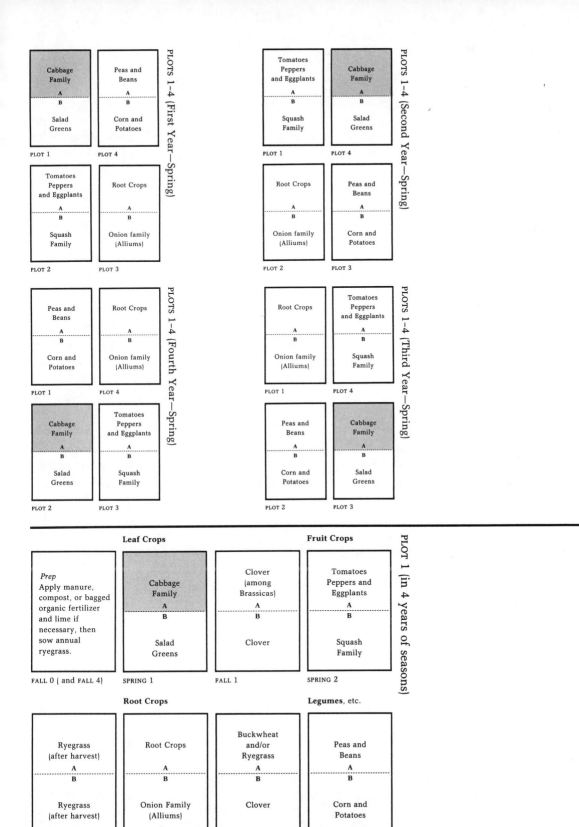

PLOTS 1–4 (First Year—Spring)

PLOT 1
Cabbage Family
A
B
Salad Greens

PLOT 4
Peas and Beans
A
B
Corn and Potatoes

PLOT 2
Tomatoes Peppers and Eggplants
A
B
Squash Family

PLOT 3
Root Crops
A
B
Onion family (Alliums)

PLOTS 1–4 (Second Year—Spring)

PLOT 1
Tomatoes Peppers and Eggplants
A
B
Squash Family

PLOT 4
Cabbage Family
A
B
Salad Greens

PLOT 2
Root Crops
A
B
Onion family (Alliums)

PLOT 3
Peas and Beans
A
B
Corn and Potatoes

PLOTS 1–4 (Fourth Year—Spring)

PLOT 1
Peas and Beans
A
B
Corn and Potatoes

PLOT 4
Root Crops
A
B
Onion family (Alliums)

PLOT 2
Cabbage Family
A
B
Salad Greens

PLOT 3
Tomatoes Peppers and Eggplants
A
B
Squash Family

PLOTS 1–4 (Third Year—Spring)

PLOT 1
Root Crops
A
B
Onion family (Alliums)

PLOT 4
Tomatoes Peppers and Eggplants
A
B
Squash Family

PLOT 2
Peas and Beans
A
B
Corn and Potatoes

PLOT 3
Cabbage Family
A
B
Salad Greens

PLOT 1 (in 4 years of seasons)

Leaf Crops

FALL 0 (and FALL 4)
Prep
Apply manure, compost, or bagged organic fertilizer and lime if necessary, then sow annual ryegrass.

SPRING 1
Cabbage Family
A
B
Salad Greens

Fruit Crops

FALL 1
Clover (among Brassicas)
A
B
Clover

SPRING 2
Tomatoes Peppers and Eggplants
A
B
Squash Family

Root Crops

FALL 2
Ryegrass (after harvest)
A
B
Ryegrass (after harvest)

SPRING 3
Root Crops
A
B
Onion Family (Alliums)

Legumes, etc.

FALL 3
Buckwheat and/or Ryegrass
A
B
Clover

SPRING 4
Peas and Beans
A
B
Corn and Potatoes

Why Bother?   Some garden books will tell you that even though the principle is strong, there is no point to crop rotation in a small garden because the effects aren't measurable. But that kind of thinking actually misses the point. By that same logic, if we can't measure the residues of a particular pesticide on the vegetables we eat, then we might as well use it on them (and by extension, on ourselves). Both imply that if an effect is small, then it doesn't matter whether it is good or bad. But good and bad are qualities, while large and small are quantities; confusing the two always seems to end with more quantity and less quality. The language of measurement is statistical, and when you subordinate solid principles to something as fluid as statistics you pave the way to delusion and disaster, because statistics don't properly represent individual reality.

I first realized this when a man from the U.S. Department of Energy came to our town a few years ago and tried to convince our community that we should allow a proposed nuclear waste dump to be built here. Of course, some people were worried about health risks, but he said that statistics show that it would only add "the equivalent of smoking a single cigarette a day" to the health risks of the community. The way the DOE man put things it sounded as if everybody would be just a tiny bit less healthy—that the difference would be too small to notice and, by extension, too small to matter. "The overall effect (of such and such a pollutant) is just a blip on the statistical horizon," we are told. That is because the statistics only describe large groups of people, not individuals.

But the "population group" is made up of us, of real people, and if the population is affected that means a person is affected. It doesn't matter if we are talking about smoking, nuclear waste, or pesticides. The reality of the situation is that when that statistic goes up, somebody, somewhere, dies; that blip on the horizon was a person slipping over it. The effect may not be noticeable unless you're the one that dies; but then you're dead, never just one cigarette sicker. By the logic of the man from DOE, each of us who remains has benefited—at no personal cost, since we're still alive—but that realization is not satisfying; it makes me feel guilty, not grateful.

This statistical confusion of the group and the individual distorts our whole economy, and by extension our society, since those who have been (fatally) affected are not here to argue for change. They have no more power to change things than the unborn children who will inherit what we leave behind, whether it be a nuclear waste dump or a basement full of half empty pesticide containers.

There is no free lunch. The bill for every one of modernity's little conveniences will eventually have to be paid by somebody, sometime; it is part of the vague, unarticulated anxiety of this age that we may be the ones. After all, we ran up the bill, and somebody has to pay it, to be the blip, the body count. Statistics is the language of generals, politicians, and mass marketers, but we humans are all individuals, and if we don't want to sacrifice our humanity to their gods, we should never forget that. We should make sure we don't run up any bills we aren't willing to pay.

So, as an organic gardener, I adopt a new technique or tool only if it actually works better, in the long term, and even then only if I'm sure its use won't cause too much harm somewhere else. And I don't stop doing something beneficial simply because my garden is small. I'm not looking to save time at someone else's expense, and I'm not trying to rush through my gardening as if it is a chore. After all, would the passionate cook buy a cake at the supermarket to avoid the "trouble" of making one? Or put ersatz bacon bits in the spinach salad simply because "nobody can tell the difference"? To follow this reasoning to its conclusion is to say "Why bother gardening at all?" and head for the television set.

SUCCESSION PLANTING

Succession planting is kind of like a relay race. Only a few crops occupy their place in the garden for a full season. Most either grow fast and are gone by mid-season, or, though they are slow to mature, also take a long time to fill their allotted space. Some are not even planted until midsummer, for a fall harvest. In all three cases, well-thought-out succession planting schemes can make sure that every square foot of the garden is as productive as possible, throughout the entire season. The smaller that garden is, the more benefit you'll get from taking the time to figure out creative ways to use the time and space that each season allows you.

There are basically two kinds of successions: those which involve multiple plantings of the same crop, and those that match up different crops growing at different times. Aside from the usual questions like fertility, pH, place in rotation, and spacing, there are a couple of other things you'll want to know about each crop you consider for mixed succession planting: its approximate days to harvest; and its preferred season. Once you know these, you can match up long and short season, fall and spring crops, to share the same spaces.

Single Crop Successions   One of the primary goals of succession planting is to stretch the harvest period. It is traditional to plant both sweet corn and peas in succession, so that their harvest periods will last more than just a few days. This is usually done in one of two ways. Either a range of varieties with different maturity periods are planted all at the same time—which I call varietal succession—or the same variety is planted periodically, say, every week or two over the course of the spring—in temporal succession—so that the plantings will mature one after the other. An example of this second kind is staggered planting of lettuce and other salad greens, to maintain a fairly regular harvest throughout the season.

In general, and for beginning gardeners in particular, varietal succession is a bit easier to manage. This is because all the varieties planted will get the same treatment and grow under the same conditions, allowing only their genetic diversity to provide the variation in harvest date. No management is required. With temporal succession, though, the situation is more complicated. As spring progresses, the days get longer and the weather warmer; usually it gets somewhat drier as well. Each of these factors affects the germination, growth, and maturation rates of the crop, and also when it will reach harvestable size. For example, two rows of peas planted two weeks apart in March will usually mature only one week apart in June, because the germination conditions at the time of the second sowing will likely be much better; the young plants will grow faster in the then longer days, slowly catching up with the first crop. But even this difference is relative, as the slightest differences in weather between the two plantings can throw the schedule off in either direction. After years of experience in a particular garden one gets a feel for the season, but for beginners the garden calendar can stretch or shrink like a weather balloon.

With fall crops, this same process happens in reverse. Even a couple of days' difference in midsummer planting dates here in Vermont, where the days begin to shorten rapidly in late August, can lead to a harvest date difference of two, or even three, weeks! To make this kind of relay planting work requires the experience to recognize subtle cues in the garden that foretell the kind of season it's going to be—even before the weatherman knows. We've all heard these kinds of tips: that corn can be safely planted when the oak leaves are the size of a squirrel's ear; or that a thick band of color on a woolly caterpillar foretells an early fall and cold winter. The years of observation that went into the creation of this kind of folk wisdom—called phenology by scientists who study the timing of bird migrations, blooming of shrubs, and the timing of insect life cycles—was done by gardeners like yourself. Your own observation, in your own garden, will eventually provide you with the best and most reliable guides to the scheduling of successions.

Even the smallest garden can use varietal succession to stretch the harvest. For example, when planting direct-sown crops like beets and carrots, mix the seed of several different varieties before planting. Grow them just as you normally would, but you'll have both the early crop and the late crop in the same row. With a slow germinator like carrots you can go even further by mixing in a little radish seed. It will germinate immediately and the radishes will be ready for harvest by the time the carrots need thinning—harvesting them will even help with the job! (See the carrot entry in Chapter 10 for the details of this one.)

Mixed Crop Successions

Succession planting two or more different crops in the same space can be more or less complicated than single crop successions, depending on how you look at it. It's fairly simple to plan a tomato crop that follows spring spinach. Spinach should be planted outdoors very early in the spring (while the tomatoes are just getting started in the greenhouse), yet it can't take heat; tomatoes need warm weather to succeed and can't be set out in the garden until it arrives, by which time spinach must be harvested or it will have run to seed. Thus the two can ideally use the same space in the garden without a scheduling conflict (though their other needs should be considered as we discussed above in the crop rotation section).

There are many other, less obvious combinations that can be worked out, and playing around with all the options can be fun, and can provide some good eating in the process. The key is to organize the information you have about the various crops and your particular garden, then "map" all these details onto the time allotted to you by the season to see what crops might fit together.

Here's one way: take the list of crops you grow and arrange it into early, middle, and late maturing crops; I call them one, two, and three monthers. Next, make a second list arranged by whether each crop favors hot or cool weather (these should have a note telling if they are better adapted to spring or fall). To do this, make a simple flow chart showing the beds and/or rows down the left side, and the weeks of the season across the top. Then take the longest maturing crops that are most essential to you and block out the time and space they'll need according to your plan. Next, look for natural combinations with other long-season crops that want the opposite set of conditions. For example we plant our peas April 15 and harvest from the second week of July to the 1st of August. Then we take up the peas and transplant overwintering leeks that were started back around the first of May. As the leeks grow and the fall frosts become more severe, the soil from between the pea rows is used to hill the leeks for blanching. We could just as easily set out Chinese cabbages or endives, or direct seed some kohlrabi. Any of these will work; it's just a matter of which fits into the overall rotation scheme we've worked out.

Once you've figured out all the fits possible between long-season crops and mid-season crops, place the leftovers in an appropriate spot on your flow chart, then fill in with the short-season crops. It's possible that you'll have some spots that will be available for multiple plantings of really fast growing "catch crops" like garden cress, radishes, or even spinach.

Another possibility to keep in mind is that if their growth habits are compatible, some crops can overlap. This is particularly true if you are using transplants (which I recommend, especially for small gardens). For example, we set out Brussels sprouts transplants in mid-May, directly into a bed of spinach that was sown a month earlier in mid-April. As we harvest the spinach, the Brussels sprouts plants are allowed more and more room; by the time they need the

CROPS SORTED BY MATURITY RATE

One Monthers (< 60 days)	Two Monthers (60–90 days)		Three Monthers (> 90 days)		
Spinach	Lettuce	Corn	Pole Beans	Garlic	Parsnips
Radishes	Beets	Scallions	Tomatoes	Shallots	Br. Sprouts
Salad Greens	Carrots	Potatoes	Peppers	Squashes	Beets
(Mesclun)	Endive	Broccoli	Eggplants	Melons	Carrots
Lettuce	Peas	Cabbage	Corn	Pumpkins	Potatoes
Kohlrabi	Bush Beans	Cauliflower	Onions	Parsley	

This is just a sample listing, based on our garden and using transplants wherever appropriate.

whole bed, our spinach is out of the ground and in the freezer. Whenever you have a situation where a large plant takes a long time to size up, you have an opportunity for mixed succession planting.

Interplanting

The natural extension of this principle of co-existence is to see if any combinations exist that can spend their entire time together, that is, that can be "interplanted." This is largely a matter of looking at their growth habits—both above and below ground—to see if they are complementary rather than in conflict with each other.

Big Sam's favorite interplanting scheme, and one of mine as well, is to plant a quick crop of spinach between the pea rows. Both of us grow our peas on widely spaced fences. He planted his spinach in the middle of the rows; I grow in beds and put a row of spinach on each side of the pea fence, which runs down the center of the bed. Either way, the space does not go to waste, and the spinach is long gone before the peas need the room. This same principle applies to many crops. Whenever you have a tall crop like peas, or pole beans, or corn, or trellised cucumbers, you can find a crop that will thrive at its base without competing. In fact, the shade created by a tall crop may well provide the best place in the garden for shade-tolerant summer greens.

Another favorite of mine is to set young basil and marigold plants on the edge of the tomato bed, alternating with the tomatoes. This particular combination—and whole range of others—are thought by many gardeners to have pest and disease control effects as well. This body of lore, known as companion planting, deals with the

CROPS SORTED BY SEASONAL ADAPTATION
(Sample—based on our conditions)

Spring (Cool)			*Summer (Hot)*		*Fall (Cool)*	
Spinach	Lettuce	Cabbage	Cucumbers	Tomatoes	Spinach	Broccoli
Radishes	Scallions	Cauliflower	Melons	Peppers	Radishes	Cabbage
Peas	Onions	Br. Sprouts	Squashes	Eggplants	Beets	Lettuce
Beets	Turnips		Corn	Pumpkins	Carrots	Endive
Carrots	Parsnips		Basil		Kohlrabi	
Kohlrabi	Broccoli		Beans		Turnips	

mutually beneficial (or detrimental) effects different plants growing in close proximity will have on one another. Basil and marigolds may well improve the flavor of the tomatoes and repel insects, but the simple beauty of the arrangement, and the convenience of having the basil and tomatoes near each other at harvest time is enough reason for me.

Tradition also has it that planting herbs in among the broccoli will repel the cabbage butterfly. But in my garden, where herbs do alternate with the broccoli, I certainly haven't noticed any effect. In fact, I've caught the butterflies mating on the sage and the dill plants. But I do get a "free" crop of herbs from the bed that was prepared for the broccoli. So whatever the reason, be it beauty, productivity, or even pest control, interplanting is a practice worth pursuing.

In fact, all three of the techniques we've discussed in this chapter—rotation, successions, and interplanting—are excellent examples of ways in which an understanding of the plants, the soil, and the seasons of your garden can lead to big gains, regardless of the size of your garden. And planning can be fun; it's great, cheap entertainment for those long winter nights when garden dreams are the only green we've got—and educational at the same time. A garden is a huge jigsaw puzzle that takes place both in space and in time, and trying to figure out better ways to put all the pieces together is a fascinating and stimulating pastime.

CHAPTER 7

Seeds and Seedlings

Care in seeding will save more than twice the time taken when it comes to thinning later on. I consider it so important to have this phase of gardening done just right that, while I have outside help at times, I will let no one plant seeds for me.

Samuel R. Ogden

SEEDS

Seeds are at the heart of vegetable gardening, yet in my experience many gardeners, especially would-be organic gardeners, misunderstand the realities of how, where, and why seed is grown, and even more, the effect that seed selection has on harvest results. Just under a decade ago, after a number of years as a market gardener, I went into the mail order vegetable seed business. A lot of misconceptions I had about seed were quickly challenged, some important, some not.

One of the first things I discovered was that while there have been enormous improvements over the years in the quality and variety of vegetable seed, home gardeners are just not as important to the seed business as it is to them. Vegetable seed accounts for only something like 10 percent of the seed sold in this country every year. The vast majority (quite reasonable once you think about it) is seed for field corn, soybeans, grain, and grasses: for pastures, lawns, golf courses, and parks (not to mention reclamation of land stripped for construction, mining, or roadways). What's more, the major buyers of vegetable seed are not home gardeners, but vegetable farmers, who plant thousands of acres per year.

This—and a couple of other economic realities—affects the seed available to us. New varieties are generally bred for commercial growers, who know the value of good seed and are willing to pay a premium for it. Many of the characteristics of these improved vegetable varieties are great for home gardeners, too: enhanced yields, disease resistance, etc., and the quality of this new seed is very high. Other aspects, though—like uniform appearance, at the expense of flavor, and shipping tolerance at the expense of good texture—are in direct conflict with the needs of home gardeners. So the wise gardener will balance these two aspects when choosing which varieties to grow.

The breeder also is forced to balance different objectives when developing a new vegetable variety. Improvement of any domesticated plant (or animal) begins with a list of desired characteristics; then follows with propagation of individual plants that exhibit the desired traits. What happens in practice is that trade-offs must be made between, say, disease resistance and flavor, uniformity of color and taste, plant habit and yield.

No variety is perfect for everybody. A vegetable bred for commercial growers in one region need not be adapted to grow anywhere else in the world. A single large California broccoli grower, for example, may use more seed of a given variety over the course of a season than even the largest of our mail order home garden seed companies! But a variety bred for home gardeners, on the other hand, must grow as well in the desert Southwest as it does on the foggy Maine coast—even if attaining this wide adaptation requires the breeder to put aside other desirable traits—because only then will it sell well enough to offset the cost of its development.

There is, of course, some cross-over among categories. Small market gardeners often grow home garden and processing vegetables to sell direct from a farm stand, because the quality of their produce is more important than shipping ability. Home gardeners often do a significant amount of freezing and canning, and so grow varieties suited to once-over harvest. But on the whole, it is a good idea to figure out what a particular new variety was originally bred for.

Another group of vegetable varieties to consider is those which pre-date the current seed production and food distribution systems we have in this country—called heirlooms. The current definition of an "heirloom vegetable" variety is one that is more than 100 years old. But I think that a better cut-off point would be 1950. Immediately after World War II, agriculture and gardening in America underwent enormous changes, and the current system was born in that period. The widespread adoption of chemical fertilizers and pesticides, the development of hybrid vegetables, the completion of rural electrification, improvements in refrigeration and our interstate transportation system, suburban destruction of urban fringe market gardens—all these changes became part of a trend that resulted in the national rather than regional scope of our mass culture and agriculture which was born in the decades following the war.

Before this current period, vegetable seed companies were smaller and often grew their own seed, regionally adapted to the climate of the area in which the company was located. In fact, many seedsmen started out as market gardeners, and simply moved into selling seed they had saved for their own use. As their businesses developed, they collected choice varieties from other gardeners—who had selected their own favorite strains—and by close attention maintained them as distinct varieties. Unlike modern vegetable introductions, all of which are deliberately developed for sale, these heirloom varieties were simply selected over generations according to the whims and preferences of individual gardeners. Thus most are strongly adapted to a particular region of the country, and have an incredible range of qualities—in taste, texture, appearance, and disease or pest resistance—all of which were, for one reason or another, important to their backyard developers.

Of the thousands of regional heirlooms a relatively small number eventually became standards; many of our modern hybrids owe part of their parentage to them. Some of these old standards are still available today, though the re-selection and propagation of any variety subtly changes its nature over time. Early Jersey Wakefield cabbage and Bibb lettuce are two heirloom varieties that come to mind immediately.

Hybrid Seed

You may have noticed the mention of open-pollinated and hybrid seed in the discussion above. Unfortunately, many gardeners don't understand the distinction, or the differences, in both seed cost and garden performance related to this. Some organic gardeners think that it means, in essence, that one is organic and the other is not, which is not at all a relevant distinction.

To over-simplify the matter, let's say that there are two basic ways that seed comes to be formed on a plant: self-pollination and cross-pollination. Pollination is the transfer of pollen (a plant's version of sperm) from an anther to the stigma of a flower, where it can fertilize the flower's egg. In self-pollinated plants the whole process happens within the flower. Lettuce flowers, for example, pollinate themselves, as the female part of the flower containing the egg, in the process of opening, passes through an encircling ring of pollen-laden anthers. In cross-pollinated plants the pollen comes from an entirely different flower, or even plant, of the same species, transported by wind or the visitation of insects or other animals.

Open-pollination means simply that the plants are left to become pollinated (if possible) on their own, naturally. To say that a vegetable variety is open-pollinated, however, implies more than that; it implies that the variety will "breed true," that is, its offspring will resemble itself in all important particulars. After all, to call a kind of plant a variety (properly, a cultivar) is to recognize that it has a particular set of identifiable characteristics, of the kinds we've discussed above: yield, appearance, disease resistance, nutrient content, etc. In a self-pollinated vegetable, open-pollinated seed will produce 90 percent or more offspring that are true to type, because virtually all the pollen comes from the same source as the egg, and so the possibility of new genetic traits becoming established is small. But cross-pollinated plants—unless the parentage can be controlled in some way—will not maintain their identity, that is, the set of characteristics that defines a variety, and which we gardeners seek to maintain. Their genetics are in a constant state of flux; that is ideal in terms of their own need to adapt to their environment, but of little use to the gardener, who wants predictable characteristics.

Largely self-pollinated plants like lettuce, beans, peas, tomatoes (and to a lesser extent peppers and eggplants) are fairly easy to maintain, because it is their natural tendency to remain as distinct varieties once they are established as such. Cross-pollinated plants like spinach, beets, carrots, corn, and the onion, cabbage, and squash families require more attention. An established variety must be grown in total isolation from other members of its "breeding family," so that there can be no cross-pollination from outside the variety itself. Otherwise a fairly high percentage of offspring in the next generation will have traits untrue to the nature of the variety, though the fruits of the current crop will not show the differences.

Hybrids are not varieties in the above sense, as they will not breed true, that is, produce another generation of plants completely like themselves. The seed from a hybrid tomato, even though self-pollinated, will produce a grab bag of types, of which a quarter will resemble the hybrid's male parent, a quarter will resemble the hybrid's female parent, and half will display various combinations of the two parents' genetic traits. Eventually, after half a dozen generations or so, any of these offspring, could, by self-pollination, become distinct varieties themselves. If they exhibited especially valuable traits, they might be worth maintaining as such. In fact, this is how many new varieties are created: the breeder takes two plants which have characteristics of interest, crosses them, and in future generations looks for individual offspring that have the proper combination of the desired traits. He or she then attempts to bring those individuals to a state where they breed true, then perhaps crosses them with others developed the same way, until a whole range of desirable features has been bred into one plant or group of plants, and the variety stabilized.

But back to the hybrids themselves: the first generation (hence the designation F-1 we see in catalogs) of a particular controlled cross-pollination will exhibit what is called "hybrid vigor"—a sort of synergistic increase in the vigor of a plant due to the combination of widely diverse genetic traits—and great apparent uniformity (though its own offspring, the F-2 generation, will belie this). Since both vigor and uniformity are desirable to breeders (and to commercial vegetable farmers) the production of hybrid seed has been aggressively pursued since it was first developed as a method of improving corn varieties in the first half of this century.

The two keys to successful and profitable hybrid seed production are (1) maintenance of pure parent plant lines which, when crossed, will produce a hybrid of particular, desired characteristics, and (2) economical methods of making the cross-pollination to actually produce the seed. While naturally self-pollinated plants are relatively pure to begin with, and need only be grown out to check on their uniformity, cross-pollinated plants are more time-consuming to work with. It may take years to breed sufficiently pure parent plants, and significant hand work is involved. To be absolutely sure that the parent lines are kept pure, each flower may need to be pollinated by hand and the seed collected, cataloged, and replanted. Then, once the parent plants are ready to cross for production of the F-1 hybrid seed that you buy, attention must still be paid to ensure that they cross with each other, rather than with themselves or some other, unknown parent. All this means that hybrid seed is expensive to produce, and so the price of the seed is bound to be higher as well. The higher price is usually worth it, though, due to higher yields, uniformity, and disease resistance.

This higher cost of production is offset, in the mind of the seedsman, by a different factor: since the hybrid plants that result do not themselves breed true, the gardener and farmer who use the seed must return to the seedsman each year for more of the original hybrid seed. Further, the seed can be produced only by crossing the two parent lines, which are the sole property of the seedsman who developed them, and often known only to him. The "natural monopoly" which results means that, given a plant which is demonstrably superior, and enough astute human marketing to convince farmers and gardeners of that superiority, the seedsman can make a very handsome long-term profit on the sale of hybrid seed.

So, in a technical sense, there is no difference between hybrid and open-pollinated seed in terms of organic gardening. Functionally though, there is, because as seedsmen stop maintaining open-pollinated lines for sale, so they can concentrate on their own private, pure lines to be used for hybrid production, diversity—at least publicly available diversity—declines, and diversity is one of the underpinnings of the organic method. Plants like lettuce, beans, and peas may never suffer this fate because they are not economic to produce as hybrids. But even there, the drive toward mass production of a limited range of varieties works toward limiting diversity. What this means is that there is a natural alliance among seed exchanges, small seed companies, and organic gardeners to favor open-pollinated vegetable varieties, and to maintain heirloom strains, even though the short-term performance of a particular hybrid may be superior.

Buying Seed How can you tell whether a given variety is suited to your needs? Read the descriptions given in the seed catalog and on the packet very, very closely. Hybrids are virtually always identified as such, either by use of the word hybrid, or by the designation F-1 or F-2 in parentheses following the name. Seed catalogs usually describe their varieties specifically in the terms I used above. Disease resistance, uniformity, suitability for processing, and flavor will be mentioned if they exist; widespread adaptation will also be mentioned, and can almost be guaranteed if the variety in question has won an All

America Award (given to new introductions that perform well in a series of trial gardens nationwide). Seed packets are usually less helpful, but give clues to the variety's nature nonetheless.

There are three main sources of seed: local shops, mail order catalogs, and seed exchanges. Most American gardeners buy their vegetable seed from a rack display at the local hardware store or garden center; about 90 percent of the vegetable seed sold to home gardeners is sold this way. This is convenient. But, unfortunately, economics dictates that only certain kinds of seeds are sold in racks. Rack seed is generally cheap—a dollar or so a packet—and seed dealers place the racks with retailers on consignment, which means that the store can return for credit all the seed that doesn't sell. That sometimes amounts to 40 percent of the seed on the rack. It follows that the seed inside the packet must itself be very inexpensive, and the scale of operations very large, or the seed house that placed it in the rack will lose money on the deal. This effectively precludes selling all but the most common varieties—either those selected for the widest adaptation, or those which can be produced so cheaply that the enormous waste in returns can be tolerated.

The consignment system also leads to problems with seed freshness, as its low cost per packet means that the supplier, rather than requiring actual return of the unsold seed, simply issues a credit and lets the retailer dispose of it. Unfortunately, many retailers without a strong sense of responsibility, or even knowledge of gardening, keep the seed and sell it the following year at a discount. Whenever I see this happening I try to alert the retailer to the problems involved, but they rarely care, as it is not their name on the packet. When the gardener complains it is to the seedsman, not the retailer.

All good gardeners know that cheap seed is an unwise economy, but nowhere is this more true than in the home garden. After all the time and energy that goes into planning and preparing a garden, it makes no sense to end up with poor plants or an expanse of bare ground in exchange for the saving of a few dollars. So always check the date stamped on the seeds you buy and demand fresh, viable seed.

There are exceptions to the rule that rack seed is cheap and uninteresting: smaller regional companies will sometimes place racks in their area on consignment, and stock them with a full range of excellent varieties; they maintain a close relationship with the retailer and re-stock the rack regularly. A few specialty companies also stock racks with rare and unusual seeds on a selective national basis; though this seed will be given more attention by the retailer, it's still a good idea to look closely before you buy.

One last retail source of seed that is still around, at least in rural areas, is the farm and feed store. Alongside the seed potatoes, onion sets, and day-old chicks, you may find bins of loose seed, a hopper scale, and plain paper bags. The seed sold this way will frequently be well adapted to the region, having been requested and then tested by knowledgeable local farmers and gardeners for many years. Reputable dealers will not sell old seed; they depend on the repeat business of longtime residents and wouldn't jeopardize this relationship to make an extra couple of bucks per bag. But don't expect to see anything new or exciting, either; this is a source for the old reliables.

Of course, my opinion may be suspect, since I operate a mail order seed business, but even the average gardener is often better served buying his or her seeds by mail. Why? For one thing a much wider selection is available by mail order. By its nature a mail order catalog is able to offer much more depth of selection to a prospective customer because it speaks to the whole nation of gardeners. Burpee distributes its seed both by rack and by mail. The racks may offer a fairly wide selection of seed, say, over one hundred varieties of vegetables and flowers. But the catalog has that many *pages,* each full of choices—the breadth of supply is much greater.

Then there are specialty catalogs. The Pepper Gal specializes in peppers; Tomato Grower's Supply and The Tomato Seed Company concentrate on tomatoes; each lists more than one hundred varieties. Our own company, The Cook's Garden, began as a specialty catalog for salad lovers. When we began, it offered nothing but seeds for salad greens, including two dozen different lettuces and a host of obscure salad plants. We now offer more than fifty lettuces and an equal number of rare salad plants, in addition to a broad range of vegetable and flower varieties of interest to cooks who like to entertain from their kitchen gardens. There are catalogs that specialize in giant vegetables, Oriental vegetables, herbs (both seed and plants), and heirloom vegetables. No seed rack can match the depth of their selections.

There are also strongly focused regional catalogs that specialize in varieties adapted to particular parts of the country with their diverse climates. There is Vesey's in maritime Canada; Johnny's in New England; Hasting's in the Southeast; Plants of the Southwest;

Garden City Seeds in the Northern Plains; Territorial Seeds in the Pacific Northwest; there is even a catalog called High Altitude Gardens for the Rocky Mountain states. In each case, the depth of selection offered is vastly superior to what can be effectively distributed by racks, except by those same regional companies.

A final reason it makes sense to buy your seed by mail order is accountability. It may seem that buying at the local hardware store gives you face-to-face contact with the source of your seed, but that contact is illusory. The salesclerk rarely knows anything at all about it, and if there is a problem won't likely care enough to help you solve it. Mail order firms, while you can't talk to them face-to-face, almost always have horticultural help lines, and are intimately familiar both with the varieties they sell and the details of garden practice. In addition, every respectable mail order seed firm offers a money-back guarantee if the seeds don't perform as advertised. Only the top few rack seed firms offer such a guarantee, and they sell by mail order as well. There is simply no good mechanism for replacement or refund within the consignment marketing system used for most rack seed distribution.

The last source of seed for your garden is to trade with your neighbors. A hundred years ago, before garden seed companies attained the size and influence they now have, this was the major source of seed—gardeners saved much of the seed they used from a few select plants in their own gardens. Today, with the near universal trade in seeds, this distribution method has become the province of seed exchanges, more or less organized groups of gardeners who maintain old-fashioned, or heirloom, vegetable varieties that commercial seedsmen no longer sell.

The number of different varieties available from seed exchanges is staggering. The granddaddy of these, The Seed Savers Exchange (SSE), of Decorah, Iowa, prints an annual listing of the seeds available from its members running to over 250 pages of condensed, single-spaced, unillustrated listings! While SSE is just a clearing house for member names, addresses, and seed offerings, some smaller exchanges operate catalogs as a method of funding their work. You cannot expect all the seed from these sources to show the same degree of uniformity and vigor as seed from commercial sources, since much of it is grown by committed amateurs in home gardens, and thus not subject to the degree of control that professional seed companies exercise. But for sheer diversity there is no better source, and the contacts, the friends, you can make through exchanging the seed of favorite varieties are worth ten times the effort and expense of joining an exchange and saving your own seed to trade with other members.

While the seed available through exchanges is collected and distributed by amateur gardeners, the production system for commercially grown seed is a highly developed industry. A common misconception is that every seed house grows its own seed, on its own farm, and that the varieties it lists, even if they have the same name as those in another catalog, must be slightly different. This is not really the case, though. Particularly with hybrid seed, but also with most open-pollinated strains, the seed offered by different catalogs or rack companies will have been grown on the same farm and then sold at wholesale to the various retail seed companies.

Some seed companies do have their own vegetable varieties that they continue to preserve, in the sense that they grow a limited supply of the seed—called stock seed—every few seasons. They rigorously select it for its essential, defining characteristics by removing and destroying all imperfect plants before maturity. The actual seed you buy, however, will be grown on contract by a seed farm somewhere else from that stock seed.

If you take the time to consider it, this makes great sense: for every species of plant there will be, somewhere, an ideal climate to produce the seed, and seed is relatively inexpensive to ship; thus the seed company can send its small supply of highly refined stock seed to a contract grower in that ideal climate to be "increased" for distribution. One pound of stock seed becomes a thousand pounds of seed for sale, and that seed, grown under ideal conditions, is the best possible. Some gardeners are concerned, say, that a cold-hardy lettuce variety grown out for seed in California will not withstand the rigors of a New England spring; fortunately, long-bred vegetable varieties do not lose their essential adaptations in a single season, so this is not a problem.

Thus, most of the sweet corn sold in this country (by all the garden seed companies) is grown in a few counties in Idaho; the beans and peas, likewise. Most of the seed for the cabbage family is grown in the Skagit Valley of Washington state; beets and carrots, too, are grown in the Pacific Northwest while America's, no, even much of the world's lettuce seed is grown in California. All over the world, certain climates ideal for the production of a particular plant are home to seed farms that grow contract crops for seedsmen from virtually every country that has a seed industry.

There are a number of ways that seed can be treated to help fight **Treated Seed**
disease or increase yields. Some of these are just fine from an organic perspective, like inoculation of legume seed with *rhizobia*
bacteria (discussed in the bean and pea sections of Chapter 10) or
partial sterilization of the seed coat by soaking in hot water to kill
disease spores. Other methods of seed treatment, though, like coating the seed with fungicides, involve the use of chemicals like Captan that are known to be hazardous to the health of the people who
use and manufacture them. You can recognize chemically treated
seed because, by law, it must be dyed; not just an occasional seed,
but every one. If just a few seeds are dyed, that is for identification,
in cucumbers of the pollinator, and in highly refined, proprietary
strains to mark the origin of the seed lot.

Captan was introduced by Chevron Chemical Company in 1949
and was until recently the second most commonly used fungicide
in the country. It accounted in 1989 for about 20 percent of all the
fungicides applied, though the Environmental Protection Agency
had proposed banning its use on food crops as early as 1985, because
it was found to cause cancer in laboratory animals. This ban on
Captan was put aside until 1990, and even once it was in effect,
exceptions were made for twenty-four specific crops, and for its use
as a seed treatment.[7]

These uses are still allowed because of a judgment by the EPA
that the benefits to growers (amounting to about $70 million per
year) outweigh the health risks to consumers. To my way of thinking this represents a subsidy to the growers from the consumers, as
well as an even greater assumption of risk on the part of the growers—or at least on the part of their workers in the Captan-dusted
field. But in terms of home gardening the idea of subsidies is a moot
point because a home vegetable gardener is both grower and consumer—he or she enjoys any possible benefits from using Captan
and runs all the risks.

Home gardeners don't get any cash benefit from the use of chemicals like Captan, though. This kind of seed treatment is used primarily to kill bacteria and fungi in the soil that attack the seed of
crops planted in cold, wet soils; what it does is temporarily sterilize
a little bit of soil immediately surrounding the seed. But there is a
simpler solution: don't plant until the soil is ready. Commercial
growers may not have the luxury of waiting out a spell of bad
weather, but home gardeners definitely do. Just as I'd rather spend

an hour of quiet hoeing than half an hour struggling with a roto-tiller, I'd rather wait an extra week for my sweet corn, than use a chemical that creates pollution and disease problems at every step of its manufacture and distribution. If the small amounts of Captan sprayed and dusted on our food to prevent rot are enough to cause laboratory cancers, imagine the effects on the workers in the factory that produces and packages it, in the warehouse that ships it to garden centers, the truck drivers that deliver it, and the salespeople who handle it day after day, along with a witch's brew of other chemicals.

In Chapter 3 we discussed the use of wood treated with fungi-cides, a compromise that involves chemical pollution in a number of places along the line of its production process as well. The nature of the chemicals used for this, the permanence of their protection, and the relatively minor dispersal that results, are far different than the case with fungicidal seed treatments. A wood post is treated only once, and the chemical stays in the post; a seed treatment is added to the soil every time you plant and can't help but disperse into the surrounding soil. The post is not in direct contact with the food you eat, but the treatment is, even though it has months to break down before harvest. Most important, though, is the fact there are other ways to protect the seed; every method of protecting wood uses some sort of chemical treatment—paint at the minimum—and there is not enough naturally rot-resistant wood available.

Speaking for a moment as a seedsman, let me say that I'd like to see all of agriculture and horticulture return to organic methods. To not buy treated seed—and demand alternatives—helps build a more sustainable horticultural infrastructure for the future. Researchers at Cornell University and other research institutions are hard at work on biological alternatives to chemical seed treatment. Why? Because gardeners have asked for alternatives.

Just as many of us who began in the organic agriculture move-ment have worked over the last decade to learn the skills necessary to build a new food system, there are people working toward the same goals in ornamental horticulture: lawn care, landscaping, care of trees, shrubs, and perennials. Within another ten to twenty years we will have the intellectual infrastructure that drives the devel-opment of new materials and methods of gardening. At that point an organic seed industry will exist along with all the other support structures of an organic horticulture. Your dollars and your de-mands do make a difference.

SEEDLINGS

To my mind, any vegetable that can be raised from transplant probably should be, especially if your garden is small or your season short. It will also greatly improve the productivity of any garden because it allows successions and interplantings to be more closely planned. As soon as one crop is harvested, you've got another set of plants ready to make use of the space. Why give each broccoli plant a foot and a half of space when it's young and only needs a couple of inches?

Not all vegetables transplant well, though. Root crops like carrots, leafy biennial herbs like dill and fennel, and the heading types of Chinese cabbages are all likely to run to seed in response to the stress of transplanting, instead of yielding a crop. Still others grow so quickly when sown directly in the garden that transplanting isn't really worth the extra effort. Greens like spinach, mustard, arugula, and cress are good examples. In the end, your own garden plan is going to determine which plants you should start indoors.

CROPS SORTED BY SEEDING METHOD

Seeded Indoors

Normal	Possible
Tomatoes	Melons
Eggplants	Beans
Peppers	Corn
Basil	Beets
Parsley	Squash
Perennial Herbs	Pumpkins
Cabbage	
Broccoli	
Cauliflower	
Br. Sprouts	
Onions	
Leeks	
Lettuce, early	

Direct Seeded

Normal	Possible
Corn	Tomatoes
Peas	Broccoli
Beans	Cabbage
Squash	Cauliflower
Melons	Onions
Pumpkins	Leeks
Spinach	Basil
Scallions	
Carrots	
Beets	
Radishes	
Turnips	
Kohlrabi	
Lettuce	

Broadcast Sown

Normal	Possible
Salad Greens (Mesclun)	Carrots
Cover Crops	Beets
	Peas

One of the biggest mistakes gardeners make is starting too soon. I know gardeners in Los Angeles who harvest tomatoes in January, but north of USDA Zone Six you shouldn't even think of starting tomatoes until February. We start ours in two batches in mid-March and again the first of April. If the weather breaks early, it's worth it; but if spring is slow, the early ones just get tossed out as they are too big when planting season arrives. That's why it's a good idea to make two sowings of seed, a week or two apart. If something happens to one set, you've got a backup. With two plantings, a week before and a week after the theoretically ideal planting date, you're ready either way. You can always give away the extra plants if things work out.

Keep in mind that all else being equal, you are better off with young, vigorous plants than older, root-bound ones. The best produce comes from plants that grow quickly, without what the pros call "checks," that is shortages of any nutrient, of water, or of temperatures to their liking. If the plants are a little small, all you've lost is a week or two in the garden; that is often made up in the good growing days of early summer. Two weeks in March is only worth a couple of days in May, or so we say in the nursery trade.

TIMING CHART FOR SEEDLINGS

Group 1 *(Start 10–12 weeks before the frost-free date)*	Group 2 *(Start 6–8 weeks before the frost-free date)*	Group 3 *(Start 2–4 weeks before the frost-free date)*
Eggplants	Tomatoes	Dill
Peppers	Cabbage	Melons
Parsley	Cauliflower	Beans
Onions	Broccoli	Br. Sprouts
Leeks	Basil	Squash
Perennial Herbs	Lettuce	Lettuce
Celeriac	Endive	Annual Herbs

Celery, celeriac, leeks, and parsley are among the first plants to be started, a good twelve weeks before their intended transplant date, which is itself two to four weeks before the last frost. South of USDA Zone Six that will likely mean early January. You should probably just wait to direct-seed them in the garden a month before the last frost, and save the seedling space for other crops. Gardeners in the North should also start seedlings of thyme, sage, rosemary, and other perennial herbs at the same time if they want a decent harvest in the first season. This is true whether you grow your plants in a windowsill or a greenhouse.

Tomatoes, peppers, eggplants, and basil need really warm conditions. But once they germinate they grow faster, and so can be started only eight to ten weeks before the frost-free date. If you have a greenhouse, you can cut another week off that, due to the increasingly great difference spring brings to greenhouses versus windowsills. We have grown great tomato transplants in only six weeks; even a month-old plant will make a good sized bush by midsummer and yield a lot of fruit.

There is a third group of vegetables that most gardeners direct-seed, but that can be started indoors if you have a very short season, or simply can't wait for spring. All the members of the cabbage family do well grown from transplant, as does lettuce. Start them only six to eight weeks before the last frost, though; because if they get too big in the flat they don't withstand transplanting as well, and are unlikely to yield a first-class harvest. Melons, cucumbers, squash, beans, and even corn can be started in plug flats, peat pots, or large soil blocks a mere two to four weeks before the frost-free date. The plants grow so fast and are so succulent that it's difficult to hold them in a tray longer than that.

Containers

There are practically as many ways to start seeds as there are gardeners. Big Sam seeded cold-hardy plants directly in the soil of the cold frame, to be set out a month later. Southern gardeners may well be able to start their seedlings right in the garden. Turn over a small part of your garden, say five or ten percent, to nursing along seedlings. This bed should receive special care during spring preparation, so that the soil is in fine tilth and the seedlings have the best possible conditions. Be ready to rig up shade during hot periods, and some sort of cover during any unusually cold weather. If you make this nursery bed in a different section of the garden each season, as part of your overall rotation, eventually you will have improved your whole garden.

Northern gardeners, who pretty much have to start some of their plants indoors, use all different kinds of containers: wooden flats, egg boxes, sawed-off milk cartons, recycled garden center six-packs, peat pots, soil blocks, and plug trays. All will work, but whichever you choose remember that the key to growing healthy transplants is consistency: all the plants of a given size and type should get equal treatment, which is difficult using a mishmash of containers in all different sizes and shapes.

One of the most common modular systems is peat pots and strips. Many organic gardeners prefer them simply because they want the benefits of individual containers for each plant, but they don't like to use plastic. Peat containers have the benefit of consistent sizing, but they are messy to work with, and unless you use the strips, their shape makes them top-heavy once the plants have reached a decent size. Once they tip over they are difficult to keep moist as the water runs off instead of sinking in. Also, peat is a nonrenewable resource in the sense that its rate of formation in the northern tundra—only 1/8 inch a year—is far outstripped by current horticultural use.

Perhaps the best system to use, from an organic perspective, is soil blocks formed by compressing a peat-compost mix into cubes of different sizes with a small, hand-held press. These blocks are then placed into special growing trays. All you need for this system is one or more of the presses, or block makers, which cost from $15 to as much as $100 (depending on the size), plus a collection of special three-sided trays. Both are available by mail order. Generally, soil blocks require a bit more practice to make and skill to maintain than a plug or peat system, as watering is more critical. Too much water can erode the blocks and make them hard to separate at transplant time; too little water may let them dry out enough so that it is difficult to get them wet again. The time required to make soil blocks must also be considered.

When we were commercial gardeners we did a detailed analysis of the different systems, and without a doubt the most efficient and least expensive integrated system is plug trays. These are inexpensive plastic inserts for the standard 10 × 20-inch plastic greenhouse tray. They are similar to the six-packs that store-bought transplants are grown in, but are slightly heavier gauge plastic and so, easily reusable. The insert is made up of conical "cells" of different sizes, according to the size of plant that will be grown in them. Commercial growers, with automatic water and fertilizer systems, often start their plants in plug inserts with 288 or even 406 cells per 10 × 20-inch tray. That gives each plant a root mass not much larger than a pencil eraser!

Low-tech market gardeners and amateurs use trays with 162, 98, 72, 50, or as few as 24 cells per tray. This makes it considerably easier to care for the seedlings, because each has a much larger amount of potting soil to maintain it. The plant plugs produced by this system are easy to transplant, because the conical shape of the cells directs root growth downward; if set out at the right stage of growth the seedlings take right off once set out in the garden. The trays and inserts are not expensive, and with proper storage in the off-season will last a number of years.

The plastic used for these trays is recyclable, though programs may not be in place everywhere to actually do so. Still, this is a better choice for the organic gardener than the similar white plastic-foam trays. The plants may not know the difference, but manufacture of most of these uses chlorofluorocarbons, the class of chemicals thought most responsible for the deterioration of the atmosphere's protective ozone layer. A number of mail order companies sell both kinds of plug kits. Before you buy you should ask how the trays are made, and of what.

What you put into the container or block is just as vital. Straight compost—what my grandfather used—is fine for open flats, as long as it is fully matured and screened. But the texture of straight compost is too dense for plugs and soil blocks. In plugs it tends to pack down and then become hard to water; in blocks it erodes and soon you have a tray full of compost instead of individual blocks. A mix that is at least half peat will allow the block to hold together until the seedling's roots have a chance to spread, binding it into a sturdy and stable package. In plug trays and recycled six-packs the peat's coarseness helps keep the surface from packing down. A good proportion is two parts peat to one part screened compost, with a cup of lime added for every four bushels of mix. If you want to put fertilizer right into the mix, and thus into the blocks, add half a cup each of blood meal, rock phosphate, and greensand per bushel. We prefer to keep the mix nutrient-poor and then fertilize as we water, because that gives us some flexibility in fine-tuning the growth rate of the seedlings to the variations of spring weather.

Another reason peat is important is that it can absorb up to 15 times its own weight in water, and its fibrous structure is able to hold that water for slow release to the growing seedling. Commercial potting mixes are available which are mostly peat, and may be a good choice for the beginner, though you should be sure to look for an untreated, unfertilized mix. Also be sure you are buying a seedling mix. What you want will be brown in color, very light by volume, and sprinkled throughout with white or grayish specks— these are vermiculite or perlite (or both), which are added to the mix to improve its aeration and drainage. A loosely packed bag the

Soil Mixes

size of a feed sack or large bag of bird seed should weigh less than ten pounds. What you want to avoid is the small bags of fine-grained, soot-colored potting soil. They are much heavier and usually don't have the perlite and vermiculite; these mixes have all of the disadvantages of compost, and none of the benefits.

An additional benefit of the commercial mixes is that they are, for all intents and purposes, sterile. If your compost was not properly made—that is, the pile did not heat up fully—it may contain disease spores from the plants that were composted. In the incubator-like conditions under which most plants are started, that can be fatal. Of course, you can sterilize your compost by heating it (to 160°F for four hours) in the oven before mixing it with the peat. Whatever way you choose, remember that the first few days of a seedling's life make a big difference to its eventual success in the garden, and it is less resistant to problems that it might shrug off outdoors.

If you are using a tray system or container to start your seedlings, fill it loosely with potting soil—until it overflows—then scrape off the excess. Don't pack down the mix, because young plant roots need air. The mix will pack down naturally as it is watered. You should moisten the mix slightly before filling the containers, though, to keep down the dust, and so that the particles will adhere to one another.

The process of making soil blocks is a bit more complex, and requires a bit of practice. The mix should be wet enough to mold well in the block-making press; when you squeeze a handful, some water should drip out between the base of your fingers. First, fill a flat-bottomed tray or tub with the mix, then grasp the block maker down around its base and scrape it across the bottom of the tray or tub that contains the mix, forcing the potting soil into it by pressing against the side of the container; it might take a couple of passes to get enough mix into the press. Once the press is full, release the blocks onto a growing tray by pushing down on the plunger. The ideal growing tray for blocks is smooth-bottomed and three-sided, so that the blocks can be moved (if necessary, but try to avoid it) by sliding them out of the tray rather than picking them up. Continue in this fashion until the growing tray is full, set it aside, and start the next tray. Most soil blockers make a small dimple in the top of the finished block where the seed should be sown.

Germination   Outdoors, seeds should be planted three times as deep as they are across. But indoors they need only be half that deep, which means

GERMINATION AND GROWING TEMPERATURE
for various vegetable and herb transplants

Crop	Germ. Temp* (°F)	Days to Germ.†	Growing Temp‡ (°F)	Weeks to T'Plant§
Tomatoes	60-85	7-14	55-85	6-8
Eggplants	75-90	7-14	65-85	8-10
Peppers	65-95	7-14	65-85	8-10
Cabbage	45-95	4-12	55-75	4-6
Broccoli	45-85	4-12	55-75	4-6
Cauliflower	45-85	4-12	55-75	4-6
Brussels sprouts	45-85	4-12	55-75	4-6
Lettuce	40-80	2-14	55-75	2-4
Basil	65-85	7-14	65-85	8-10
Parsley	50-85	14-28	55-75	10-12
Onions	50-95	7-14	55-75	6-8
Leeks	50-95	7-14	55-75	6-8
Celeriac	60-70	7-14	55-75	10-12

*This is a range; optimum temp. is somewhere in between (high middle)
†Lower number is at optimum temp; higher number at high or low temp.
‡Best is a variation of night and day temps at levels shown.
§This depends on both light and temp levels, and is a range.

less waiting for them to break ground. Why? Because while depth brings consistent moisture and temperature, seeds also need to be near the surface to get oxygen, and in some cases, light. Indoors you can control temperature, moisture, oxygen, and light, so it's just a matter of balancing these needs.

Each seed is made up of a tiny genetic model of its parent and a supply of food. This package is dried for storage, but as soon as conditions permit, it springs back to life, though many species of plants have a built-in dormancy lock to keep them from germinating during the wrong season.

The first stage of germination sees the seed swell with water, and activate stored enzymes that start digestion of the seed's food supply. As this process accelerates, oxygen is needed, which is why, although seeds want moist conditions, you shouldn't drown them. Just soak the medium once after planting, then cover the flat with some sort of moisture barrier until the plants break ground.

After a few hours (or days, depending on the species of plant) the first seedling root, called the radicle, emerges and both water intake and food consumption level off. Then the seedling starts to actively grow new cells. As the radicle begins to grow, the metabolic products of the seed's consumption of its starch and sugar reserves are sent to the growing tip. Tiny feeder roots begin to spread throughout the soil. Soon the plant breaks ground and finds the last vital growth factor it needs: light. If you haven't added fertilizer to the soil mix, then you will need to start both watering and fertilizing soon after. From this point on the seedling becomes dependent on the nutrients its roots can find in the soil, the moisture that makes them available, and the quality of light its leaves receive. Without the right amount of each—in proper proportion to each other and the temperature—no plant will prosper.

Temperature now sets the pace for change in the plant. Optimum temperatures vary from plant to plant, but most vegetables will thrive in temperatures of 65–75°F. If your house isn't this warm and you don't have a greenhouse, you can start your seeds on top of the refrigerator or in the wash room. But keep a close eye on the flats, because the moment they break ground they need all the light they can get.

Seedling Growth

For all practical purposes the flats should be kept at 55°F or above. Many species of vegetables will germinate at temperatures below that, but they will take so long you'll use up your seedling space nursing them along, and I've never met a gardener who didn't feel short of both time and space. Also, premature bolting (formation of a seed stalk and flowers) may be triggered in some biennial vegetables if they are exposed to extended periods of cool temperatures.

Since heat and light fuel plant growth, the relationship between the two is critical to growing healthy, vigorous seedlings. A common mistake among gardeners without a greenhouse is to keep plants at too high a temperature for the amount of light they receive. Not only is the light from a south-facing window more short-lived than it might seem (rarely exceeding eight hours a day), but the glass in house windows screens out parts of the sunlight that plants need. What often happens is that the gardener tries to compensate for slow growth with more fertilizer and higher temperatures; both of these make the problem worse, since they increase the imbalance between light levels and the other factors necessary for good growth. The result is limp, leggy seedlings that are hard put to cope with outdoor conditions when planting time arrives.

It's also possible for the temperature to be too high in a greenhouse. On cloudy days the experienced gardener lowers the temperature in the greenhouse to compensate for the lower light levels. Despite the temptation to keep the temperature high and catapult the plants ahead, it will only put them out of touch with the season as it is developing, and cause problems later. While every plant has a range of temperatures that it likes best—and which should be provided—within that range the cooler you keep it the better off the plant will be. Don't take things too far, though. The combination of low temperature, low light, and overwatering are ideal for the development of the damping-off fungus, which can level a whole flat of transplants before you know it. If any plants start showing the symptoms (withering of the stem at the soil line and collapse of the plants) remove them from the flat and destroy them. Then get the flat out into the sun as quickly as you can; high light levels and fresh air will do wonders for the remaining seedlings.

Fertilizer and water also need to be kept in proper proportion. To grow, plants need nutrients, and without enough moisture, they'll not only be unable to take up those nutrients, they'll wilt and die. But too much water washes away the nutrients in the tray or pot and the plants will starve. The conventional wisdom holds that you should feed the plants every seven to ten days, but really it should be every certain *number of waterings,* not every certain number of days. That way the amount of fertilizer is based on the amount of water that the plant has taken up, not some abstract calendar date. One compromise solution is to fertilize every time you water, at one-quarter strength. That way you don't need to keep track of when you last fertilized, and the plants get an even, constant supply of nutrients.

Keep an eye out for signs of under- or over-fertilization. Leaves that curl under are a sign of overfeeding; discoloration, though, is usually a sign of underfeeding. If the plant is pale, that is likely a sign of nitrogen deficiency; leaves with purplish undersides indicate a shortage of phosphorus; leaves with bronze edges show a shortage of potassium. Since seaweed and fish fertilizers contain balanced amounts of all these, the solution is just to increase or decrease the strength or frequency of feedings.

The mix we've used, both for growing bedding plants to sell, and for our own gardens, works out to a tablespoon each of liquid fish fertilizer (or fish emulsion) and liquid seaweed per gallon of water. This is the full-strength formula and should be diluted 4:1 if you fertilize with every watering. Because we had a lot of trays of plants to water—sometimes a thousand or more—we mixed it up in a bucket at sixteen times the normal strength, and then watered with a hose that had a siphon proportioner on it. Even with only a dozen trays or so you might find this more convenient than using a watering can. If so, check the equipment section for a description of how a proportioner works and where you can get one.

Hardening Off   It's not enough to raise vigorous, healthy seedlings if they are so pampered that they can't survive the sun and wind and rain and the seesaw effect of day and night temperature changes. Here in Vermont we can get a spell of hot humid weather followed immediately by brisk sunny days that peak in the 60's and fall back into the 30's only a few hours after sunset. But frosty nights aren't the only enemy to tender transplants. Wind can be just as hard on young plants raised in the still of a greenhouse or windowsill, snapping off brittle stems or flattening them to the ground, where they can fall prey to all kinds of fungi and insects. Even the sun on which they are so dependent can be dangerous; plants grown indoors develop extra photosynthetic cells in the leaves, and a sudden increase in available light can cause them to literally overload, then shrivel and fall.

All of these problems—changes in temperature, wind, and light—can be solved by hardening off the seedlings. As planting day approaches, help them adjust gradually to outdoor conditions. This will give them a chance to develop their defenses. At first, just move the flats outside for a few hours in the afternoon; then gradually increase the time they spend in the open air, exposed to the sun and wind. Hardening off is one of the best uses of a cold frame: put the plants in the frame after the first few days, and then leave the lid off for longer and longer periods each day until it is no longer needed. This process could last as long as a week, but doesn't have to; if good transplanting weather comes along (see the next chapter), by all means set them out.

Buying Seedlings   For those gardeners who lack the time and space to start their own plants, the local garden center may be the only source of seedlings. If you do buy started plants, be sure to examine them closely. You could bring more problems home than you'd care to deal with. Forewarned is forearmed.

Obviously, the seedlings should be free of insects and their eggs; be sure to check the undersides of the leaves, and look closely where the leaf branches meet the stem and at the growing point of the plant—where the youngest, tenderest leaves are—as those are favorite congregating places of many feeding insects. But also check underneath the flats themselves: night-feeding pests will crawl up between the sections of a six-pack container to spend their days safe from harsh sunlight and the prying eyes of the greenhouse proprietor.

Second, buy only young, vigorously growing plants. Just how to recognize over-age transplants is difficult to describe; probably the two surest visual cues—beyond the presence of flowers or fruit—are the color and the shape of the leaves. For example, seedlings of the cabbage family all start out looking quite similar, but as they age the leaves take on different shapes: Brussels sprouts are round and cupped; broccoli leaves are spreading, with a slight ruffling of the edge; cauliflower leaves are quite upright, with a more distinct ruffling. The appearance of these leaf characteristics, combined with a change in the leaf surface to a leathery texture, signals that the plants have been held too long. With fruiting plants like tomatoes and their relatives, or members of the squash and cucumber family, avoid seedlings that are in flower, or worse, which have small fruit present—they are over-mature, and they won't produce as well as younger plants!

Third, the plants should be well proportioned and well fed. Greenhouses are expensive to operate and the garden center operator needs to fit as many plants as possible into the space he has available. This means that the seedlings are too often crowded, and so consequently their tops are developed all out of proportion to their side branches. The smaller your garden the more money it is worth to buy larger plants that have been grown with more space to develop. The rule-of-thumb is that at planting time a seedling should be as wide as it is tall. If you are unsure that the plant has been properly fertilized, look back at the discussion of nutrient deficiency symptoms earlier in this chapter, so you will learn how to recognize the signs of both over- and under-fertilization.

CHAPTER 8

Preparing and Planting the Garden

Now all is ready for the preparation of the seedbed, but before we start we have a few chores to perform in preparation for the actual seeding. First we check our garden tools and ready them for use; we get the pea wire out of storage and prepare the compost pile, for we will have to use compost in the planting of peas.

Samuel R. Ogden

Taking a barren piece of ground that has lain fallow all winter and planting it is profoundly rewarding. I love the smell of the frost-loosened soil. As I work, I occasionally stop to lift a handful and crumble it gently between my fingers, take the last small bit up to my nose, and give it a sniff. Our soil can be just a bit astringent in its natural acidity, and if I detect too great a bite I'll spread a bit of lime before going any further. That astringency wakes the nose, though, to a complex fragrance. There is really no one smell that a healthy, long-worked soil exudes, no one overriding odor, but rather a myriad of scents from all the seasons gone by and all the crops that have grown there.

As I rest on my fork in the early morning light and sniff, I can imagine farmers and gardeners from all over the world, and their crops, their families, their lives; I can smell the ancient, fertile soils of Mesopotamia, Chichan Itza, China. I can sense their toil, their sweat, their tears, but also their joy, and the warm satisfaction they must have felt at harvest time. That vision—that my work is part of a continuous, human tradition spanning so many centuries—doesn't come while struggling against the balance of a top-heavy, overpowered machine, or from inside a layer of protective clothing; it comes from close-up contact with the soil, the air, the plants, the animals: the whole community of the garden, stirring in anticipation of another day's warming.

Others think that spring soil preparation is too much work and spend their hard-earned money on power equipment to hurry through the job. Not me; the work I'd have to do to pay for a tiller is much less enjoyable than the garden work it replaces, and wrestling with a tiller makes gardening itself into a job, not a joy. I had to use one when I was a market gardener—there was so much to be done and so little time—but now I'd rather listen to the thrubbing of the partridge off in the woods than a struggling engine. And there is no worry about revolving piston-powered parts that can get out of hand to interfere with my contemplation. My four-year-old son can help me, digging with his own trowel, examining with delight the worms, grubs, and beetles we unearth. I can stop my work to enjoy his proud display of small rocks he's found and lugged to the edge of the garden.

At planting time everything is so new, so clean, so full of promise; as yet there is no drought, no disease, nor any other problem; no neglect has lessened the cornucopia to come, and in the mind no effort is required to produce it, harvest it, or prepare it for the pantry; it is still perfect and ideal.

If you insist on using a tiller there are few considerations to take into account beyond what was noted in Chapter 3. With the small, high-speed cutting-type tillers you will be able to work fairly well within a bed system, as I recommend. Simply stand on the established path and allow the tiller to work back and forth, perpendicular to the path. This is a bit more of a strain on your back than walking behind the machine, but it won't leave footprints of compaction across the bed.

With a larger, tine-propelled or wheel-driven tiller, you can minimize the damage caused by footsteps in the newly turned soil by treading the straight and narrow. If you look closely at the tiller's tines, and then examine a newly turned area closely by feeling around with your hand in the soil, you'll notice that the center of the row (where the main armature of the tiller is) never gets as well prepared as the two strips on either side, which are directly in line with the tines. So, unless you can walk completely outside the path of the tines, tread instead in the center, and then do your planting in the better prepared side strips. With root crops in particular, this will make sure that there is the least effect from compaction.

When preparing a bed by hand with a spading fork, no such concerns are necessary, because you work backwards across the bed, and so don't step on the newly prepared soil. If you really want to do the best possible job, work from a planting board, which is simply a piece of 2 × 12 lumber as long as the bed is wide. If you stand on the board while working you decrease soil compaction even further, and as compaction of the topsoil is one of the primary inhibitors of root development, you'll be doing the plants a real favor.

While little things like never stepping in the growing beds might seem inconsequential, the fact is that, combined with a whole repertoire of other methods of increasing your garden's productivity, they create a very noticeable difference. One accomplished gardener and writer on the subject calls these little details "one percenters." Each by itself may only boost your yields or reduce your problems by one percent, but if you keep looking for little ways to improve your gardening, eventually those "one percenters" will add up to a much more productive, healthy and satisfying garden.

How do you know when the soil is ready? Clayey soils in particular must be worked at the right time, or they harden into brick-like clods after digging; and sandy soils don't hold up in beds if they're too dry when prepared. Big Sam believed the soil could be worked only once the "sogginess" was out. What does this mean? Pick up a loose handful of soil, then close your hand and slowly squeeze it into a fist; no water should come out between the bases of your fingers. Unclench your fist. The handle-shaped clod of soil on your palm should be moist enough to hold together but not slick or shiny; the wrinkle and print lines of your hand should not be visible. Poke the clod with a twig. It should break apart into smaller clods, some of which will collapse simply from the shock of falling off the main clod. That is soil at the proper moisture content for spring planting.

Once conditions were right, Big Sam, who planted his four-plot garden in rows, would begin.

So, no matter what the plot plan says, start working the plot which is ready first, at the side which is least moist. Spade or plow under the manure (spread the previous fall). This must be done carefully so that all of it is turned under. Throw off all the rocks and stones. The new surface should be smooth, friable dirt. The plowing or spading should be done crosswise to the slope of the garden. The conventional procedure is to follow plowing by harrowing . . . but in my experience, once the soil is in good condition it will not be necessary to harrow after plowing. . . .

In lieu of harrowing, I go over the whole plot carefully with a potato hook. Starting at the upper edge of the plowed piece and working backwards so that all footsteps are worked over in the process, I move at right angles to, or across, the furrows left by the plow, smoothing out the inequalities, breaking up lumps, and removing clods, stones or what-have-you as I progress.

I plant in beds, so the process I've developed for spring preparation of an established garden is a little different. First off, I use a spading fork to prepare the plot. Here's how: I start at the uphill corner which has dried the most and work sideways across the top of the bed in a strip. Standing in the path, I push the fork into the ground with my foot, like a shovel. The fork should be facing the interior of the bed, that is, it should be digging with the inside of the curve of the tines. I work the fork back and forth just a second, then pull way back on the handle and pop a bit of soil out of the ground. I continue this "edging" across the width of the bed.

Next, I step over this line of disturbed soil and face the opposite direction. Ideally, one should stand on a board while working, to distribute the weight and avoid compacting the soil in the growing bed, but it is not necessary. I stick the fork into the ground parallel to the first strip I worked, but four to six inches into the undisturbed area. I loosen and remove this slice of soil, lift it on the tines of the fork, then flip it just an inch or so into the air and quickly, with a twist of the wrist, lift the fork so the tines hit the slice of soil I've removed and shatter it into a pile that lands right back where it started. I continue this process grid-wise across the bed until I've done the whole area I'll be planting. I don't get ahead of myself because the soil should be prepared only a few days ahead of planting.

If the beds are boxed in, it is then a simple matter to rake the surface to remove any rocks or stubble and break up any clods that are left. You can lay boards from side to side to make any necessary paths, or rake out paths just as you would in an open, unboxed

To prepare a permanent bed for planting, work across the bed using a garden fork. Standing on a board distributes your weight and reduces compaction.

To prepare temporary beds mark the boundaries with lines, then rake the soil from path areas into the beds, raising them.

bed. Beds less than four feet across are unlikely to need any paths at all.

To put an open garden plot into temporary or seasonal beds, use stakes and string to mark the edges of the beds, then rake loose soil from the path areas into the beds to make an extra loose, compaction-free place for your vegetables to grow. You might want to get a bedding rake, which differs from a normal rake in that it is a bit stouter, and on the back side of the tines has a straight metal edge that is very handy for scraping soil up into the beds. Start on the uphill side and reach to the far side of the first bed. Rake clear a path there, pulling the loose soil uphill into the bed. Then walk down that lower path and rake the soil from where you previously stood into the bed as well. When you're ready to plant the next bed, move the stakes and string down there. Preparing the area this way really takes no more time than simply raking it, and the plants in the beds enjoy an extra few inches of richly prepared garden soil.

Either method will work just fine, and neither will be a lot of work at any one time, as you shouldn't prepare the soil until you are ready to plant. Try to avoid binge gardening, or as we call it here in Vermont, Memorial Day Madness. Big Sam described it this way:

It is possible, of course, to wait until all danger of frost is over, then plow the entire garden plot, harrow it, and, in a great burst of energy, get all the planting done and over with in one fell swoop. This might seem to be the simplest way, and I know that in many instances it is the way taken. But even though it seems to be simple, such a procedure results in complications later on, for all the weeding, thinning, and cultivating operations would have to be done at once as well, and inasmuch as these later operations are more laborious and exacting than the planting, the result would be that they would get done only in part, and not properly at that. In the end, therefore, what appears to be the simple way is in reality no way at all.

Once again: why hurry? Gardening is a bit like juggling, and to succeed the balls must be thrown up into the air one by one, so they don't all come down at once. But to hurry through the planting not only makes more work and worry later on, it means you miss the birth of the garden that soon will be.

SETTING TRANSPLANTS

With the garden ready and the trays of seedlings fully acclimated to outdoor conditions (see the previous chapter), we are ready to set them out as soon as the proper planting date has arrived. Because Big Sam grew his tender transplants like tomatoes and peppers in open trays and started hardy crops like lettuce and broccoli direct in the soil of the cold frame, he had to wait for ideal weather to set them out.

With the first overcast day, preferably with mist or light rain falling, I start setting them out. If the weather can be caught at the right moment, the whole procedure is simplified for it will not be necessary to water the plants as they are placed in the ground. If the weather continues lowery and wet for a few days afterward, there will be no need of watering the plants after they have been set out; otherwise they will have to be watered until the roots get a good start.

If you can wait for these conditions, by all means do so. But for us the procedure is simplified by the use of plug trays or soil blocks, and it is possible, even if not preferable, to transplant in less than perfect conditions. Specific information about the handling of each vegetable, its proper planting date, spacing, and any special attention required, can be found under its entry in Chapter 10.

As we have discussed, light is absolutely essential to garden plants. But too much sun, particularly just after setting the plants is hard on transplants. When indoor-grown plants are first brought outside for the season, they aren't prepared for the strength of the sun. Glass filters out part of the solar spectrum, and indoor plants, to compensate, develop extra layers of light-gathering cells on their leaves. Moved outdoors suddenly, they will drop a portion of their leaves to reduce the level of photosynthesis.

Wind can be just as hard on the plants as sun, and in many actual cases compounds the stress. The good transplanting days here in Vermont often accompany the passage of a front. If it is a warm front, the days immediately following will be hot and steamy; even though the sun may be swathed in haze, the high temperatures raise the level of biological activity in both plant and soil to a point where the plant's recently disturbed roots—on which it depends for water—just can't keep up and it goes limp, like a person suffering from heat exhaustion.

Cold fronts are even worse, because after they pass our Eastern weather turns bright and blustery even if not cold. The combination of crystal clear skies, bright sun, and strong wind really puts a strain on the plants. The sun revs up the photosynthetic engine of the plant at the same time that the combination of low humidity and strong winds literally sucks moisture from the leaves, leaving them gasping for water that the limited root structure of the transplant is ill prepared to provide. After all, the roots draw moisture from the soil by osmosis, and the amount they can provide to the leaves is limited by their surface area. Established plants draw an enormous amount of water from the soil; fully two-thirds of the rain that falls on your garden is returned to the atmosphere by transpiration by plants. While water is essential both to carry nutrients within the plant, and for photosynthesis, the vast bulk of it merely serves, by its passage through the plant, to keep the leaves upright, and only about one percent of it actually remains in the plant.

So if the weather is forecast to change to bright and sunny, or just hot and hazy, figure out a way to rig up some shade for the plants. Partial shade is obviously better than total darkness for getting them used to life outside, so if you use a basket or a box, make sure it isn't solid. Ideally it should be about fifty-fifty shade and sun, though even something as skimpy as brush stuck into the soil around the newly set plants will help soften the sun and wind a bit. If you want to get high-tech you can lean screens together over the row or bed; though if your garden is in a windy spot like ours you'd better fasten them down somehow. A row of cinderblocks on each side of the bed, the corners of each screen resting on a block with another block on top to hold the screens down, works well. Commercial shade cloth that can be installed on lightweight hoops is the system we use now, but for a small number of plants individual protection may make more sense. If transplant day itself is sunny, wait until late afternoon to set them out; then the strength of the spring sun will be a bit less overpowering, and the plants will have overnight to adjust.

The process of setting the plants is fairly straightforward. While I use the same general techniques as my grandfather, I use the intensive method of spacing transplants within a bed. This means that—rather than lining the plants up in a row, with a large space between the rows—I plant the entire surface of the bed, with the seedlings set equidistant from one another in a hexagonal pattern. Thus, once the plants grow to full size their leaves touch and they cover the entire surface of the bed. This arrangement lessens weed competition and makes the absolute best use of the space available.

We use different spacings according to the mature size of the plants. But all the patterns share the same principle: alternating odd and even rows running across the width of the bed. To visualize how this works, take a handful of pennies and set them on the table. Put three across, then two nestled in between but next to the first. Take three more and nestle those next to the first pair, then nestle another pair next to the second set of three and so on until you run out of pennies. Those rows of twos and threes are the rows of, say, lettuce.

The way we set the location of the plants is simple. Our beds are thirty inches across at the top, and our plan is based on this measurement. But the principle is the same for any size or shape bed— it is one of the beauties of equidistant spacing that you can use it to fill any space, not just a rectangular one. Taking the first two plants and starting at the end of the bed to be planted, we put one

Equidistant planting makes the most of your garden and allows high yields from small spaces. These lettuces are planted in a 3:2:3 pattern.

Planting beds in a 3:2:3 pattern is easy: set one plant in each corner, another halfway in between them, then a pair equidistant from them and each other. Repeat that process of threes and twos until the bed is full.

in from each corner. Since it borders the edge and won't be completely surrounded by other plants, we space it half the distance from the end and side of the bed that it needs to be from the other plants, which puts it at a 45° angle in from the corner. Assuming that this will be a 3:2:3 pattern, like that of the coins and lettuces above, we then set the third plant in the center of the bed, equidistant from and in line with the first two. From that point all the figuring is done, and we set the remaining plants by eye. The next two go equidistant from the three in the first row and from each other, just like the first pair of coins on the table. The next three are set equidistant from each other and the first pair, and then another pair goes in, then three more, another pair, and so on, until all the plants are set or the bed is filled.

The process is the same whether you are planting onions in alternating rows of 5:4:5, or cauliflowers on a 2:1:2 pattern. Each plant gets an ideal amount of space, with little wasted, and cultivation (see below) is much more efficient than by any other method that we've tried that offers similar yields per square foot. With plants that get the wide spacing of 2:1:2, a smaller companion plant can be set on both sides. With the cauliflowers above, for example, we can set small herb plants all along the row, which will make the planting even more efficient, as well as beautiful.

I should add that we don't use any measuring or digging tools in this process. I don't lug anything along the row; it's just the planter (me) and the plants. If the lettuces, say, want to be eight inches apart, well that's the distance from the tip of my thumb to the tip of my little finger when my hand is outstretched. Eighteen inches is from the tip of my longest finger to my elbow; my foot, luckily, is a foot long. Your body may be a different size, but it isn't going to change suddenly, and once you know how far across your fingers and hands are, and how long your feet and arms are, you can leave the ruler back in the shed and save a lot of time and trouble. I don't use a dibble to make the transplant holes either. The soil in our beds—as in any well tended, highly fertile organic soil—is soft enough that my hand works just as well. For small seedlings a poke with the finger is enough. For larger plants, a quick scoop with the hand is all it takes. Big Sam often put a shovelful of compost wherever he was going to set a plant; when I'm doing the same I simply go along ahead of time and prepare each spot; then when I plant I can be free and easy about it.

One thing I will do, though, if the weather isn't cooperative at transplant time and I want to get the seedlings off to a fast start, is to "shoot" them in with a jet of water. Take a hose with a trigger grip nozzle on it out into the garden, aim the nozzle at each spot where a plant is to go, and pull the trigger for just a second. The blast of water will burrow a small hole and temporarily fill it with soupy soil; plop the seedling quickly into the hole before the water drains away; it will set the roots for you and create the closest possible bond between root and soil, which is the key to getting those disturbed roots growing again. After setting, draw some soft, dry soil from around the spot loosely over the moist area, leaving the final depth of the plant the same it was in the flat—unless it was too leggy and it is one of the crops, like tomatoes, that respond to deep planting. The same effect can be had with a watering can from which the sprinkler cap has been removed.

You can also mulch the plants to lower the evaporation rate of water from the soil, and generally temper the soil climate. You should be sure to choose the proper mulch for the season and climate. In warm to hot climates use a thick mulch of some organic material to insulate the soil from the hot sun; in cool climates black or clear plastic is preferable because it lets the sun

"SHOOTING" TRANSPLANTS
Above, loosen the roots a bit if
necessary; *right*, shoot a stream of
water where the plant is to go;
below, then set the plant and pull
dry soil around its base.

warm the soil. Don't use field hay as mulch unless you *know* that it was cut before the pasturage began to set seed, or you'll just be spreading weed seed around your garden. With an organic mulch, be sure not to spread it until the soil is warm—unless you are trying to keep the soil cool; I've seen more than one beautifully mulched, weed-free garden here in Vermont without a single ripe tomato— even by September—because the soil never had a chance to heat up. With plastic mulches, remember that the clear type will warm the soil more efficiently, since it lets the sun through, although it will also allow weeds to grow, which black plastic won't. Neither lets rain through directly; so don't put it on dry soil or you'll create a mini-desert that will harm the plants; the soil should be moist, but not soggy when the mulch goes on.

If spring fever got hold of you, and despite our best arguments against starting your seedlings too soon, you have a bunch of over-grown, leggy plants come setting time, here are a few things you can do. Keep one thing in mind, though: roots can grow new leaves, and a healthy top can grow new roots, but the stem is the bridge between the two; if anything happens to the stem there is no way for the two ends of the plant to move nutrients back and forth. Therefore, always hold seedlings—whatever the size—by their root ball or by the leaves, never by the stem.

While details specific to each plant can be found in the vegetable listings, here are a few general principles to helping overgrown seedlings adjust to transplanting. If it is a plant like tomatoes or broccoli, that sprouts new roots when the stem touches soil, it can be buried deeper than normal to reduce the amount of top exposed to the sun and wind. Carefully remove all leaves on the portion of the stem to be buried, and any fruits or flowers that have formed. Except for broccoli and its relatives, you should lay the stem in a shallow trench rather than drop it into a vertical hole. Broccoli family plants should not be trimmed, and can only be buried up as far as the first leaves.

If the seedlings are root-bound, that is, if their roots have filled the container and started to circle around the bottom of it, they'll need to be "woken up," or the plants will never amount to much. With plants that have thick, fleshy roots, dig a larger hole and spread the roots out until they are not doubled over each other. Cut out any damaged or diseased sections. After partially filling the planting hole, water them in thoroughly so that there are no air gaps trapped around the roots. If the plant is large, stake it. Sink the stake on the

156

"TRENCHING"
TOMATOES

Plant on right is well
grown, plant on left
much too tall and
spindly.

Knead the pot-bound
roots a bit to stimulate
new growth . . .

then remove all but the
top four to six leaves on
the plant with knife or
shears.

windward side and tie the plant to it with soft strips of cloth or other nonbinding material. Do not use a slip knot, or you'll strangle the plant as it grows.

Fibrous rooted plants can't be treated the same way, as you can't spread out the tightly formed root ball. Simply knead the root ball in your hands like clay to break loose a portion of the tiny root hairs. That signals the plant to send growth hormones back to the roots, something it had stopped doing when the roots reached the sides of the pot. Don't be shy: it's like waking a friend from a bad dream; if you're too gentle it won't work.

DIRECT SEEDING

Over his many seasons in the garden, Big Sam developed a sure-fire method to guarantee quick and vigorous germination of crops sown direct in the soil of the garden.

My procedure in planting is as follows: Starting at one end of the row to be planted, I work over a strip of soil about three feet wide, along the direction of the row, using the potato hook. When I finish the row, I walk around the garden so as not to trample on the soil,

Lay bare stem in six-inch-deep trench along the row . . .

then angle top of plant to a vertical position at desired spot and firm the soil.

and, taking my hook with me, I return to the other end of the row, lay down the hook, and pick up the rake. With a penknife I have already cut a notch on the handle of the rake marking the distance between rows. Now I work over the same strip of soil with the rake, working along the direction of the row this time (as well), smoothing the soil. When I reach the end of the row, using the mark on the rake handle, I set one of the stakes of my garden line, then return to the other end of the row walking around, taking the rake with me and again avoiding walking across the garden. Now I carefully measure and set the other stake, drawing the line taut along the surface of the ground. I have the seed at this end of the row, and a small shallow bowl into which I pour some of the seed. Stepping out a good stride on the garden soil, I squat, setting the bowl down beside me, reaching to my left with my right hand I make a shallow furrow along the line with my finger; then, with seeds taken from the bowl between my thumb and forefinger, I sparingly scatter the seeds in the drill I have made. Next I just barely cover the seeds with fine soil and with the back of my hand or fist firmly compact the earth on top of the seeds I have just planted. Picking up the bowl, I take a long stride or two, squat, and seed another four or five foot section of row.

Since he is discussing small seeds he only barely covers them, but as long as every seed is buried at a depth 2–3 times its width, depending on season and soil moisture, the same good results can be expected. All seeds have the same basic requirements for successful emergence: proper temperature, sufficient but not excessive moisture, and air. In early spring the soil is still cool and moist, so we should not plant as deep as later in the season when the top few inches of soil is hot and dry.

At varying depths you trade off among these three needs of the seed, and the relationship can be altered to help certain plants get a good start when they normally wouldn't. A clear or black plastic mulch will raise soil temperatures and keep off spring rains, thus lowering soil moisture and making it possible to start some heat-loving plants early; laying a board over the row if mid-summer will lower soil temperature and conserve moisture, allowing the direct seeding of cool weather crops. Each of these methods is discussed in Chapter 10.

The process for planting in beds is essentially the same, with some minor differences. Since the seedbed was prepared during the

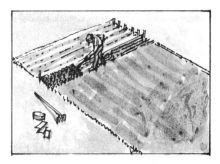

Working backward, level
and prepare area with
hook, then rake smooth.

Mark rows with garden
line using rake for a
measure,

then seed using the taut
line as a planting guide.

process of making the beds, or during spring preparation of the bed, I start right in with marking the rows, which is done in a slightly different manner. Instead of using the garden line, I have a marker board that can be dragged along the bed, and teeth, which protrude from the bottom of the board at whatever interval I want between the rows, do the marking for us. In a thirty-inch-wide bed like ours, this may be as little as three or as many as five rows. Alternatively, I may use a narrow-bladed or pointed hoe. If I wish to plant only a bit of each crop, the rows can run across the bed rather than along its length. The most important factor in determining the distance between rows—aside from the eventual size of the vegetable—is the size of the hoe I will be using to cultivate the bed. By choosing a spacing that works well with your hoes you can save an enormous amount of effort later on.

Since there is an established path, I don't need to walk around the whole plot, only back along the path. Having carried the seed in my pocket, I put down the marker and proceed to plant the first row, tapping the seed from its packet as I go at a rate appropriate to the particular vegetable I am sowing. Each row is labeled immediately after sowing with the date and the vegetable sown, using a small wooden tag marked with a weatherproof laundry pen that I carry in my pocket.

Some crops may be broadcast sown—that is, sprinkled evenly across the surface of the bed—and for this the procedure is slightly different. Salad greens, spinach, bush peas, even carrots (though I don't recommend this last, as they are too slow to germinate, and weeds will have a chance to become established) may be planted this way. Cover crops and green manures are almost always planted broadcast, so the coverage of the bed will be complete, with no inter-row spaces in which weeds can get a start. Here's how we do it. First I work over the surface of the bed with our hand harrow, the spike-toothed rolling cultivator described in Chapter 3. You can use a fine-tooth rake, but you'll have to be a bit more careful about moving soil (and later, seed) around the bed rather than just roughing it up. This process leaves the surface of the bed in a multitude of small ridges and fluffs up the soil.

The seed is then sprinkled on the surface. A small grass seed spreader or a jar with holes poked in the lid can be used, but I just do it by hand. I've found that after a little practice you can get even coverage if you mimic the action of the seeder with your hand. I grab a handful of seed from the bag, and then hold my hand upright with the fingers curled upward in a loose grip, and shake back and forth horizontally. By changing the amount of spread between my fingers, the distance back and forth that my hand travels, and the suddenness with which I change its direction, I can alter the density and pattern of the spread.

Once the seed is distributed to my satisfaction, I take the hand harrow again and go over the bed to settle the seed down into the fluffed-up surface that I created during my first pass with the tool. With all but the smallest seed you'll be able to tell visually once you've buried it. With large seed like peas you may want to add a thin layer of compost on top to assure that the seed will be fully

SEEDING
IN PERMANENT BEDS

Above: Make furrows running across
the bed.

Above: Then make planting tags and
place at end of each row.

Right: Sow the seed. To avoid
confusion, don't cover rows until all
are done.

covered. The thing you are trying to avoid is moving the seed around after it's been scattered—if you do, it's probably going to bunch up in certain spots, leading to uneven growth across the bed. Once the seed is covered you can tamp it by standing on a section of plywood placed on the bed, or as I do, by watering. Either way should put the seed into sufficient contact with moist soil to assure prompt and complete germination.

CHAPTER **9**

Cultivating the Garden

With good soil, good seed, and proper planting, the garden will be up and off to a good start, and then will come the necessity of caring for it. The number of poorly cared for gardens seen about might lead one to the conclusion that this is a formidable task, but such certainly is not the case. If the size of the garden is within our means as far as expendable time is concerned, and we are on hand to give it care when care is needed, the results will measure up to all expectations, and the demands on our time will not be excessive.

Samuel R. Ogden

The old saw "a stitch in time saves nine" could have been invented by an observant gardener. The two cardinal points to learn about garden care, if you want that care to be as easy as possible, are timing and consistency.

Though many improvements have been made in both tools and techniques of cultivation over the twenty years since Big Sam last revised this book, the principles remain the same: (1) Cultivate promptly, so the weeds are small and easy to uproot; and (2) plant your crops a consistent distance apart so that the cultivation may proceed as quickly and efficiently as possible. Many gardeners think of efficiency as the ability to get a lot done in a short time—a line of reasoning that leads direct to the equipment dealer's showroom. I disagree; to me efficiency is the ability to get a lot done with a minimum of work and worry, an understanding that leads instead to an enjoyment of the gardening itself.

Big Sam seeded his plants quite close together by conventional standards, though still in rows, and he did all cultivation by hand, with a potato hook.

In spite of what the authorities may have to say on the subject, my objective is to get the rows as closely spaced as possible. There is a tendency to get the rows widely spaced, believing that this makes for easier cultivation; they are either very far apart to permit the use of horse or power drawn cultivators, or slightly less wide so that a wheel hoe pushed by manpower can be used. I do not agree with either of these procedures. It is a waste of land and of productivity to use horse or motor drawn cultivators on anything smaller than a commercial market garden. As to the wheel hoe which is pushed around by hand, I believe I can demonstrate that its use involves extra labor and time as well as a waste of valuable garden space. In the first place, the design of the implement requires that the energy be applied in the most inefficient manner possible. The handles are high so that all the push is from the arms and shoulders, whereas the push should come directly from the legs, as any football player knows. The result is that, in order to make progress with the machine, it is necessary to proceed by a series of jerks and pushes, which not only wastes energy but makes it difficult to control the cultivator blades with any accuracy. Consequently it is impossible to cultivate close to the row without the hazard of ripping out some of the plants, and after all that energy has been spent, one still has to get down on hands and knees and weed by hand in order to do a good job. If a machine could be devised which could be pulled instead of pushed, the result would be one more in line with human mechanics, and to cultivate by pulling is the method I advocate.

For the first four years I had my market garden I used Big Sam's potato hook as well, though I used a vise to bend the two outside tines in so I could get closer to the plants without harming them. I still have this hook, but now I rarely use it for cultivation. Instead I use the stirrup hoes described in Chapter 3, which are sort of like a hand model of a high-tech wheel hoe.

Wheel hoes have been vastly improved in the last twenty years, but they are still hard on the back, and they have other problems. First, because of the jerky motion caused by the combination of pushing with the arms and shoulders while stepping forward (which is the natural result of the rhythm you establish working with one), a wheel hoe tends to scallop the ground, digging deeper during the middle part of the push than at the beginning or the end, when the arms are pulling back. This leads to inconsistent results.

Second, a wheel hoe can only cultivate where there is room for the wheel in front of the blade. This means that it can only get close to plants that are beside it, and that makes it suitable only for rows, which we demonstrated in the planning and design sections are wasteful for small gardens of the type most gardeners have. There are offset blade models available, but they are very expensive. Even so, they are unable to work in any way but a straight line directly behind the wheel; if you wish to deviate even a bit from the course the wheel has taken to catch a stray weed, you have to tilt the hoe, and that makes it dig unevenly again. If you struggle to jerk the rear end around a bit, there is imminent danger of it going too far and gouging up one of the plants.

Third, since you can't use a wheel hoe to work backwards, due to the design of the tool, there is no way to cultivate your footsteps, and every weed seed you compact with your foot is given a new line on life.

I own a very high-tech Swiss wheel hoe but—the hundred or so dollars it cost me, notwithstanding—it spends most of its time in the barn. There is, it seems, a law of interaction that binds us practically with the power of physics, which is that the level of equipment determines the level of work. The larger the machine, the larger *quantity* of work it can do, but with lower *quality*—in the sense that there is a quality of work, just as there is a quality of life.

To put it in more concrete terms, consider the difference between walking, riding a bicycle, and driving through a new countryside. If you walk you don't see as much of the country on a given day, but what you do see, you truly experience—the sounds of birds, the rustling of leaves in the wind, the sounds of voices from houses set back from the roadway; the scents of farmyards, wildflowers, even the small streams you pass over. In addition your mind is free to contemplate each of these. If you ride a bicycle you still see and hear many of these things, except that the wind in your ears may obscure the more delicate sounds, the scents will pass more quickly, and you must keep your mind focused on the bike and the road. You become very aware of the sounds of the bike and your own breathing as you labor up the hills; there is no forgetting the hills and dales you traverse, but your experience of them is quite different.

In a car, you are aware of what? The speed limit, the yellow line, the sound of the air conditioner if you have one, or the rush of air past the windows if they are open. You smell upholstery and gasoline fumes; the countryside—of which you do see more than if riding or walking—is so fleeting and flat it might as well be on a television screen. I don't call that traveling, and I don't want that same shallow hurry to reduce my experience of the garden I've managed to finesse from the land I call home and the time I call mine. So, while cultivation is considered drudgery by a lot of gardeners, perhaps that is just because of the way they do it.

The one thing my Swiss wheel hoe does have, that I like, is a kind of blade that really takes care of the weeds quite well. Instead of being a miniature moldboard plow blade, or a foursome of forward-arched cultivator tines, or even an arrow-shaped duck's-foot blade, this blade is a single, thin hoop of spring steel mounted to skim along just below the surface of the soil at a slight downward angle. This skimming process—when you can keep the wheel hoe level—very neatly cuts off the weeds just below the surface. So once I noticed that the same Swiss company made three sizes of hand hoes with a similar blade—called stirrup hoes—I bought all three immediately. Now that I use these stirrup hoes, cultivation is not only good, moderate exercise, but it is also a quiet time, a contemplative time. The roto-tiller and the wheel hoe come out only when they're really needed.

Big Sam cultivated working backwards, straddling the rows, so he could work both sides of the row in one pass; this way he covered both sets of footprints. I have found that he was right to say that once you've gotten the knack of it, you won't need to do any hand weeding until it is time to thin, and then you can do both the thinning and the weeding at once. I also agree that his method was faster than using a wheel hoe. But by planting in beds and using a stirrup hoe, I think that I have developed an even quicker method than he had, so that, when we had our market garden, I could cultivate five hundred feet of carrots in about fifteen minutes. Now that I no longer have to hurry, the efficiency of this technique makes maintenance a snap.

Let's use carrots as an example. We plant our carrots in beds thirty inches wide, with five rows, six inches apart. (This and other planting methods are detailed in Chapters 8 and 10.) Since Big Sam taught me to mix a little radish seed in with the carrots so that the rows would show quickly, I am able to do my first cultivation only a week later, thus setting back any quick-sprouting weeds.

Here's how I go about it. I stand beside the bed, and because I am right-handed, it is on my left. I hold the hoe with the five-inch blade beside me, my left hand thumb up, fingers out, about halfway down the handle with my right hand fingers in, thumb up, at the top. This grip allows me to control precisely both the depth and the direction of the hoe. Placing it between the first two rows of carrots, I walk along briskly, looking at the head of the hoe and guiding it with my two hands. At the end of the bed I switch to the other side of the bed and return in the same fashion. With five rows there are four passes to make, two in each direction, to cultivate the interior of the bed. The outsides are done last, using a wider blade, and I walk backwards to cover my tracks. Regardless of the size of the garden, there is no way that a wheel hoe can go this fast, or do as thorough a job, and there is considerably less danger of uprooting the plants by mistake.

For transplants spaced on hexagonal centers in the beds there is a similar and equally efficient method. As I described in the last chapter, equidistantly planted beds are like orchards, and the plants are accessible from all sides. What this means in practice is that you can quickly cultivate all sides of a plant from the path, without ever stepping in the bed, or compacting the soil. The trick is to cultivate on the diagonal, not along the run of the bed.

Holding the stirrup hoe in the same way as above, I work backwards, starting with the first diagonal row of plants. I put the hoe down at the far side of the bed and pull it toward myself, lift it while taking a step back along the path, then repeat the process for the next row. Once you have the timing of your step and the movement with the hoe worked out, you'll find it easy to proceed smartly down the bed. When I reach the other end, I turn around and work my way back up the same path, working the other diagonal, which gets the other two sides of each plant (except the ones on the edge of the bed). After I've done these first two passes I switch to a wider hoe and—just as with the carrots—do the edge, plus the path if necessary, covering my footprints as I go.

As the plants grow toward each other over the course of the season, and the amount of open soil between them decreases, you simply switch to a narrower hoe. I feel that for any garden of a quarter-acre or less, there is no need for a wheel hoe; all that is needed is a little planning, a set of stirrup hoes, and the hands and feet you were born with. Time spent cultivating will no longer be wasted time, but a chance to enjoy your garden and watch it grow. The close observation that accompanies this kind of hand work will also help you see ways you can improve your garden.

One of the hardest jobs facing the new gardener is thinning, and it's one of the most difficult to justify (to yourself), because it seems to involve destroying your own work. Don't think of it that way; every crop needs room to grow, and we want to maximize yields, not numbers of plants. Prompt thinning to recommended spacings is absolutely necessary. With some crops it can be done successively, and the thinnings brought to the table. In fact, many of the tastiest harvests you'll get from your garden will come from thinnings: crunchy finger-sized carrots, baby beets steamed with the tops still on, tender spinach and lettuce thinnings; so don't think of the time spent at it, or the plants removed when thinning, as wasted. Specific guidelines for each crop are in the next chapter.

Finally, a note about weed control, a topic of no importance if you have been diligent and complete in your cultivation. As we all know, a weed is simply any plant growing in a place we don't want it, at a time it shouldn't.

I have spent a good deal of time on the subject of cultivation precisely so you won't need to think about weeding as a separate item in your garden agenda. Weed when you thin your crops, and when you harvest your crops; when you walk past a weed that has escaped the hoe and grown to flower, grab it and toss it to the side of the plot after shaking the soil from its roots. Your time is never wasted doing so! If the weeds do manage to take over a plot, sow a fast-growing cover crop to choke them out; the details are in Chapters 4 and 6. As long as you maintain a regular program of cultivation and plant cover crops during fallow periods, you'll keep the soil occupied with the plants you want to grow, and keep out the weeds that want to grow.

IRRIGATION

In Chapter 3 we discussed the different kinds of irrigation systems, but now we need a word about their use. As with seedlings, water in the garden can be either a blessing or a curse, depending on how much there is and how it is used; too much is as bad as too little. While it is absolutely necessary for good growth, there are times when it should be withheld if the crop is to live up to expectations. When he wrote the first version of his book, Big Sam felt irrigation was unnecessary except during severe drought; but by 1971 he had decided, on the basis of his own observations, that just about any garden, in any climate, could be improved by making sure the plants never went without.

Most garden crops, be they leafy, or roots, or fruits, consist primarily of water. And if a cucumber is, we will say, ninety percent water, how can one expect to obtain perfect fruit if at any time there is a lack of moisture? In fact cucumber fruits, in their shape and size, offer a convincing record of the amounts of water which have been available to it (them). Cucumber growers will all have noticed a fruit small at the stem end which suddenly swells out to normal size, or one which starts out nobly only to be squeezed into a miserable pointed end, or even those which swell and shrink and then swell again, thus giving visible evidence of the dry and rainy spells. Good fruits and leaves and roots will result if the plants are never allowed to suffer from lack of water, and the measure of this is the condition of the soil.

How often and how much to water, though, seems to be a matter on which it is impossible to get agreement. Some gardeners insist that frequent light waterings are best; others are convinced that light waterings cause the plants to develop root systems which are shallower than normal—making them less tolerant of drought—and that plants should only be watered when they are on the verge of wilting, and then deeply and thoroughly. Big Sam, as I mentioned above, has held both positions himself, and I must admit that, to a certain extent, I do as well.

When the plants are young, I water frequently; their roots are limited to the surface regions of the soil, and without water they will never develop. I water very shallow-rooted crops and fast-growing leafy greens frequently, right up until a week before harvest. But with most plants, once they have reached their full size, I water only if absolutely necessary. I feel that pampering them after that point lowers the quality of the harvest: whether it be corn, herbs, or carrots, tomatoes, melons or beets, I want the flavor of that vegetable to be expressed fully, to be concentrated. Since vegetables are largely water, it stands to reason that to give them extra as they approach maturity will only dilute their essence, that is "water down" their flavor.

So, there are certain critical times when particular plants either should or should not be watered if you want the best results. For example, peas and beans need plenty of water during pod development, or they will not fill out properly. Tomatoes must have a consistent water supply during fruit formation, or they may crack; the same is true of carrots and radishes as the roots enlarge. All these details will be found in the vegetable section under their respective headings, but there are a few rules-of-thumb that the beginning organic gardener would do well to know.

The general rule is that growing gardens need an inch of rain a week, and if this is not forthcoming, you should make up the difference. In order to track the rainfall you can purchase an inexpensive rain gauge, preferably one of the kind that you simply stick into the ground (away from obstructions that might distort the rainfall pattern). Then when you water you can place this gauge within the spray pattern of the sprinkler, to measure what you are adding to the equation. Or you can simply use a container from around the house.

To choose an example: we use agricultural impact sprinklers in our gardens. These are the rotating brass kind you see on a golf course, and with sufficient water pressure they will cover an eighty-foot circle. We have found that it takes four and a half hours to apply an inch of water on the garden with a hundred-foot run of ¾-inch hose at normal household pressure. If you have a small garden and water by hand, you can time your watering to determine the appropriate times and amounts: figure the gallons per minute of your own hose by timing how long it takes to fill a gallon pail, and then multiply by the area you want to cover. One inch of water on 100 square feet comes to about 65 gallons.

When you should water involves two separate questions: how often, and what time of day. I decide when to water the same way I decide when to plant, by taking a handful of soil from the bed and squeezing it in my hand; if it will not hold together in a lump, it's time to water. Some times are special, though: unless water squeezes out between my fingers, I always water immediately after transplanting or seeding; and unless the plants are physically wilting, I never water just before harvest. To check the depth of dryness dig a small hole and look at the cross-section view of the top six to eight inches of soil.

The best time of day to water depends on the situation. If you are in a hot, dry climate and water is precious, water in the evening (or the very early morning) so losses to evaporation are kept to a minimum. In humid areas it is a good idea to water only on sunny days, and always by lunchtime so that the plant leaves have a chance to dry off before evening; otherwise you are creating a good environment for bacterial and fungal infections to develop. If you can make sure the foliage dries completely at least once every 18 hours they will have a hard time getting established. This is especially true in greenhouses and cold frames, which are shut tight overnight.

In cold climates like ours it makes sense to water early in the day for another reason: the soil is cooled down by the irrigation water—especially in early spring, when soil and water are at their coldest—and if the sun has a chance to heat the soil right back up, the plants will suffer that much less. This is even more important when watering seedlings: professional nurserymen often heat their greenhouse irrigation water to avoid temperature shock on their seedlings.

PESTS

Like weeds, pests and diseases are simply organisms that are pursuing their lives in a way that is inconvenient for us. That may sound awfully dry, but it's true. As mentioned in Chapter 4, there are more microbes in a double handful of soil than there are people on this earth, and yet most of the time our gardens thrive; obviously only a few of them, on fairly rare occasions, cause us any disease troubles. When you consider that there are something like a million insect species on earth, the fact that a few thousand of them have become pests (to us) seems like a miracle more than a plague. Unfortunately, this statistic can't keep the blight off your tomato plants or stop the leaf miners from tunneling in your spinach. There are, however, some basic practices that can help keep pest and disease problems to a minimum—without resorting to dangerous pesticides. (Specific methods of combating particular pest and disease problems can be found in the next chapter, and discussion of the different kinds of pesticides in Chapter 3.)

Your most effective defense against both pests and diseases is brain power. Get to know the problems, then figure out solutions. Observe how and when the problems begin; that requires that you know the garden, the soil, the plants, the weather, all the variables that make your garden the challenging and wonderful gestalt that it is. Careful observation will almost always provide a clue to control.

Let's consider the cabbage root maggot. Without some sort of control, spring plantings of cabbage, broccoli, and cauliflower here in New England, as well as early turnips and radishes, are frequently ruined by these small white maggots.

Big Sam found a solution to this pest in his garden by focusing on its parent:

This is a fly, the actual identity of which I have been unable to determine. It lays its eggs in the ground near the stem of any one or all of the vegetables in the Crucifer family. The eggs hatch into maggots which promptly wiggle their way into the stems of the plants in question. If the infestation is severe the maggots will kill the plant. . . .

To combat them, I have found that wood ashes are highly effective; in fact I believe that, if used with care, they can be one hundred percent effective. In cases where the vegetable in question, like broccoli, is set out in the garden as a plant, once the transplanting has taken place and the roots have had a day or two in which to become established in their new environment, take a small handful of dry wood ashes and spread it on the ground so that all the area around where the stem emerges from the ground is covered. . . .

If high winds or heavy rains disturb the layer of ashes, I suppose it would be wise to give the plants a second application. As nearly as I can tell, the early part of the season is the worst; at least later plantings . . . do not seem to be as badly afflicted as early ones.

Aside from the obvious pleasure that he took in solving this little natural science mystery, the case of the cabbage root maggot provides an excellent example of just how many different ways a particular problem can be solved. The first step in controlling any pest, whether an insect, a mole, or the neighbor's dog, is to get to know its life cycle, and then find a way to interrupt it so your garden is no longer affected.

One of the first ways is to alter the conditions in the garden so they no longer favor the pest. When Big Sam spread wood ashes around the base of his broccoli plants, it seems he either made the site unattractive to the fly, or so altered the soil that the eggs didn't hatch. This could be because of the dryness of the ash, which would desiccate the eggs; or their caustic chemistry—wood ashes and water yields lye—which would kill the eggs, while at the time marginally raising the pH at the base of the plant and providing extra potassium for good root growth. Either way, the wood ash trick is a simple and effective solution.

Another simple method of pest control is to time your plantings to avoid periods of heavy pest pressure. This strategy, based on Big

Sam's observation that later plantings weren't bothered, would mean holding off planting until the major spring hatch of cabbage flies is past. I found in my research some years ago (when I had more broccoli than I did wood ash) that in the Northeast this fly finishes laying her eggs about two weeks before the frost-free date. Unprotected plants set out in our garden before this date are almost always attacked by maggots; those set out after almost never. The solution was clear: wait two weeks, and no control was necessary.

A third approach is to physically prevent the pest from reaching the plant. There is an old-time organic gardening trick to beat cabbage root maggots that works quite well: make flat cardboard collars three inches or more in diameter and set them about the base of the broccoli plants. The mechanism here is obvious: the fly can't reach the soil to lay her eggs. Even easier is to put a floating row cover on the bed immediately after transplanting. Not only will the fly be kept out, but so will flea beetles, and the plants will benefit from a milder microclimate under the cover.

Three other methods that work in some cases (but not this one) are physical destruction of the pest, that is, hand picking and killing them; physical avoidance by crop rotation, so that the plants are not where the pest expects to find them; and the use of predators, say, the introduction of ladybugs to prey on the eggs of leaf-eating insects. A fourth, additional method is interplanting: you can confuse or repel pests by mixing in plants unattractive to them with those they feed on, so they have a more difficult time finding their favorites. I have not found this to be totally effective in preventing pest problems, but it will lessen the damage.

What is the alternative that we have avoided by taking the time to know the natural history and culture of our garden? The standard chemical pesticide used for the control of cabbage root maggots is Diazinon, an insecticide first put on the market in 1952.[8] Diazinon is one of about a hundred organophosphate insecticides,[9] the first of which were developed as part of the nerve gas research done by Nazi Germany in the years before and during World War II.[10] The normal methods of application are as a liquid soil drench, or in granular form, mixed with the soil around the base of the plant, much the same way Big Sam used wood ash. Unfortunately, this chemical can be taken up and moved throughout the plant, though it is thought to be partially metabolized in the process.[11] These metabolites, however, may be even more potent as nerve agents than the Diazinon itself.[12] Evidence from incidents of organophosphate poisoning indicate that although humans have bodily enzymes that can break down Diazinon, sensitization may occur which will prevent this detoxification from occurring if exposure is repeated. Also, there is direct experimental evidence that Diazinon exposure causes birth defects in birds.[13]

Diazinon persists in the soil up to three months.[14] If surfactants—used in most pesticide formulations to enhance their penetration, but not required to be identified on the label—are present, persistence may be much longer, though soil pH, moisture content, and temperature also affect its degradation rate.[15] Diazinon is also mobile in the soil by leaching, though the presence of large amounts of organic matter can restrict both its effects and its mobility.[16]

If all this seems needlessly complex, I agree, so let me summarize: a man-made substance invented as a result of chemical warfare research can be used on the food you grow (and then eat) in place of wood ash to prevent infestations of cabbage root maggots. Unlike wood ash, however, Diazinon is expensive to buy, dangerous to use or store, contributes nothing to the fertility of the soil, and may cause long-term nerve damage and birth defects. That's progress?

Oftentimes at our garden center, customers looking for a quick fix solution to some garden problem would say, after I explained the background, say, of cabbage root maggot infestation and how they could solve it, "I just don't have the time to learn all that organic gardening; it's too complicated." But look again at the discussion above; which approach is the complicated one?

Managing a garden may be a complex activity, but it is a rewarding one, and one that brings us closer to the natural world. In contrast, the apparent simplicity and ease of use with the Diazinon treatment masks not only a great complexity, but a host of dangers both to us and our gardens; it quite possibly creates more problems than it solves, though we don't know for sure. And that uncertainty is its biggest problem, to my way of thinking. The hidden chemical complexity, the smokescreen of unperformed safety experiments that the chemical salesmen and their regulatory agents hide behind, when they say a particular pesticide "has no known dangers," is simply not open to our observation, or our analysis. We have to depend on them, and they are in it for the money . . . our money. All we will ever have if we use their products is ignorance or anxiety, not bliss nor a concrete knowledge of the problems and their solutions.

I have yet to figure out how we as a people came to believe that every new product must be progress, and why the burden of proof should fall on those who suspect a product may have dangers rather than on those who created it for their own profit.

DISEASES

When discussing sick or weak plants it is essential to distinguish between disease and deficiency. Without proper care your garden will not thrive, and if there is either too little or too much nutrient in the soil, the plants cannot be expected to remain healthy and produce well. Following the practices in Chapters 4 and 5, the gardener should face few problems with fertility, but keep an eye on the plants nonetheless—we discussed the visual cues to major nutrient deficiencies in Chapter 7, and they are generally the same for older plants as they are for seedlings.

If the plants begin to show symptoms of nutrient deficiency, don't hesitate to side-dress with some immediately available yet organically stable fertilizer like fish emulsion. There are critical phases of every plant's development, and if not given good care and ample nutrition at those times, they will be weakened, and weak plants are more susceptible to both pests and diseases. As organic gardeners we work toward the goal of letting the soil feed the plants without our direct intervention, but in practice it takes time to build the soil to a high level of fertility. Just don't panic and jump on the chemical treadmill. Plants fed synthetic fertilizers on soils devoid of organic matter may develop deficiencies in a wide range of minor nutrients, ranging from boron to zinc, but using an organic fertilizer or compost makes it very unlikely that such deficiencies will ever develop.

Diseases, on the other hand, involve specific infections, and have more diverse specific symptoms. While details concerning the diseases various plants are susceptible to are discussed in the next chapter, some general notes on disease prevention are appropriate here.

Where do diseases come from? Many are already in your garden among the billions of bacteria and fungi always in the soil; others are brought in from elsewhere on seed, on the roots of purchased plants, even in the soil clinging to the shoes of visitors. Given susceptible plants and the right conditions, disease can spread rapidly. Gardens are not sterile places nor should they be, so the best we can hope to do is to keep the plants in top condition, exclude known sources of disease, and try to control conditions that favor their spread.

To avoid seed-borne diseases, buy seed only from reputable dealers, and save your own seed only from healthy, vigorous plants;

store seed in a cool, dry, dark place. Also, if particular diseases are especially prevalent in your area, search out resistant varieties of the crops you want to grow. Read catalog descriptions closely; specific resistances are almost always mentioned if they exist. With tomatoes, for example, resistance to Verticillium wilt is noted by a capital ''V'' after the variety name; Fusarium wilt resistance by a capital ''F''; and so on. A major part of most vegetable breeding programs is developing disease resistance; take advantage of that fact and you'll have fewer problems.

My grandfather bought field-grown onion plants by mail, but I can't recommend that—the source of the plants concerns me, and some soil-borne diseases like pink root of onions could be unintended passengers. Pests or their eggs can also be brought in on plants purchased at garden centers. If you do buy plants, examine them carefully for any sign of disease or pests. Flying insects can come in on their own, or may be blown in by the wind, bringing disease with them. Many bacteria and fungal spores are also carried on the wind, and may lie dormant on plants or in the soil for long periods, until conditions are right for them to grow and reproduce.

Once present, what these micro-invaders need to establish a foothold on your plants is moisture. Humid, still air and standing water on the plant leaves provide an excellent place for them to thrive. A typical problem is that of early blight in tomatoes: first the bacteria is splashed by rain from the soil to the lower leaves of the plants; once established on the leaves, it can spread in subsequent rains from leaf to leaf. You may spread it yourself if you work in the garden during wet weather, by brushing from plant to plant with wet hands and clothes. Thus, irrigation can also work against you if it is ill-timed and helps the spread of bacteria.

In addition to buying clean seed, inspecting plants brought into the garden, timing irrigation properly, and staying out of the garden when it's wet, you should practice basic garden sanitation: don't leave dead or diseased plants in the garden where they can serve as a breeding ground for diseases; and don't put them on the compost pile unless you're sure it will heat up properly and kill the spores and bacteria on the diseased plants. If you aren't going to take the time to build a proper ''hot'' pile, burn the plants instead; you can put the ashes on the pile. Finally, practice the kind of crop rotation discussed in Chapter 6, so that any diseases that do get a foothold in your garden don't persist.

CHAPTER 10

Vegetables for
the Garden

A garden grown as one should be, without chemical sprays or fertilizers, will produce vegetables which are superior in taste and quality. These attributes take color from the soil in which the vegetables are grown to an extent that is little recognized.

Samuel R. Ogden

ASPARAGUS

Asparagus is a perennial and therefore should have its own, permanent space in the garden. Well-established beds will continue to produce for decades, so the soil should be deeply prepared and totally free of perennial weeds. A well-drained and only slightly acid soil (pH 6.5–6.9) is best. The most important nutrient according to recent research is phosphorus, and an application of 5 pounds per 100 square feet of either rock phosphate or calcium phosphate will make sure this element is abundant. On acid soils the second of these is preferable, as its natural alkalinity will help raise the pH of the soil. In either case one application at the time the bed is established should be sufficient, as both of these materials break down slowly. On a continuing basis, a fall application of 1–2 inches of compost or well rotted manure will provide enough nutrients to keep the bed flourishing. You'll probably want 10–12 plants per family adult.

Asparagus can be started from seed, but in most cases it makes more sense to plant established crowns bought from a reputable nursery. The seed is very slow to germinate, and must be nursed along in a holding bed through one whole season before it produces a usable crown for the following spring. Crowns are planted as early in spring as the ground can be prepared.

To plant the crowns, dig a 6–8-inch-deep trench a foot wide, and place a shovelful of compost every 15–18 inches; set out the crowns on these compost mounds with the roots fully spread out (not doubled over). The side of the crown with the buds (from which the spears will grow) should be pointing up and 4–6 inches below the surface of the bed. Cover the crowns with a few inches of soil and compost mix, and leave the remainder of the soil from the trench heaped between the rows. Rows should be 18 inches apart in beds, or 4–6 feet apart if you want a path between the rows. The plants can also be set equidistant in beds 15 inches apart for intensive gardening, but make sure the bed is in top-notch condition. In humid areas wider spacings will help avoid disease problems.

As the first season progresses and the ferns grow, gradually fill in the trenches until the soil surface is level again. Avoid covering the foliage at any point, as you will slow fern growth and thus lower future yields. New asparagus beds should be watered regularly, at least weekly, unless there is regular, ample rainfall. In following years they can go without if necessary.

Plant asparagus crowns atop a mound of compost so that the top of the crown is 4–6 inches below ground level. Cover the crowns with 1–2 inches of compost, then fill the trench gradually over the season, as the plants grow.

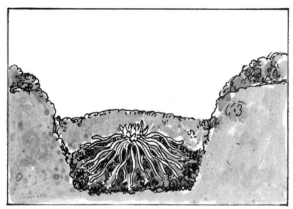
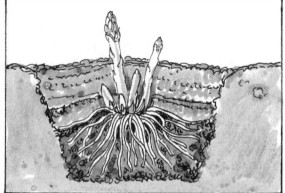

The most significant disease problems in asparagus are fusarium rot and asparagus rust. Most new varieties of asparagus are resistant to both. The major pest of asparagus is the asparagus beetle, a ¼-inch-long black-and-gray beetle with a cross right on the middle of its back. They lay dark, shiny eggs no bigger than a speck on the emerging spears each spring. The larval form is ⅓-inch long, olive green to dark gray with black head and legs, and wrinkled like a mummy. Both the adult and the larval forms eat the foliage of the plants and will disfigure the spears. Since they hibernate in garden trash, the best control is to cut back the ferns after the first hard fall frosts, clear the bed, and re-mulch with new material. To keep beetles from returning, cover the beds with a floating row cover until harvest. There is also a spotted asparagus beetle, slightly larger, which is reddish brown with six black spots on each wing. These and the occasional cucumber beetle that finds its way to the asparagus bed can be controlled the same way. Serious infestations can be dusted with rotenone powder, but this is not a long-term solution.

Keep the bed weed-free, either by hand weeding or mulching. Cultivation is not a good idea, as it harms the shallow crowns and lowers yields. Mulching can also be used to extend the harvest season. Simply pull back the mulch on part of the bed early in spring. That section will warm up sooner and bear sooner, too. On the still-mulched part, let the first few spears grow tall enough to begin unfolding their ferns before you cut them; that will slow down that section of the bed and stretch the season on the tail end without lowering overall yields.

The standard recommendation for asparagus in my grandfather's day was to trench deeply, manure liberally, and wait two years before beginning to harvest the bed. All three of these recommendations have been altered in the face of recent research. It has been found that overall yields and total spear count can both be increased by a light harvest the first year after planting established crowns. Nonetheless, it makes sense to limit the first year's harvest to only a couple of weeks. In later years it can be continued for 4–6 weeks, or until the spears start to decline in thickness to the diameter of a pencil.

Harvest before the tips of the spears begin to open, either by cutting the spears on an angle, at or just below soil level, or by grasping them at soil level and snapping them off with your hand. If you'd like to try the European trick of blanching asparagus to produce tender white spears, heap more soil up over the plants—or better, apply an 8–10-inch ridge of fully matured compost over the row—and harvest just as the spears break through.

Asparagus should be eaten or frozen as soon as possible after harvest, though it can be stored, standing upright in a shallow tray of water for a few days. After harvest, allow the ferns to grow throughout the summer until hard frost kills them, then cut them back to the ground and burn or compost them.

The standard varieties for home gardens over the past forty to fifty years have been the Washington strains. Asparagus is a dioecious plant (which means there are separate male and female plants) and the females normally waste a fair amount of energy producing mixed-up, cross-pollinated seed, and littering the bed with it each fall. Unless the resultant seedlings are weeded out in spring, they will eventually compete with the mother plants, though it is unlikely they will ever bear as well, because of their random genetic background. But a 35-year breeding program at Rutgers University in New Jersey has now resulted in all-male strains of asparagus that yield 3–4 times as much as the Washington types. Jersey Giant is adapted for heavy soils and is generally considered the best all-around home garden variety; Jersey General does particularly well in the mid-Atlantic region, and Jersey King is best for southeast and desert regions. As of this writing, which cultivar is best for California had not been determined. The newest release is Jersey Jewel, which, because of a "persistent green" gene, is the best selection for edible landscaping, as the plants stay green and bushy longer than the other cultivars.

BEANS

For garden purposes there are two types of beans: bush beans and pole beans. Bush beans grow on small, self-supporting plants while pole bean plants will climb anything that they can wind around, not just poles. Within these two types there are an incredible range of different cultivars, some grown for the pods, which are eaten fresh or frozen; the immature shelled seeds, eaten fresh; or for fully mature dry shelled beans, which are stored for winter use.

Those grown for their pods are the common "string beans" of our childhood, though only a few kinds, like the French "filet" types, still have strings running along the seam of the pod (and must therefore be "filleted" before use if allowed to mature). These days they are usually called "snap beans" because of the way, at the proper harvest stage, they snap in two when bent. Snap beans can be green or purple-podded—or even yellow, but then they are called "wax beans." If the pods are flattened instead of round they are called "Romano" beans, and you will find that there are purple and yellow Romanos as well as the green. All of these variations exist in both bush and climbing types.

The pods of any bean can be allowed to mature, and the beans shucked out for fresh use, but the most common cultivars bred especially for this purpose are the French "flageolet" beans, Lima beans, and Fava, or broad beans. These last two are different species from all the others we've discussed, and have much larger pods and beans. Limas come in both bush and climbing forms while Favas exist only as bush beans. We will not deal with either of them here.

Any of these, plus a myriad of others, can be allowed to mature fully and dry for shelling and winter storage. Every region of the country has its traditional favorites: there are Vermont Cranberry beans, Soldier beans, Jacob's Cattle beans, Yellow Eye beans, Case Knife beans; the range is endless and fascinating. And then there are heirloom favorites from other parts of the world: the Bush Blue Coco of France, the Cannellone beans of Italy, the Adzuki bean from Japan; of these exotic foreign beans 90 percent can be grown in American gardens. Only a few of the hottest or coldest regions cannot grow one or the other kinds; we, for instance, do not have a long enough season to mature most kinds of Lima beans, or the Mung and Adzuki beans from Japan.

All beans are legumes, which means that their roots play host to a kind of soil bacteria capable of extracting nitrogen from the air— itself about three-quarters nitrogen—that makes up almost one-quarter of the soil by volume, and "fixing" it in small warty nodules which form on legume roots. This symbiotic relationship between legumes and the *rhizobia* bacteria not only helps the beans themselves grow, but stores nitrogen for later crops; this makes beans (and peas) a valuable part of any crop rotation scheme. Dusting the seed with a purchased bacterial inoculant (available from most seed houses) just before planting will make sure that there are plenty of bacteria available to do the job. For more on this process, see "Peas."

Beans are a warm-weather crop, and cannot be planted until after all danger of frost. We plant bush types an inch deep, two rows to the bed, 18 inches between the rows, and 6 inches between the plants. Sow a seed every two inches and then thin out the weakest plants as soon as they have four leaves. For equidistant spacing, poke three seeds into the soil 6 inches apart each way, and thin out the two weakest in each group, The average family will need 5–10 feet of beans (10–20 plants) per person, as each plant yields about a quarter pound of beans. Bush beans will set one or two flushes of pods, but should then be removed and replaced with another crop. To lengthen the harvest period, either replant the same cultivar more than once (temporal succession), or a range of cultivars of different maturities (varietal succession).

For continuous crops from a single planting, or if space in the garden is limited, grow pole beans. You can set stout poles 10 feet long, 2 feet deep, and plant 6 to 12 seeds, an inch deep, around the base, then thin out the weakest plants at the four-leaf stage, leaving four to six plants. Rough surfaced poles work better than smooth, planed lumber. Another method, especially popular with kids, is to make a bean tepee. To do so, either lean together the tops of four 12-foot poles set in the corners of the bed, or set a single post in the center of the growing bed, drive stakes in a ring around the outside, and then run twine from the stakes to the top of the pole. If you use the twine method you can control the shape of the teepee more closely and fall cleanup will be less trouble (see below).

We plant our pole beans in a single row down the center of bed, just as if they were bush beans, and then erect an untreated twine

Pole beans grow just as well on a trellis as they do on poles, and are easier to harvest.

trellis for them to grow on. The trellis is made from 8-foot-long 2 × 2 posts sunk two feet in the ground, ten feet apart. A 10-foot-long piece of electrical conduit, flattened at the ends and drilled to accept a wood screw, is used to join the two posts at the top. Next we connect the bases of the posts an inch or two above ground level with a run of twine, then run a criss-cross of twine back and forth up to the conduit, with cross ties running from post to post every foot or so. Once the beans are up, have been thinned to one plant every six inches, and have started to ramble, we wrap each plant around an upright string of the trellis. That gives them the idea, and from that point on the vines climb on their own. Because untreated twine decomposes quickly in contact with the ground, fall cleanup is a snap with this kind of trellis: just cut the lines loose from the posts, roll up the whole affair and throw it on the compost pile.

Once the plants are up, keep the bed clear of weeds. Since beans are shallow-rooted, mulching or close planting works better than too frequent and vigorous cultivation. Close planting can cause problems in wet years, though, as under wet conditions it can foster development of blights and rots. Try to keep bush beans upright, and the pods off the ground. Stay out of the bean patch during wet weather or after watering; you'll spread whatever disease spores are present from plant to plant on your tools, hands, and even pant legs.

Many of these diseases are seed-borne, so buy seed grown in the western United States, where the dry conditions make it easy for seed growers to prevent disease. Most of the bean seed sold by seed retailers, both mail order and on seed racks, is grown there. If you save your own seed, be sure not to save any seed from plants that show signs of disease on either the leaves or the pods. An excellent guide to vegetable diseases is *Identifying Diseases of Vegetables*, published by Pennsylvania State University and available from a number of mail order seed houses. (See Bibliography.) Also be sure to rotate the bean patch, so that any spores or bacteria left in the soil don't have a ready host the following spring.

Diseases can also overwinter on your permanent trellis parts, so if disease has been a problem you should sterilize your stakes and posts or use them for some other crop the following season. One of the beauties of a cut-and-compost, untreated twine trellis is that there is no place for disease and insects to overwinter but on the posts, and they can be easily treated with a bleach dip or spray. This is made by mixing with water at a 10:1 ratio and then either dipping the stakes, or spraying the solution on the posts.

The major insect pest of beans is the Mexican bean beetle. They look like large ladybugs: up to 1/3 inch long, with an oval body that is yellow to brown and eight black spots on each wing cover. The eggs are laid in yellow clusters of four to five dozen on the undersides of leaves, and after hatching grow into 1/3 inch long yellow grubs, with six rows of spines that make them look almost fuzzy. In the process they make a lacework of the bean leaves. Once they've grown to full size they attach themselves to an unhurt leaf, which they may roll around themselves, and pupate. After they emerge as adults the whole cycle starts over, and may repeat two or three times a season if time permits. The time from egg to adult is about a month, so there is plenty of time for the attentive gardener to interrupt the process. The major defense is the simplest: pick off the beetles and crush them; the same applies to the eggs and the larvae. If the infestation is severe you can dust with rotenone. The surviving bean beetle adults overwinter in gardenside debris, so keeping the place tidy will help break the cycle as well.

Harvest snap beans promptly as soon as the pods begin to swell with seeds; this signals the peak of flavor. If you leave them on the plant after that point, the plants will stop producing and move into a seed-ripening phase. This is particularly important for pole beans, which, if you keep them picked off, will produce over a very long period. Yellow-podded beans should be left long enough to develop their characteristic color; purple-podded beans are colored from the start.

Filet types should be harvested very young, and unless you are growing the newest "faux filets," they will need almost daily attention during the harvest period. The pods should be harvested as soon as they reach 1/8 inch in diameter, regardless of the length, though it will usually be 3 to 5 inches. There should be no swelling, and when snapped in half, the two pieces should break cleanly, rather than remaining connected by a string along the pod seam.

Fresh shelling beans such as flageolets and Limas should be harvested as soon as the beans themselves begin to separate from the pods. You can feel this by squeezing the pod—there will be a tiny bit of give before you feel the bean inside. Open a pod. The beans inside shouldn't be moist on the surface, and should have shrunk back a bit from the pod. Color is not a good indicator of maturity, as shell beans come in many colors. To harvest as dry beans wait for the pods to dry completely on the plants, then cut the plants off at ground level and hang them upside down in a dark, dry, airy place. Check a few pods periodically, and once the beans have hardened you can take the plants and beat them against a tarp on the ground to loosen the pods. Shuck them and store the beans in glass jars.

There are literally thousands of bean cultivars. Our favorite pole bean is one called Emerite, but the old standbys in my grandfather's garden, Kentucky Wonder and Romano are great, too. So is Blue Lake. A bit more exotic, but just as easy to grow, and plenty prolific, are the Italian heirlooms Green Annelino and Golden Annelino. They are flat-podded, full flavored, and curl around like a crescent moon. There is also a purple pole bean called Trionfo Violetto that is exceptionally beautiful as an ornamental vine, as well as a prolific producer of tasty pods. A new one that we discovered only last season is Frima, a yellow flat-podded pole bean from Austria that has exceptional flavor.

For bush beans the cultivar Tendergreen—also one of Big Sam's favorites—and its descendants are good because they are resistant to many bean diseases. For filet beans we grow one of the new "faux filet" types called Finaud, which does not need frequent harvest like the original Fin des Bagnols and Triomphe de Farcy; others of this type are La Belle and Astrel. Our favorite purple bush bean is Royal Burgundy, and among the yellow wax beans we grow both Golden Rocky (Beurre de Rocquenfort) and a new French cultivar called Dorabel which colors up earlier than any other wax bean we've tried. There is a bush Romano that has very good flavor, and then we also grow a flat bean that is yellow with purple stripes, called Dragon Tongue, that is exceptionally productive, has great flavor, and is not at all demanding.

With shelling beans the number of varieties is so great that probably the best way to proceed is to try a few each year and see what you like. Personally I don't much care to eat them, so I haven't tried many, and the ones I have, I've grown for fun more than food. There is a lot of history in these traditional American crops. Some of the classics are Soldier, Jacob's Cattle, Black Turtle, Vermont Cranberry and Red Peanut bean. Once you're hooked you may want to exchange seed with other gardeners to get some of the rarer cultivars. For example you could grow the pole bean Mostoller's Wild Goose, the original seed of which—according to the 1990 Yearbook of the Seed Saver's Exchange, a nationwide network of gardeners who maintain and trade open pollinated cultivars—was found in the craw of a goose shot in Pennsylvania in 1867. Believed by the hunter to have gotten the seed from Indian villages near Lake Erie, the goose was eaten, but the seed saved. Planted the following season, this bean cultivar was then maintained by the Mostoller family of Somerset County for over 120 years. It is said to be quite flavorful and productive, but that's barely the point; just knowing you are part of a tradition that stretches back that far makes it a bean worth growing. Some of the traditional foreign beans are the French Chevrier flageolet, the Italian Cannellone bean, the Japanese Adzuki and Mung beans, and the Swedish Brown bean.

BEETS AND CHARD

Beets and chard are actually the same species, drawn toward different ends by generations of gardeners who selected some plants that had especially broad stems and vigorous foliage, and others with larger, sweeter, more deeply colored roots. The first of these became the plant we call chard and the second eventually became the garden beet, or as the Europeans say, beet root.

Chard, or leaf beet, is one of the gardener's best bets for a season-long supply of fresh greens from a single planting. There are several colors of chard—golden yellow, bright scarlet, green, and white—but really only two types. Stem chard, usually known as Swiss chard, has more or less broad stems and large, tough leaves. The stems have a crunchy texture and a mild, clean flavor; they substitute nicely for celery or pac choi where those two vegetables are not grown. Leaf chard, called leaf beet in Europe, has tender leaves and much smaller stems; its common name is "perpetual spinach" as it will produce spinachlike leaves over a long period. The leaves of both kinds make a good boiling green, but the leaf chard is better for salad.

The earliest beets had long, carrot-shaped roots, and ranged in color from reddish black to bright yellow orange, and even white. Until a few hundred years ago, yellow beets were preferred, but over time the now familiar round red beet gained ascendancy.

Both chard and beets are biennials. During their first season they increase in size, and under favorable conditions store their excess food reserves in a swollen root; then in their second season this food reserve is used to produce a central stalk on which flowers, and then seed, are borne. Most gardeners simply plant them as annuals, of course, buying new seed as needed.

The best soil for beets is nearly neutral, has ample organic matter, and is well drained; cold, wet, acid soils won't grow good beets and the foliage will show it—the areas between the leaf veins will be pale yellow with a mottled appearance. They love well prepared raised beds, but too rich a soil may cause forking and hairiness in the roots and increase the chance that the plants will run to seed without forming usable roots. Therefore we put beets, along with the other root crops, in the third part of our four-year rotation, immediately preceding the legumes, which will restore high levels of soil nitrogen for the replanting of nutrient-hungry leaf crops.

Beets are a cool-season crop, and in hot climates are grown spring and fall; matured during hot weather, they will often be tough and woody, with an unpleasant flavor. Here in the North, however, we can grow them right through the summer. The first sowing of beets should be in early spring, as soon as the ground can be worked. On rare occasions a late cold snap will fool them into thinking that they've already endured a winter, and they will run to seed; but if this happens the second planting (we sow every two weeks or so) will quickly fill in the harvest gap. You'll want to plant about ten feet of beets for each adult family member over the course of the season.

The seed of both beets and chard is actually a small, withered fruit containing four to eight seeds, so it should be sown sparsely to avoid later thinning. Set the seeds ¼- to ½-inch deep depending on soil type, moisture, and temperature conditions (see Chapter 7 for details); they should be placed half an inch apart in rows 8–12 inches apart, depending on the cultivar and its size (see below). Equidistant bed spacing is 8 inches; the two or three seeds sown in each spot can later be thinned to the strongest plant. Leaf chard can also be planted on an 8-inch spacing, but stem chard should have a foot per plant.

Once the plants are an inch or two high, thin the seedlings to ½-inch apart. About three weeks later, thin once more. Give carrot-rooted beets a final spacing of 2 inches; 4 inches is enough room for the standard round beets, and 6 inches apiece will allow the large, late storage beets to fulfill their genetic potential. This time you can eat the thinnings as baby beets. Keep the bed free of weeds, and if the beets start to grow up out of the soil, hill them a bit to keep their shoulders from turning green and tough. The carrot-rooted types are most likely to do this.

The worst pest we have with beets and chard is the spinach leaf miner, the larva of a small fly which lays a mass of small, white, cylindrical eggs on the underside of the leaves in late spring. After hatching, the larvae burrow into the leaves and then chew passages in between the upper and lower surfaces of the leaves, hence their name. Papery gray areas on the leaves are a sure sign of leaf miners, and infested leaves should be removed from the plants and burned to destroy the larvae. In our garden this pest has a relatively short damage cycle, basically from mid-May to mid-June, and if we can protect the plants with a floating row that keeps the fly from laying her eggs, the cycle can be broken. An equally easy method is to delay planting until after the active season of these ¼-inch, two-winged gray flies.

Western gardeners may have more problems with the beet webworm, a yellow or green segmented caterpillar ½ inch or more long, with a longitudinal black strip down its body and small black spots on each segment. What you are likely to see, though, is its hideout, a leaf that has been rolled up and secured with webbing. Snap off the leaf and crush or burn it.

The major disease of beets is leaf spot, which is favored by cool, wet soils or seasons. It shows up first as small circular tan or brown spots with purplish borders scattered over the leaf surface; eventually whole leaves may yellow and fall off, leading to elongation of the plant's crown. Pick off the leaves and mulch the plants to control the disease, as it spreads through rain or irrigation splash. Burn or turn under all plant residues at the end of the season and move your beets to another bed—good garden cleanup and rotation will prevent most beet disease from ever getting a foothold. Beet cultivars resistant to leaf spot are now available, as well.

You can harvest beets or chard at any time. Beet roots are best harvested once they have reached ½ inch or more in diameter, but for storage the roots can be much larger, up to 4 or even 6 inches in diameter. Use special varieties adapted for storage and plant 90 days before the first fall frost, so that they are ready just as the weather cools down in fall. After harvest, cut the tops ½ inch or so above the crown of the plant, and store the roots in damp sand or sawdust just above freezing. Under good conditions they should keep 3–4 months.

Beets can be overwintered in the ground for early spring use, but should be harvested before growth starts in spring. Once the plant breaks dormancy, the root becomes increasingly bland and fibrous, as the support structure of the seed stalk is constructed by the plant from the accumulated sugars in the root. In cold climates a deep mulch will be necessary to prevent freezing of the crown.

Aside from the new commercial hybrids there are relatively few beet varieties. What we do have is a lot of variations on a few basic types. The long, carrot-rooted beets are represented by the varieties Cylindra, Formanova, and Forono. They grow to about 1 inch in diameter and 4 to 8 inches long, with as much as half their length above ground. These types are excellent for canning because of their shape, and are also especially easy to peel after cooking; the roots slip easily from its skin with a little finger pressure at the tapered end.

Early round beets come flattened or globular; the flat ones are mostly descendants of the old Egyptian strains, while the round cultivars will have names like Little Ball or Dwergina. Both types mature early but don't hold well; harvest promptly to get tender, fiber-free roots. Main crop types are commonly descendants of Detroit Dark Red or its variants; they mature larger and hold longer, and have stronger tops than the early beets. The rough-rooted late-storage types like Lutz Greenleaf, Winterkeeper, and Long Season can grow to enormous size without losing their sweet taste and fine texture.

The only generally available golden beet these days is a globe-shaped cultivar called Burpee's Golden, and while it is not a vigorous plant, the roots are a beautiful golden yellow color that does not bleed when cooked and which is oh-so-sweet. There is also a white beet that goes variously under the names Albina Vereduna, Albino, and Snow White. It is a large, vigorous plant that has good texture and is very sweet. Even more interesting, though, is a variety named Chiogga, which has alternating concentric rings of pinkish purple and white in the root. It is also known as the Candystripe beet. One last unusual cultivar is MacGregor's Favorite, thought to be of German origin but long cultivated in Scotland, and grown as much for its leaves as its long tapered roots, which are slow to develop and a bit rough. Also known as the Victoria or Dracena beet, it has thin, straplike leaves, with a deep metallic purple color that becomes brighter in cold weather. The leaves are used to add color to salads, or the plants are simply used as an ornamental.

Chard varieties range from very broad-stemmed varieties like Lucullus and Monstruoso d'Ingegnoli, with ribs the width of your hand, to leafy varieties nearly indistinguishable from spinach, such as the old English heirloom known simply as Perpetual Spinach. For those who like a little bit of color, there is Ruby Red or Charlotte Swiss chard.

BROCCOLI

Broccoli is not a very glamorous vegetable; not even politicians will claim it. It is one of the most nutritious vegetables you can grow, yet though the average family eats some twenty-six pounds of broccoli a year, only about half of American gardeners grow it. In fact, it is ranked sixteenth of the top twenty vegetables grown in American gardens.

There are basically two types of broccoli cultivars, those which are adapted for production of a single central sprout, and those that will produce a lot of lateral shoots after the terminal shoot is cut. Since the part of the plant we eat is its flowering shoots, you might think it would belong in the "fruits" part of the rotation. But all the members of the cabbage family—known as the brassicas—including broccoli, are relatively nutrient-hungry plants, so we put them in the first year of our rotation, when nutrient levels are at their highest. Also, since the soil-borne diseases to which all brassicas are susceptible are able to survive long periods in the soil, we want to keep all the brassicas in the same part of the rotation so that the time between repeated plantings in the same plot is maximized.

Broccoli is a cool-season crop. Here in the far North it is grown as a spring-sown, summer-harvested crop, but south of us it can be sown both for a spring and fall crop. In the deep South, spring plants must be started before Christmas and set out by Valentine's Day so that they have a chance to head up before the weather turns hot. Perhaps the best climate for broccoli (and its relatives) in the United States is in the Pacific Northwest, where the combination of cool summers and mild wet winters make broccoli almost a year-round crop.

Plant breeders and growers have made enormous progress with broccoli over the past ten years or so, and new research has led to three different methods of growing broccoli, depending on what kind of harvest you want.

If you want to go for those big, blue-ribbon heads you've seen in the catalogs, select a cultivar like Super Dome, start your plants 6–8 weeks before the last frost, and set them out two weeks before the frost-free date, two feet apart in rows three feet apart. In intensive beds, that is a single row down the center of the bed. Set the plants with their first leaves just above ground level and water them in well. A month or so later, when the central bud begins to form, side-dress the plants with a bit of extra fertilizer; we use a tablespoon of fish emulsion in a gallon of water. Let the head grow to full size and cut just before the florets open to yellow.

If what you want is a long harvest of small, eminently usable side shoots, choose a cultivar like Bonanza or Green Comet, and treat it the same way, but cut the central head as soon as it reaches three inches across. That will shift the hormonal balance of the plant and send its growth energy to the side, or lateral shoots. Cut that first,

GROWING BROCCOLI

For large heads set the plants two feet apart, side dress with fertilizer just as the heads begin to form, and delay harvest until just before the florets show yellow.

For continuous harvest set the plants two feet apart, cut the central head up high when only 3 inches across, and harvest side shoots at the same size.

For maximum yields set the plants 6–8 inches apart or direct seed in "clumps" two feet apart, or in rows, thinning to 6–8 inches apart. Side dress as buds form and harvest small heads before florets show yellow.

early head up high on the stem, to keep from shocking the plant, and do the same with the side shoots so the plant is stimulated to produce as many laterals as possible. In both these cases you need a big plant, so start early and make sure that nothing slows its growth.

But if you want to get the most broccoli in the least space, with the least effort, though, you should take the opposite tack. Commercial growers set their plants a mere six inches apart in rows eighteen inches apart; their total yields are double that of the methods above. The individual heads are much smaller, and the crop is ready all at once, but if you are freezing broccoli, that's a boon. Proven cultivars for this method are Southern Comet, Premium Crop, and Emperor. In intensive beds you could set the plants on eight-inch equidistant centers; just make sure that there is no shortage of nutrients, and be prepared to side dress with fish emulsion at bud formation time. This third method also works well if you are direct-seeding spring broccoli. You can either sow the seed ¼-inch deep in rows and thin at the four-leaf stage, or place a few seeds in each spot where you want a plant and then remove all but the strongest once they are established. I'm going to try growing it in hills: I'll sow eight to ten seeds per hill, two or three feet between hills, then thin to the strongest five.

In the North, seed fall broccoli 10 to 12 weeks before the first fall frosts, but by mid-July at the latest. In mild winter areas of the South, August is the time, but you'll probably need to shade the beds to help with germination and nurse the plants through their first few weeks. If you wait until the weather cools down, they won't set buds before temperature and day lengths get too low to mature a head. October is planting time in the desert Southwest, where much of the country's winter crop is grown.

We cover our spring broccoli with a floating row cover immediately after sowing or setting, to temper the weather a bit and to keep off flying insects. Flea beetles can decimate tiny, sprouting seedlings; but the real danger to transplants is from the cabbage root maggot. These are the larvae of a small housefly-like insect that appears around the time dogwood and shad trees are in bud. It spends about two weeks laying its eggs at the base of young plants. When the maggots hatch they tunnel into the roots of the broccoli, and in the process do enough damage that the plants wilt or, in severe cases, break off at the ground. Once the plants are infested, it's hard to do much for them, as removing the larvae involves digging up the plants. The row cover prevents the cabbage fly from reaching the plants to lay her eggs.

My grandfather, gardening before the advent of row covers, used wood ash to control this pest. A few days after transplanting he would sprinkle dry wood ash around the base of each plant so that the area was completely covered, out to a distance of four inches or so. He didn't have an explanation as to why this should work, but his garden was proof that it did. My guess is that either the ash, which is highly alkaline, changed the pH of the soil so radically in the exact area where the fly lays her eggs that they won't hatch, or that the ash is so powdery and dry it desiccates the eggs. It is possible, though, that the ash simply supplied enough potassium that root growth on Big Sam's broccoli was vigorous enough to withstand some resident maggots. At least that was the conclusion reportedly reached by a Washington state researcher who studied the problem some years ago. In fact, he was said to have found that the wood ashes actually attracted cabbage flies!

The other traditional methods of interrupting this fly's life cycle are collars and mulch. Collars are three-to-four-inch circles cut from tar paper or cardboard, that have a slit from the edge to the center, so that they can be placed on the ground at the base of the plants, completely surrounding the stem and preventing the fly from reaching the soil to lay her eggs. This is the same idea as mulching. While you could simply mulch the entire bed, the most effective material seems to be sawdust. As a whole-bed mulch, sawdust is too acidic and nutrient hungry, but placed in a 6–8-inch circle surrounding the stem, at a depth of 1–2 inches, it prevents the fly from reaching the soil. Hay is not as effective, perhaps because its porosity allows the fly to climb down through it to the soil.

Once the plants are up and growing, their major enemies are the cabbage worm and the cabbage looper. Both of these are pale green caterpillars, an inch to an inch-and-a-half long, that eat everything cabbagelike in sight, including broccoli.

Big Sam had a great method for controlling cabbage worms: me. My brother and I (and an occasional friend) were given old, warped tennis rackets and paid a bounty of a nickel each for the dead, dusty white butterflies that are the adult form of the cabbage worm. This may still work well if you have energetic kids, or need the exercise yourself; but it's not the most efficient method out there. You can also handpick the eggs before they hatch, but while they are easy to recognize—they look like tiny, ridged, yellow-to-pale-orange footballs stuck end-first to the undersides of the leaves—they are very small eggs, and laid singly, which makes effective control just as time-consuming as swatting the butterflies.

Hand picking is more effective after they hatch, though it means you'll have to put up with some damage to the plants. Young worms seem to prefer the upper side of the leaves near the midrib, so that's the easiest time to find and crush them. Later they work their way down the leaves, and they eventually hide inside the head, at which point they are really difficult to control. You can expect to see the first young caterpillars about a week after you notice the butterflies have arrived in your garden.

Probably the most effective method of controlling these pests is by the use of what old-time organic gardeners call "bug spray," an unappetizing concoction that uses statistics the way they ought to be used. Here's how to make it. Once the caterpillars appear, find a few that look abnormal or that seem more sluggish than the others—what you are after is sick or parasitized individuals—plus a dozen or so normal ones; if you can't find any sick ones gather three of four dozen total, the more the better. Here's the revolting part: take the caterpillars and put them in an *old* blender with a cup of tepid water and make bug soup. The water should not be chlorinated; if you are on a community water system, use water from a pond, stream, or mudpuddle. If you don't have a blender you're willing to sacrifice for this purpose, you can crush them by hand or with a mortar and pestle. Add another cup of tepid water, pour the "soup" into a mason jar and set it in a warm place, say the laundry room, for a couple of days. Then take the contents of the jar, dilute with a further amount of water appropriate to the size of your garden, and put it in a garden sprayer, straining it if necessary. Use this spray to thoroughly coat the leaves of the plants affected. With any luck, the majority of the caterpillars will soon sicken and die.

Why? Because you "cultured"—using a kitchen table form of genetic engineering—whatever disease or parasite the sick and dying caterpillars you selected had, and then spread it all over the food supply of the remaining caterpillars. The reason for getting a large number of individuals if none of them look sick is that it is statistically likely that some of them were ill, but just not showing the symptoms. By giving the existing disease good conditions to spread—warm, unsterilized water with crushed caterpillar bodies in it—you helped along a thoroughly natural process, and that is the essence of organic gardening. The principle involved here is simple, and applicable to any number of garden pests, as long as you can catch them at the feeding stage. If this method is too down and dirty for you, there are commercially prepared biological pesticides available.

Timing is also critical when using these. *Bacillus thuringiensis* is a naturally occurring bacterium that infects, and eventually kills, a wide range of soft-bodied caterpillars. It is harmless to other kinds of animals, including people (but also to adults of the same species as the caterpillars). If you use this spray, which is sold under a number of trade names such as Dipel and Thuricide, you need to begin spraying within a few days after the butterflies appear, and repeat the sprays every week or two while the butterflies are around, to make sure that none of the eggs hatch onto uninfected leaves. Once the caterpillars catch the infection they stop eating, but it takes three or four days for them to die.

There are several seed-borne diseases of the whole cabbage family that affect broccoli, but if you buy quality seed from a reputable seed house they won't concern you. Club root, however, is a soil-borne fungus that can be brought into your garden on the roots of purchased transplants, or with a load of manure from livestock that fed on infected plants, or even on the soles of your shoes. Its first symptom is wilted plants in the heat of the day that recover overnight. Pull one of the affected plants and look at the roots; the deformity associated with this disease will quickly explain its name! The best way to avoid a repeat (if you do see the symptoms) is to destroy any infected plants and keep all brassica family crops out of that area for at least four years. Seven years is better, though impractical for home gardeners. You can help prevent club root with an application of wood ash around the base of the plants, as that will raise the pH of the soil beyond the range that supports the fungus. For this use, mix the wood ash into the soil instead of just dusting it on the surface.

As mentioned earlier, broccoli should be harvested just before the florets open. Cut with a sharp knife, preferably at an angle so that rain or irrigation water can't collect on top of the cut stem, which could lead to stem rot if the season is wet. Keep the buds cut off if you're trying to extend the harvest, because once the plant begins to flower, it forgets about you and your freezer!

I mentioned some of the good new broccoli varieties earlier, but there are also a number of unusual types you might want to try. Romanesco broccoli is a sort of cross between broccoli and cauliflower, and one of the most beautiful crops I know. The heads are chartreuse, and resemble the ascending spiral of a conch shell, with each individual floret made of tightly closed buds in this same arrangement. Seen from above the florets interweave like ripples in a quiet pool. And the taste is fantastic; richer than cauliflower, but without the mustardy greenness of broccoli. For a large plant that produces large heads, grow the original, called Romanesco; for smaller, more uniform heads try the cultivar Minaret. Both are long-season plants and should be grown like Brussels sprouts. The other two interesting broccoli are the ancient purple and white sprouting types. These never really form a central head at all, but grow into large bushes that are covered with small sprouts. They, too, should be grown like Brussels sprouts. The cultivars used are called simply Purple Sprouting and White Sprouting, though you may see early and late strains listed in some specialty catalogs. Purple cultivars that form a large central head include Burgundy Queen and Violet Queen. These are usually listed in seed catalogs as purple cauliflower, but for my money they are broccoli.

BRUSSELS SPROUTS

Brussels sprouts are one my favorite garden plants. Sure they take up a lot of room and they're slow-growing, but they share those characteristics with two of my other favorite crops: leeks and celery root. All of these crops are at their best just when the garden seems empty, done, kaput—and winter is ready to close in for good. I admit that Brussels sprouts aren't ever likely to make the vegetable top ten, but they are beautiful, relatively carefree plants and if you've eaten only store-bought sprouts you don't know what you're missing.

The first time I saw a Brussels sprouts plant, I thought it was some kind of mutant, with its little topknot of foliage perched on a leafless stem packed with miniature cabbages. It's actually the same species as broccoli and cabbage, but over the few hundred years it's been in cultivation, growers have selected plants that sprouted readily at the leaf joints, called axils, instead of heading up, and saved the seed from those. If you've ever harvested a tall cabbage and then been pleasantly surprised to find a ring of little heads sprouting from the bare stalk a few weeks later you'll understand how this important characteristic was discovered.

Soil preparation, seedling care, and most of the other cultural rules for Brussels sprouts are the same as for broccoli, except that they need more time and space. The seedlings should be started two weeks later than the other spring-planted brassicas, and set out two weeks later as well, once the weather has settled. Harvest will be in late fall, instead of late spring. There isn't much point in trying to rush the season, as the sprouts shouldn't be harvested until after the first fall frosts have sweetened them up. That's why store-bought sprouts don't taste as good: 90 percent of them are grown along the California coast just north of Santa Cruz, where the weather is cool year-round, but rarely frosts; that makes for very productive plants, but bland flavor.

Once ready for the garden each plant should be allotted four square feet apiece to prosper; no one has yet come up with an intensive trick to coax more sprouts out of smaller plants the way the commercial growers have with broccoli. If you are planting in beds, set the plants two feet apart each way; in rows they can be a foot-and-a-half apart in the row, with the rows three feet apart. With good fertility they'll fill the space. We plant a single row down the center of a thirty-inch bed and grow a quick crop of spinach along the edges; the spinach is up and gone long before the sprouts need the space. Pests and diseases are the same as for broccoli, too, and while there are plenty of them, it's a simple task to take care of the sprouts at the same time. While the rest of the garden grows, bears, and then dies back, the sprouts just keep plugging along, waiting their turn.

When they differ from their cabbage family relatives is at harvest time, usually September through October here in Vermont. Brussels sprouts can be harvested anytime after the sprouts begin to form, but flavor and vitamin content both improve if you wait until at least the second significant frost. Though they are rich in vitamin C to start with, their content of this important nutrient is highest if the sprouts are harvested when the temperature is at or slightly below freezing.

Brussels sprouts mature from the bottom of the plant to the top because the top, or apical, bud (the plant's growing point) produces a sprout-inhibiting hormone; the farther from the apical bud a given sprout is, the weaker that hormone is. As the plant grows taller, the lower sprouts begin to form, and when it reaches its mature height production of the hormone stops and sprout formation proceeds up the stalk. This gradual maturation is fine if you want to harvest your sprouts a little at a time, over a long period; but if you want a concentrated harvest you should cut off the apical bud to stop production of the hormone earlier than would happen normally. This will change the plant's hormonal balance and allow all of the sprouts to ripen at once.

Left alone, Brussels sprouts ripen gradually, from the bottom up; cut off the top six inches of the plant if you want all the sprouts to ripen at once.

Timing is important for this "topping," though. If you take out the apical bud too soon, the sprouts may mature before frost has had a chance to enrich their flavor; if you wait too long, the lower sprouts may become over-mature. A good rule-of-thumb is to top the plants six to eight weeks before your intended harvest date.

If hard frost threatens—below 25°F—you can pull up the plants, with a generous soil ball, and put them in a more protected place. A shed or cold frame should be enough, but you could put them right on the dirt floor of a root cellar, and they'll continue to ripen for a few weeks. If the plants have already been topped, and the sprouts are just about ready, you can simply cut them off a few inches below the lowest good sprouts, remove any remaining leaves, and put the resulting "sprout logs" in the root cellar. Sometimes farmers even take them to market like this and sell them to knowledgeable cooks by the piece.

When it comes to cultivars, there are two basic kinds of Brussels sprouts. Dwarf varieties like the old Jade Cross have closely spaced round (or even flattish) sprouts that cling tightly to the main stem of the plant. In general this type is hardier and matures earlier. But the sprouts hug the stem so tightly it's difficult to get them off, and if you cut them off you'll lose a lot of leaves because there is almost no stem on the sprout. The taller, later varieties like Long Island Improved have smaller, teardrop shaped sprouts perched off the main stalk on short stems—which makes for an easier harvest—but they are not as hardy. One of the first cultivars to combine the best of both was Jade Cross "E" (the "E" stood for "extra internodal length"). Since then small specialty seed houses have begun to import a whole range of European cultivars. Some of the best are the early hybrid Oliver, Dolmic hybrid, which is two weeks later, and Lunet hybrid, which is two weeks later still. Another good sprout with more of the dwarf in it is the Japanese bred Prince Marvel hybrid.

Perhaps the most interesting, but also one of the slowest growing Brussels sprouts is Rubine, a deep reddish purple cultivar that is an exceptional ornamental plant as well as a tasty producer. Try it: I can guarantee you that a triangle of Rubine plants surrounded by half a dozen lower-growing hardy ornamental kales is a sight to behold in the cool gray mist of a November morning. And when you're done looking at it, bring the tasty red sprouts to the dinner table!

CABBAGE

Cabbages are often classified as early, late, or overwintering types. But for this discussion let's divide the clan into ball-headed, flat, pointed, and savoy cabbages, as this gives a clearer idea of the choices we gardeners have. Most of the cabbages in cultivation are ball-headed; that is the standard, and there are both red and green cultivars that will perform well at some season in every region of the country. Flat-headed cabbages were once widely grown, primarily for storage, but are rarely seen anymore except in heirloom seed lists. Pointed cabbages are early types, and to date I have seen only green cultivars. Some of the older ones are still available, and new hybrids are still being developed; pointed varieties are generally quite small, which makes them ideal for intensively planted home gardens. Savoy cabbages are recognized by their curly, crumpled leaves; there are early and late types, though in general a savoy will be later than an equivalent smooth-leaved type.

Cabbage's place in our garden rotation is the same as broccoli, as are its disease and insect problems. As with both broccoli and Brussels sprouts, young cabbages take up only a fraction of the space they'll need at maturity; a quick "catch crop" of some other type can be grown in that extra space until it is needed. Scallions, spinach, lettuce, and other fast-growing greens make good candidates.

Cabbage itself should be grown quickly, and without checks, if it is to be as tender and tasty as possible, so if you will be interplanting make sure that the bed is sufficiently fertile, well watered (yet well drained) enough to support the growth of all the nutrient-greedy plants you put in it. To avoid problems with splitting and tipburn (discussed below), the nutrients should be easily available at the early stages of growth, and less so as the heads mature. A bed that has had manure applied the previous fall, at a rate of two to three bushels per hundred square feet, and then been turned under and planted to a cover crop, is ideal.

If you wish to harvest over the longest period, either plant a varietal succession of different types in mid-spring, and again in late summer, or plant every two to three weeks, using a quick-growing fresh-use cultivar harvested promptly as each planting matures in temporal succession.

The different types of cabbage require different spacings. Early cultivars, including virtually all the pointed types, can be set as close as 8–12 inches apart. Most ball-headed cabbages need 12–18 inches apiece, depending on what size head you want. Except for a few of the newer hybrids, savoy and storage cultivars will need 18–24 inches apiece to develop mature heads. If you want to grow really large heads, space the plants 24–36 inches apart. In each case, rows should be 30–36 inches apart to allow a path between the plants at maturity; you can also plant double rows with a path between each pair, or as we do, set the plants equidistant in semi-permanent beds.

Cabbages can either be grown from transplant or direct-seeded where they are to grow. The details of the process are described under "Broccoli" and apply equally to cabbage, though some elements are more and some less important.

Timing, for example, is not as critical to success with cabbages as it is with broccoli. But to get the best taste and storage qualities in your cabbages it still helps to pay attention to how the plant responds to the changing seasons in your garden. Spring-set plants should be set out before they reach the six- to eight-leaf stage (when the stem is about the diameter of a pencil), unless the weather is fully settled. If they have to endure more than a few days of temperatures below 50°F (after they have reached that size), there is a significant risk that they will run to seed without forming a head. Fall crops planted for storage or sauerkraut should not be planted more than about 10–12 weeks before the first fall frost. The tang of good homemade sauerkraut is directly related to the level of sugars stored in the leaves of a cabbage head; it takes time, plus a period of cool weather, even a bit of frost at maturity, to get a good supply of these sugars. Cabbages for storage need to harden off and slow down their growth before harvest, and the change to lower temperatures and light levels that accompanies the approach of fall is essential to this.

The two major problems that afflict cabbage, but not broccoli, are tipburn and splitting. Both can be prevented by a combination of good practices and proper choice of cultivars. Tipburn is a condition where the margins of interior leaves in the head die back. In moderate cases the bad parts can be cut out and the cabbage used, but in severe cases the head may be ruined. Tipburn is caused by a calcium deficiency—leading to a dieback of growing tips in both roots and tops—but in most organic gardens, it is a result of too heavy a manure application, which raises nitrogen and potassium levels in the soil beyond the balance point and sets the stage for later problems.

Tipburn is triggered by a hot, dry spell, which causes a slowdown in the quick growth allowed by the high nitrogen level. Combined with the tendency of potassium to displace calcium—most plants are ten times as efficient at absorbing potassium as calcium—that leads to a dieback of recent growth at the leaf tips. The new growth of a cabbage is inside, close to the growing tip of the plant, and so the damage is not immediately visible.

Each of these nutrient and weather factors interacts with the others and will lead to problems with a number of other vegetables besides cabbage. To balance the nitrogen and potassium in this given example, an application of calcium phosphate (also called colloidal phosphate), or ground phosphate rock—at a rate of about five pounds per hundred square feet at the same time as the manure—should work. The phosphorus will bring the nutrients of the manure into balance, as most manures are low in phosphorus, and both calcium levels and the pH of the soil will be raised. Calcium availability rises and potassium availability drops as this happens; so the balance of nutrients picked up by the plant will change in favor of less tipburn.

The key element here is balance. Using organic fertilizers, instead of commercial synthetic ones, does not mean you can just ignore what you add to the soil, though it does mean you won't have to worry about those additions coming back to haunt—or bankrupt—you. Organic gardening is not some hocus pocus psychotherapy for the land. It is a skill, and a craft, and an art like any other, and it repays the care and attention that the gardener gives to it many fold. (After all, it is the depth and complexity of our interests that makes them satisfying; we'd be foolish to ignore that complexity.)

Split heads are also the result of an interaction among nutrient availability, weather, and the susceptibility of the particular cultivar planted. In general, splitting is triggered by fluctuations in growing conditions—the most common cause is a period of cool, dry weather followed by a spell of warm, wet weather. What happens is that during the cool, dry spell plant growth slows, and the tissues harden up to conserve moisture and resist the cold; then, if the weather suddenly turns favorable, these tissues can't expand fast enough to accommodate new growth, and they rupture. In carrots it is the root which splits, in tomatoes it is the fruit, and in cabbage the heads crack right open, soon followed by rot unless the weather dries out again.

One way to avoid splitting is to keep growth continuous by making sure that water is available to the plant at all times, so the tissues of the plant stay supple. Since cabbage is a leaf crop, excessive nitrogen levels will aggravate splitting problems, too. Choice of cultivar helps because some cabbages have a shorter core, or stem, than others. We don't usually see the stem of a cabbage until we cut it open, but it's a fact that pointed cabbages, which have a longer core than other types, are more likely to split than ball-head and flat cabbages. Unfortunately, the better tasting cabbages are more likely to split; taste has been found to be connected with a tender leaf structure, and those delicate leaves are less able to restrain a rapidly expanding core stem.

Cabbage harvest couldn't be simpler. Cut the head as far up the stem as you can without losing too many leaves. Given time, a second crop of mini-cabbages will form at the base of the plant, just below the cut, a sure sign of its relation to Brussels sprouts! If you'd like a single larger head for your second harvest, remove all but one of the sprouts. We often pull the plants after harvest to make room for another crop, but you could simply plant the other crop in the open space around the sprouting stalk.

One of my favorite cabbages is the pointed heirloom Early Jersey Wakefield. This cultivar has been around over a hundred years and is still one of the best tasting cabbages you can grow. It is also small—so that they can be grown close together to save space—and resistant to tipburn. Spivoy is a good pointed, savoy-leaved hybrid.

Golden Acre and its relative Red Acre are two of the best tasting non-hybrid ball-headed cabbages, but neither is very resistant to splitting. Stonehead is, but the leaves are tough. Many new hybrids are introduced each year, and the catalog descriptions will almost always tell you if they are resistant to splitting and tipburn, as well as to some of the other common cabbage diseases. One of my favorites is the early, loose-headed Japanese hybrid Salarite. The red ball-head hybrid Ruby Ball has been around a long time (for a hybrid) but is still tops in my book, and it is widely adapted to different climates around the country.

Not much has been done with hybridization of flat-headed cabbages, and so those available are mostly heirloom cultivars.

One I have tried and been happy with (though I don't have much actual use for it as it grows too large) is an English variety called Robinson's Champion Ox, available through the Seed Saver's Exchange as Robinson's Drumhead. In our garden the heads themselves reach 18–24 inches across and the whole plant can be three feet from side to side.

Most of the savoy cabbages I am familiar with are hybrids, and good choices include Savoy King, Savoy Chieftain, and Savoy Ace.

CHINESE CABBAGE

The plant we Americans call Chinese cabbage isn't really a cabbage at all, but from a different, though related species, *Brassica rapa*. An ancient Indian oil and spice plant, it spread east to China and Japan, where over centuries of cultivation it was developed into a vegetable crop that is now of central importance to the diet and cuisine of those countries. There are two basic kinds of Chinese cabbage: a heading kind, which is what we will call by that name, and then a kind which has highly developed stems and is known as celery cabbage or *pac choi*.

There are four types of heading Chinese cabbage. A given cultivar can have a wrapped-over head, not unlike a European cabbage though taller, or a joined-up head, which is more open-hearted. Furthermore, each of these can be either a short, stocky barrel-shaped plant, or tall and cylindrical. Aside from their shape, though, all four kinds are remarkably similar. They have pale green leaves with a diaphanous crepelike texture, and are lightly savoyed, or ruffled, at the edges.

Chinese cabbages grow best in cool weather, and thus like most European cabbages are adapted to either spring or fall planting, but not mid-summer. In general, though, the wrapped-over types are more heat-tolerant and earlier to mature, while the joined-up types tend to be less compact, later to mature, and more cold-tolerant. From this we can deduce that the former are better for spring and the latter your best bet for fall planting.

Pac choi is a non-heading plant with highly developed petioles (leaf stalks) and relatively small spoon-shaped leaves that begin about halfway out the petiole rather than right at its base. The leaves are smooth, shiny, and more succulent than Chinese cabbage, more like a Chinese chard than anything else. Here again, though, there are four basic types. One type has narrow petioles with a round, celerylike cross section. This is thought to be the original, ancient form of the plant. Then there is a type that has wide, flat petioles. Within each type are cultivars with either green or white petioles. *Pac choi* is generally more heat-tolerant than Chinese cabbage, though the types do differ: those with white petioles are generally grown for fall harvest, while the green petiole types are slower-bolting and therefore better adapted to spring planting for summer harvest.

Both Chinese cabbage and *pac choi* like the same rich, well drained, slightly acid soil as the other members of the cabbage family. The basic problem you'll face in growing either kind is that although they prefer cool weather, they will almost certainly bolt if regularly exposed to temperatures below 50°F when young. The rule-of-thumb in this case is that more than a week of cold weather when they are in the four- to six-leaf stage will cause the plants to run to seed. While new cultivars can take considerably more temperature variation, you still need to pay close attention to the weather in order to set the proper schedule for planting and harvest.

Spring crops, due to the regimen of early cool temperatures, increasing day length, and warm-to-hot temperatures at harvest, are more prone to failure than fall plantings. In our experience the keys to success are: (1) start from transplant, but only in individual cells or soil blocks so as to avoid shocking the plants when they are moved to the garden, and (2) fight your spring fever; that is, don't start too soon. Both Chinese cabbage and pac choi should be started around the same time as Brussels sprouts (about a month before the last spring frost). The same timing applies if you are sowing directly in the garden, but never plant before the soil temperature reaches 50°F; that is almost certain to cause bolting. You can check this with a soil thermometer; make sure the probe is at the level the seed will be placed by the planter, not deeper or shallower. For fall planting start about 60 to 70 days before the first fall frost (or the onset of cool weather if you live in a hot climate). Gardeners in cool summer climates can likely grow pac choi right through the summer, planting every two weeks or so for a continuous harvest. Whatever the schedule, the seed should be set ¼ inch deep in cool moist conditions, and up to ½ inch deep if the weather is hot and dry.

Chinese cabbage and pac choi share the same diseases and pests as other members of the cabbage family, though in our garden they are especially attractive to flea beetles. I cover the first spring crop with a floating row cover. That both keeps out the flea beetles and helps moderate temperature and moisture to lessen the chance of bolting.

Spacing for these two crops are quite different, as the plants are radically different in size. For Chinese cabbage, allow 18 inches per plant in rows two to three feet apart. If you plant in beds they can be set 18 inches apart in an equidistant pattern; on our three-foot-wide beds that is a 2:1:2 pattern. Pac choi can be grown much closer, with row spacings as little as six inches, in rows 18 inches apart, or 6 inches equidistant in beds. In the same three-foot bed this would be a 5:4:5 pattern. Pac choi can also be broadcast-sown in well-prepared beds and harvested as a seedling or salad crop a scant two weeks after germination, when the plants are only 4–6 inches tall.

Chinese cabbages can be harvested anytime after the heads firm up. They should be solid in response to a hand squeeze. Spring crops need to be harvested promptly to avoid problems with bolting or head rot; fall crops need to be picked before hard frost. Pac choi is ready for harvest anytime after it has four or five leaves. The stalks can be harvested individually, or the whole rosette cut off below the crown. Thinnings make a great addition to salads. With both kinds the flowering sprouts are themselves edible, so even a bolted plant is worth having. Just don't let it set seed or you'll be pulling young plants as weeds for years to come.

Some good Chinese cabbages for spring and fall planting are Dynasty, Two Seasons, and Spring A-1, all squat, barrel-shaped cultivars, and Green Rocket, Monument, and Jade Pagoda, which are tall and cylindrical. My favorite pac choi is a dwarf green hybrid named Mei Quing Choi, by far the best tasting and slowest bolting of all the ones I've grown. Two decent white-stemmed cultivars are Le Choi and Prize Choy. They are quite similar in appearance, but Le Choi has a much stronger mustardy flavor. One last Chinese brassica I like is Tatsoi, which is a close relative of pac choi and looks like a very dark green, cabbage-leaved, loose-leaf lettuce. It is the most bolt-resistant of all these greens, and should be grown 18 inches on center and harvested stem by stem like parsley.

CARROTS

Carrots are among the most productive crops you can grow, and to my mind, one of the best tasting. There are a few basic types: round, or short and stubby carrots like the Chantenay types; Amsterdam and Nantes carrots, with blunt-ended cylindrical roots ranging from finger size up to 1 × 8 inches and both sweet and succulent; the long, pointed Imperator types that we see in the supermarket; and Danvers or Flakee types, which have a drier, more solid root that stores well.

Each type has its use. The round and Chantenay types are good for very early crops, containers, or hard, shallow soils; the Amsterdam and Nantes types are best for fresh eating and juicing; and the long, solid types can be grown for a fall crop that, once dug, can be buried in damp sand in the root cellar for winter eating.

Carrots go in the third part of our rotation, after the leafy crops and fruits have lowered nitrogen levels, and our applications of phosphorus and potassium-containing rock powders have enriched the beds. The bed is also relatively free of weeds after two years of clean cultivation, so we can be sure that the carrots will have a good chance to outrun any returning weeds. Carrots grown in nitrogen-rich soils can grow quite large, but they'll taste awful, and the roots will likely be hairy and misshapen.

In cool areas you can sow carrots throughout the growing season in temporal succession, planting a new crop every two to three weeks. In areas with hot summers, it's best to limit yourself to spring and fall crops, as carrots grown and harvested in mid-summer are likely to have a bitter, resinous taste.

Carrots do not transplant well. Sow the seed ¼ inch deep in rows 6 inches apart. If you want a path between each row, add another foot. But carrots are one of the best crops for raised beds, because the freedom from compaction that a permanent bed gives them really helps their growth. Our three-foot-wide growing beds allow five rows per bed, running lengthwise. You can just as easily run the rows across the bed, which will make it easy to sow only as many feet of row as you'll want to harvest and eat each week. Sow the seed as thinly as you can. I learned from Big Sam to mix in a small amount of radish seed with the carrot seed, and sow them together. That not only makes sowing the small carrot seeds easier, but the quick-germinating radishes break up the soil surface when they emerge, which is a real help for the slow-sprouting carrots.

It also makes it possible for me to cultivate the rows even before the carrots are up, and that means less weed pressure. Carrots do not compete well against weeds; by getting in early with the hoe you can make a big difference in the amount of weeding you'll have to do later. Harvesting the radishes a few weeks later also helps thin the carrots, normally one of the least satisfying garden jobs. By using this radish interplant I am not only able to get a "free" crop of radishes, but also able to completely avoid thinning my carrots until they are the size of a pencil, and so, fit for the table. Then I can at least get something for the time I put in: sweet, tender baby carrots to snack on!

Carrots are not bothered by many pests and diseases. We occasionally have problems with the carrot rust fly on early crops (planted before May 15, two weeks before the last frost), but it is easily controlled by putting down a floating row cover immediately after sowing. Leave the cover on until the radishes are ready to harvest, then harvest, weed, and thin all at once. From there on care is a snap: just an occasional hoeing until the carrots close over their tightly spaced rows. Sometimes we'll see a brightly colored parsley worm, but that is an easy pest to hand-pick and crush underfoot.

Carrots will sometimes split if the weather goes from a prolonged dry period into a wet spell. Regular watering during drought will prevent this; it is more of a problem with spring and summer carrots, as the fall varieties are more fibrous and less succulent, so less affected by variations in the water supply.

My favorite of the short types is a round-rooted cultivar called Parmex, though a new introduction, Thumbellina, is its equal. Of the cylindrical-rooted types I like Minicor and the old heirloom Touchon; there are also some new hybrids of this type, and of these I like Mokum, Napoli, and Ingot. For the long fall crop carrots I recommend the high Vitamin A and beta-carotene hybrids A-Plus and Lucky B. For fun you might find it interesting to grow one of the large storage carrots like Kuroda—they are surefire ribbon winners at the local fair!

CAULIFLOWER

Cauliflower is grown essentially the same way as broccoli, but it is more sensitive to variations in growing conditions, and more prone to failure if stressed. Transplants should be started at the same time as broccoli, and not be exposed to temperatures below 50°F; I grow them right in with my tomato transplants.

Many people buy started cauliflower plants because of their delicacy, but unless you know the grower and can trust his or her methods, this is unwise. Most commercial growers of bedding plants have a hard time giving plants the precise care that cauliflower requires, and unless you inspect the plants carefully before buying you may be disappointed at harvest time. Obviously the plants should be free of insects and disease. But look at their general condition, too. The stems should be green, less than a pencil thickness in diameter, the leaves soft and satiny, and the plant's roots should not have started circling the edges of the container. Ideally, look for a tag in the flat that has the planting date; if it was more than a month previous, pass by those plants.

Cauliflower plants should not be set out until the weather can be counted on to stay above 50°F in the daytime. Light frosts won't hurt them, but extended periods of cool weather will lead to buttoning—the formation of tiny, bitter heads on otherwise normal plants. It is necessary for all the members of the cabbage family, and especially cauliflower, to be grown quickly, without interference from low temperatures, lack of moisture or fertility, or any kind of insect damage. To minimize transplant shock, we water-in our newly set cauliflower plants with a fish fertilizer solution (at one tablespoon per gallon of water) and then cover them immediately with a floating row cover.

Spacing for cauliflower is equally important. The plants should have a minimum of 18 inches square, and 24 inches square is better. If grown in rows, allow a full three feet between the rows; in beds we run a single row down the center, just like Brussels sprouts. You can grow cauliflower 18 inches equidistant in beds; but be prepared to pamper the plants and keep a close eye out for any nutrient or water deficiency. Purpling or paling of the leaves means they are getting hungry and should be fed immediately with a fish fertilizer mix such as they had at transplant time.

Cauliflower should be blanched (bleached) before harvest, beginning when the curd (partially developed, edible flower head) is about the size of an egg. You can do it one of three ways: tie the leaves up over the curd with twine as my grandfather did, tie them with a rubber band as I do, or break the mid-ribs just above the level of the curd and layer the leaves over the curd to block the sunlight. Harvest promptly when the curds are just beginning to separate, before they take on a ricey texture. Unblanched cauliflower curds turn a pale purplish yellow or tan color, and are not as tender as when properly blanched.

The best, most widely adapted cauliflower I know is the Japanese hybrid Snow Crown. If you buy plants that is almost certainly what you'll get, because this variety is resistant to most of the problems of cauliflowers. There are a number of European hybrids that do well in the Pacific Northwest, and others developed for the prime cauliflower-growing areas of Long Island and the Salinas valley of California, but most gardeners will want to stick with Snow Crown.

CELERY AND CELERIAC

Both these plants are biennials, and related in the same way as beets and chard; that is, they are two varieties of the same species: *Apium graveolens.* Stalk celery is a relatively difficult plant to grow well, and might be best avoided by beginners; root celery, though, presents no problems to the average gardener except the amount of time it requires to mature, which is only a matter of patience.

Because they are grown for different parts of the plant, we put celery and celeriac into different parts of our rotation: the former is treated as a leaf crop since it is a notoriously greedy feeder; the latter is treated as a long-season, early-feeding root crop like leeks. Both, however, are started from transplant at the same time.

Both stalk and root celery are started in flats 8 to 10 weeks before the frost-free date. The seed is very small, so it should just be pressed into the surface of the potting soil, watered, and the flat covered to preserve moisture until the seed sprouts, which is likely to take a week or two. If you don't need a full flat, put your parsley and other slow-growing herbs in the same tray. To sow thinly enough, you can use a pen or pencil to pick up the seed: just touch the tip of the pencil to your tongue, then into the seed; the moisture will cause a few seeds to stick to the pencil tip; then you can push them off into the waiting flat with your finger. During their time in the tray, keep the plants above 50°F to avoid triggering their biennial bolting reflex. As soon as the plants have their first true leaves, thin to the strongest plant per cell of the tray, or to an inch apart if you are using an open tray.

Set the plants out 12 inches apart once the weather has become reliably mild. An occasional light frost won't hurt them, but persistent daytime temperatures below 50°F will cause them to bolt, or at the minimum slow down their growth enough to hurt the quality of the final harvest. If planting in rows, allow 2 feet for a path. We give both root and stalk celery a shot of fish fertilizer at transplant time to get them off to a good start. The stalk celery will continue to receive periodic side dressings of this type, while the root celery, after its initial feeding, will be left to fend for itself. I don't blanch celery; the tight planting will take care of that to the extent necessary.

Stalk celery can be harvested once the stems reach usable size, either by cutting off the entire plant at ground level, or by pulling individual stalks from the outside of the plant and letting the younger, inside stalks continue to grow. There is usually little time to do this in our garden, as the crop isn't ready until fall, and it is not hardy enough to withstand frequent frosts. Root celery, on the other hand can be hilled with soil and will survive even a hard frost. In our garden it is harvestable from the middle of September until Thanksgiving. To get the smoothest celery roots, pull away the soil once the knobs have reached an inch or so in diameter, and rub off the small feeder roots above ground level with your finger, then hill the plants.

The most common cultivars of stem celery are variants of Utah 52-70, but there are also some Pascal types, which are more bolt-resistant. So-called "self-blanching" celery is really just a yellow petiole type, which some gardeners prefer, though it is not as vigorous as the green petiole types. Some catalogs list red cultivars, mostly from England, that are quite hardy, but only slightly red. Southern gardeners can grow celery in the fall and winter, and should choose the "Florida" cultivars that have been developed for their winter conditions.

The old standard cultivars for celery root are Alabaster and Giant Prague, but they are not nearly as vigorous or reliable as the French cultivar called Diamant. There are also some cultivars of celery that are grown for the leaves, which are dried and used for seasoning. They are listed in most catalogs as "cutting celery" and are grown just like parsley.

CHICORY AND ENDIVE

These two salad greens ought to be more widely grown than they are. Chicory is a short-lived perennial, while Endive is a biennial somewhat resembling lettuce. They are closely related, but the endive is grown as a leaf vegetable, while only some chicories are grown that way. One form, called witloof, or Belgian endive, is grown as a root crop. We place each in our rotation accordingly. All are cool-weather plants, and are grown as spring or fall crops.

Spring endive can be direct-sown as soon as the ground can be worked. Set the seed ¼ to ½ inch deep in rows 2 feet apart and thin after emergence to 8–12 inches between plants (depending on the cultivar). You can also start from seedlings and set out three-week-old plants in the garden at the same spacing, either in rows, or equidistant in beds. I grow endive just like lettuce; it is subject to many of the same problems, but is generally hardier.

Endive is a bitter plant by nature, and most gardeners will want to blanch the heads before harvest. Perhaps the simplest way is to wait until the heads are the size you like—and the weather is dry—then gather up each head with one hand and slip a rubber band a third of the way down over the head. That will hold the leaves upright and, after 7–10 days, blanch the inner part of the head. If rainy weather arrives, remove the bands or the heads may rot.

Cool weather also tempers the flavor of endive, so for the very best crops combine a fall growing schedule with a week or two of blanching. Fall crops should be sown about 70 to 90 days before the first fall frost. They may need some help to germinate in warm soil; we sow the seed, water thoroughly, and then lay a 2 × 6 board over the row to insulate it from the sun. As soon as the seed germinates we remove the board.

Radicchio, the beautiful burgundy-leaved, white-veined salad seen in expensive gourmet shops, used to be a difficult crop to grow in America, but with the introduction of new Dutch cultivars over the past few years, it can now be grown just like endive. Only about 75–80 percent of the heads will form properly, though, so be sure to plant a few extra. You can tell when the heads are ready by thumping or squeezing. They should be firm, but not hard. The exterior will be green, but once the outer leaves are removed you find the characteristic, bright burgundy inner heart. Radicchio can also be grown and forced like Belgian endive, which is another member of the same species.

Belgian endive is a salad crop that is grown first as a root crop, stored for a few months, then forced to send out new shoots which are harvested for mid-winter salads. Direct-seed 60 to 90 days before the first fall frost, ¼ to ½ inch deep in rows 8–12 inches apart (add another foot between rows if you want a path). Thin to 8 to 12 inches apart in the row, and allow the plants to grow for the summer, removing any seed stalks that may form.

After the first frosts have slowed growth of the plants, carefully dig the roots and let them dry for a day in the open; then cut off the tops an inch or so above the crown. Select uniform, well-shaped roots 8–12 inches long and about an inch across at the crown. Smaller roots will not produce vigorous sprouts, and larger roots may produce multiple sprouts instead of a single, full-size one. Store the roots in damp sand in the cellar or a pit, where they can be kept just above freezing. After a month or so of curing, remove enough from storage to fill a one-foot-deep flower pot with roots, tightly packed shoulder to shoulder, standing upright. Put the pot full of roots in a totally dark spot, with a constant 50°–60°F temperature, water enough so that the bottom of the roots are just barely under the water (use a tray under the pot), and wait three weeks. Sprouts will form and can be cut just above the crown and used for salad; strong roots will produce three crops before needing replacement. If you don't have a dark spot in which to force Belgian endive, you can rig up a support with bent coat hangers and cover the flower pot with a black plastic garbage bag. Be sure to poke a few holes in the bag for ventilation or the sprouts may rot.

To force Belgian endive, bring roots out of storage and plant in a pot. Keep the pot in total darkness, at 50°–60°F for three weeks.

Some of the other chicories you might want to try include Spadona, Ceriolo, and Radichetta. They can either be sown in late summer for spring harvest—yes, they are hardy even here in Vermont—or direct-sown in early spring and harvested at the seedling stage. Either way, blanching will temper the bitter flavor if it is too strong for you. Blanching is easiest on the summer-sown, spring-harvest schedule because as soon as the plants begin their regrowth in spring you simply place a fiber nursery pot over them, and harvest a week to ten days later.

My favorite endives are the small, thin-leaved ones known as *frisée* in Europe. Très Fin Maraichère and Fin des Louviers are two of the originals, and many new descendants of these have been developed; look in the catalog description to see if they are listed as a forebear of the cultivar you are considering. Broader-leaved endives that are more resistant to fall weather include Salad King and Frisan. The best radicchio cultivars are Dutch, and there is getting to be a full range available. For ball-headed Chiogga or Verona types try Giulio, Augusto, or Medusa. The elegant, pointed Treviso types are a bit more difficult to grow, but new cultivars like Early Treviso and Nerone should work well. The two best available Belgian endive cultivars for home gardeners are Zoom and Toner hybrids.

COLLARDS
AND KALE

Collards and kale are best thought of as loose leaf cabbages. They are the closest of our modern garden brassicas to the original wild cabbage from which all were developed. They are easier to grow than cabbage, more nutritious than broccoli, and in the opinion of many, better tasting than even the best Brussels sprouts. Collards are grown primarily in the South, and kale in the North.

Both are normally fall crops. Seed in mid-summer and thin to 18 inches apart so the plants can grow to full size. Pests and diseases are technically the same as for the other members of the cabbage family, but few seem to bother the kale if its more refined cousins are around. Harvest single leaves, starting at the bottom of the plant. The taste, like that of Brussels sprouts, is greatly improved by frost, so there is no real point in hurrying the season. My favorite variety for taste and hardiness is Red Russian, a relatively smooth-leaved non-hybrid variety. For high yields and a curly leaf with excellent flavor I grow Blue Surf, an improved Winterbor type from Holland. The standard varieties of collards are Morris Heading and Vates.

CORN

Sweet corn was my grandfather's trademark crop, largely because it was so difficult to grow here in the Northern mountains. There has been a lot of change in the corn world since his time, and while it has made growing sweet corn easier, it's also made choosing the right variety more difficult. There are both more kinds of sweet corn, and more cultivars within the established kinds, each with important advantages, disadvantages, and cultural requirements. I hope we will be able to clarify this cornucopia (if you'll excuse the pun) and rescue a plan from the plethora of details needing your attention. Keep in mind that if your garden is small you may not want to give sweet corn the space it demands. If you do, though, read on.

Where once there was simply field corn and sweet corn, we now have three distinct kinds of sweet corn. Breeders have worked long and hard to manipulate the genetic triggers that control the balance of starch and sugar in sweet corn kernels in order to bring gardeners new sweet corn cultivars which are not only sweeter and tenderer, but hold those qualities longer after harvest.

The standard sweet corn which, when picked at the peak of ripeness and transported immediately to an already boiling pot of water for a quick—not too long—dip, is the peak of all summer produce, surpassing in my childhood memories even the taste of that first, ripe, red tomato. That, to me, is sweet corn. Then there is sugar-enhanced sweet corn, which has a variant gene that adds new tenderness to the species, and often extra sweetness as well; but what is most important about this sugar corn, as I call it, is that it holds its sweetness much longer, and doesn't have to be cooked within five minutes of picking to have that good old-fashioned sweet corn flavor. Finally, there is super sweet corn, the product of a slightly different genetic arrangement that nearly doubles the sugar content of the kernels, as well as slowing conversion of that sugar to starch.

The process of growth and maturation in corn involves three stages. First, the vegetative growth of the plant takes place. Then, the plant tassels, and ears begin to form; plant sugars that have accumulated in the stalk of the plant are rapidly translocated to the developing ears, and peak at a stage that gardeners call ''full milk.'' Finally, growth slows and the ears begin their final maturation; from that point on the sugars in the kernel begin a one-way, irreversible conversion to starch that will allow the kernels, which are, after all, the plant's seeds, to store the energy they'll need to germinate when the time comes. It is this last step that breeders have tried to change, slowing down the conversion of sugar to starch as much as possible.

CORN CULTIVARS SORTED BY TYPE

Standard (su)	Sugar (se/eh)		Supersweet (sh2)
Earlivee	Alpine	Platinum Lady	Early Xtra-sweet
Golden Cross Bantam	Burgundy Delight	Sugar Buns	Honey 'n Pearl
	Clockwork	Seneca Arrow	How Sweet It Is
Golden Jubilee	Kandy Korn EH	Starshine	Illini Xtra-sweet
Jubilee	Kiss & Tell	Tuxedo	Northern Xtra-sweet
Seneca Chief	Miracle		Starstruck
Seneca Horizon			
Silver Queen			

One of the differences between the two kinds of improved sweet corn is critically important for home gardeners, especially those with limited space: what I call sugar corn can be grown right next to traditional sweet corn without worry; but the super sweet cultivars must be isolated, or they will cross with other types and the ears will revert to a tough, starchy texture without the flavor that makes them super. Since corn is wind-pollinated, this isolation needs to be at least twenty-five feet, and if the garden is in a windy area, fifty or even one hundred feet is best. You can limit yourself to one cultivar, or at least one type to avoid crossing. But if you live in a densely populated area with neighbors close on both sides, their planting plans may affect you, whether you like it or not.

There are other differences as well. Both the sugar corns and the super sweets have a different texture than traditional sweet corn. Some people consider them crisp, but others watery, while just about everyone agrees that traditional sweet corn, picked at its peak, is creamy or milky. This is apparently due to a lower level of polysaccharides in the juice of the new kinds. Which you might prefer is a matter of taste, and I won't presume to dictate to you which is better. But the difference affects garden performance.

When the seeds of sugar and super sweet corn cultivars mature (and their abundant sugars are finally converted to the starch that the seeds require for storage of energy for later germination), the kernels shrink and take on a shriveled appearance. This is especially true of the super sweets, and the effect is that when super sweet corn seed is planted it needs to take up much more water than traditional varieties before it reaches the state—"imbibition," as botanists call it—that triggers germination. That takes time, and in the spring, seeds that don't germinate quickly often rot, which is just what will happen to the seed of these new cultivars if the soil isn't fully warmed up before planting.

In most corn cultivars the different stages of growth are triggered by a sort of accumulation of good growing weather, and once each stage is reached, there is no going back. Scientists and breeders use a measure called heat units (HU) to quantify this accumulation. Heat units are measured by taking the number of hours each day when the temperature is above 50°F, then multiplying that by the number of degrees over 50°F. The earliest varieties might have a heat unit requirement for harvest of about 1300 HU, while late maturing varieties might require as much as 2000 HU to ripen.

While most of us don't have the time or interest to measure the heat units on a daily basis, understanding how they work makes it clear that corn yields are going to be a matter of how big a plant you can grow by the time the cultivar's heat unit break point is reached.

Whichever type of corn you decide to grow, put it in the richest part of your rotation, as corn is a greedy feeder. In some cases it could go in the second part, with an extra bit of rotted manure or compost added to the bed. This would be done if the corn was interplanted with cucumbers, melons, pumpkins, or a trailing squash of some kind. That makes good use of the growing space, though it puts very strong demands on the soil.

The sex life of sweet corn makes one more demand: that you make sure the wind will be able to move enough pollen from the tassels to the silk. The standard recommendation is that all types of sweet corn should be planted in hills or in blocks of at least four rows. That way, no matter which direction the wind blows it will be able to pick up pollen. We plant three rows of small, early varieties in a three-foot-wide bed, with the plants a foot apart in the rows, and simply plant two adjacent beds. If you've got to make the most of a small space you can plant hills of 4–6 seeds in a 2:1:2 pattern; but ideally you'd still want to have two beds planted next to each other. Larger, later cultivars need more room, or so we are led to assume. But studies have shown that at plant densities of two- to four-square-feet per plant, yields were up to one ear per square foot. In our garden—with only a square foot apiece—the average early corn cultivar yields just one ear per stalk, with a second, smaller ear to follow if time allows. Though the ears are smaller, on a square foot basis this is better production.

As noted above, corn, especially the sugar and super sweet types, should not be planted until the ground is fully warmed. How warm? The absolute minimum soil temperature is 55°F, but 65°F is better and 75°F is ideal. Here in Vermont we don't really have the luxury of waiting for the ideal, so we plant just after the frost-free date and hope for the best. You can actually plant up to 7–10 days earlier if you use a cool soil–tolerant variety (usually noted in the catalog description). That is because the growing point of a corn plant doesn't actually break ground until the plants are almost 6 inches tall; if a late frost knocks back the top of the plant, it just grows up out of the soil and keeps going.

You can stretch the harvest period by planting the same cultivar more than once, or by planting two or more cultivars with different maturity rates. In my garden I plant three different corn cultivars: Earlivee, a regular sweet corn that is listed at 55 days; Seneca Arrow, a sugar corn listed at 65 days; and a white-kerneled sugar corn called Starshine, listed at 80 days. By not growing any super sweet varieties (they are too sweet for my liking anyway) I avoid having to isolate the different plantings. The first is my insurance, the second my main crop, and the third a gamble, since our frost-free period is rarely more than 90 days long.

The seed should be sown an inch deep, four seeds per foot of row, and thinned to one seed per foot when the plants are 3–4 inches tall. If you are planting in hills—which are really just clumps of plants, not actual raised mounds—put 4–6 seeds per hill and thin to the strongest four. Big Sam, who planted in hills, always removed a shovelful of soil from each spot and replaced it with a shovelful of compost. If I planted in hills I would, too.

Once the seed is up, the corn should be kept weed-free until it is knee high. At that point you should stay out of the corn patch until harvest time. Most of a corn plant's root growth takes place between tasseling and harvest, and you compact the soil whenever you walk on it. Either mulch the rows, sow a cover crop, or train the squash or cucumber plants to work out into the plot to shade out any later weeds. In terms of moisture, the mulch is probably best; in terms of soil fertility, the cover crop—especially if it is a legume. But in terms of efficiency, the interplanting is best. I've tried the squash–corn combination, and there is no question that it works, but I'd only do it if I was planting in beds. If you interplant the two in large plots, getting in to harvest is a real pain. I have no doubt that the rough and tumble vines keep out raccoons, as companion planting fans claim: I barely want to thrash my way through the abrasive tangle myself to harvest the corn, and I planted it!

Corn cultivars are very specific to different regions, and so a blanket recommendation is hard to make. The best way to decide which corns to plant in your garden is to ask knowledgeable local gardeners for advice, and to read seed catalogs carefully. Be sure to alter any "days to maturity" numbers you see to account for the difference in your local climate relative to that of the seed company. In my garden, for example, what is listed in a catalog from upstate New York as a 55-day cultivar will take more like 70 days; this difference diminishes for later cultivars as our summers eventually catch up with the rest of the world. Regular sweet corns (see chart page 214) will usually have the letters "su" in parentheses somewhere in the description; sugar corns will be described as "Everlasting Heritage" or "sugary enhanced" types and have the code "EH" or "se" or "SE" (the last of these codes means even sweeter);

and super sweet corn will have the code "sh2" in the description, which stands for "shrunken two," the name of the gene responsible for its sweetness and holding quality.

CUCUMBERS

Cucumbers are tender annual vines, first domesticated in pre-history in tropical Asia. They can't take the slightest bit of frost; in fact, even a moderately long spell of cool, wet weather is all it takes to steal their vigor and make them lapse in a downward spiral. But given rich soil, warm weather, and a place to run, they'll outgrow just about any other garden plant.

We put cucumbers in the second part of our rotation. Before planting we add some extra compost to their bed to help get the early growth going. Once the last spring frost is gone and the weather settled, the seed can be sown, 3 seeds to the foot, ½ to ¾ inch deep in a single row down the center of the bed, or in rows 3–6 feet apart. Here in the North it helps to start the plants indoors in large soil blocks or cell trays, a couple of weeks before sowing— but not sooner—because rootbound seedlings will never amount to much. The plants are then set out one foot apart in a row down the center of the bed. At transplant time I make a small depression in the soil with my hand, fill it with an organic mixture—made with a tablespoon each of fish fertilizer and liquid seaweed to a gallon of water—plop the plant's root ball right down in it, then pull a bit of dry soil back over the spot. Since the roots are so tender I let the liquid settle them instead of packing the soil with my hands. Whether we direct-sow or set transplants, we cover the bed immediately after planting with a floating row cover, to keep off cucumber beetles. If they find the seedlings at this stage—and they always seem to hatch right at cucumber planting time—they can kill the plants within a matter of days. Keep the cover on until their first reproductive cycle is over and you'll lessen the damage quite a bit.

Unless you're going to grow them in with the corn, I'd recommend trellising cucumbers. It increases yields, decreases disease, and helps with both pest control and harvest; to me that's a convincing list of advantages. When the plants begin to run (or flower, whichever happens first), we take off the row covers. By then the plants are growing fast enough so that the remaining cucumber beetles can't really hurt them physically, though the bettles still carry disease. Then we set up the same kind of trellis we use for pole beans and tall peas (described in Chapter 4), rigged with a vertical line for each plant and horizontal lines every foot or so. Gently lifting the vines, we wrap each around one of the vertical lines and then leave them to their own devices. Within a week they're headed for the top.

Probably the worst thing about cucumber beetles is that they spread bacterial wilt and cucumber mosaic. Bacterial wilt dries up the leaves and causes them to wilt. You can check suspicious plants by cutting across a stem; if it oozes a sticky white juice, pull it up, destroy it, and replant. Cucumber mosaic causes the leaves to mottle, curl, yellow, and eventually fall off. If there are fruits on the vine they'll be small, light colored, and warty. Many new cultivars are resistant to these diseases. Still, try to control the beetle if it causes you problems. Cucumber beetles can be killed with a mixture of rotenone and pyrethrum, but I've found it isn't worth the trouble. Here in our part of Vermont we are not much affected, because from the time we take off the covers until the first frost kills the plants there is hardly time enough for these diseases to develop.

Cucumbers are more than 90 percent water, and so they shouldn't be allowed to suffer for lack of it. Since trellised crops need more water than sprawling plants, and are more difficult to water by overhead irrigation, cucumbers are an excellent candidate for drip irrigation. (See Chapters 4 and 8 for irrigation details.)

The first few flowers that appear on your cucumber plants will be male flowers, and will not produce fruit. They are generally borne in clusters, while the female flowers are single and borne at the end of a small fruit (which is the ovary). The single most important thing you need to know about harvesting cucumbers is that they have to be kept picked; if any fruits are allowed to ripen, the plant will stop producing fruit. A mature cucumber is yellow, and if you see one turning that color pick it and toss it on the compost pile or into the chicken yard.

Cucumbers are ready for harvest at any point after the female flower falls off the end of the fruit. You don't need to grow a special variety for pickling, either. Just harvest the tiny fruits and pickle them whole. At that point they are ideal for pickles because they haven't yet taken up a lot of water, and when you put them in the pickling syrup they can absorb that instead—with no need for salting first. Once the vines begin to bear, the fruits seem to grow almost overnight, and should be checked frequently. For fresh use, harvest just as the dimple that contains the spines fills out. At that point the cuke will be swollen and juicy, but the seeds and skin won't have begun to harden.

There are many productive, disease-resistant hybrid cucumbers available. My recommendation is simply to avoid the so-called gynoecious types that have all female flowers, as keeping track of the pollinator plants is too much trouble for the home gardener. Likewise, I consider the parthenocarpic cucumbers—which will bear without pollination, and in fact need to be protected from it the way super sweet corn needs to be protected from regular corn—an unnecessary complication. Personally, I prefer the long, thin, Burpless hybrid cucumbers grown on a trellis. And I always plant at least one trellis full of Lemon cucumbers, an heirloom variety that bears tender juicy fruits the size and shape of a small lemon.

EGGPLANT

Eggplant is a tropical perennial shrub, a relative of the tomato and the pepper, and like them, one that gardeners here in North America grow as an annual. It is a warm-weather crop and demands a long, hot, growing season to be truly productive. Yet, grown on a spring-planted, summer-harvest schedule it will succeed just about anywhere in the continental United States, with the exception, perhaps, of coastal Washington and Oregon.

We put eggplant in the second part of our rotation, where the soil is mellow and well endowed, but not loaded with nitrogen. High levels of that essential nutrient lead all members of the tomato family to produce luxuriant foliage but little fruit. Like its relatives, most gardeners will need to start eggplant indoors to guarantee the conditions young eggplant seedlings need. If there is one plant you would buy, this might be it, because the seedlings need both high temperatures and plenty of light to thrive.

Start eggplant seedlings 8 to 10 weeks before the frost-free date. Germination temperature should be above the normal 72°F (our compromise level for the range of kitchen garden vegetables). Seedling growth is also much faster at higher temperatures. Each time the leaves of adjacent plants touch they should be transplanted to a larger container, finishing in a 4- to 6-inch pot.

Two weeks before transplanting prepare the bed by covering with black plastic to help raise soil temperatures; if you have 18-inch O.C.

drip irrigation tubing, lay it along the center of the bed first, and dump a shovelful of compost on each emitter. That way once the plastic is in place you'll be able to locate the emitters and place each plant right next to one. The plants should be hardened off gradually—they are more sensitive to transplant shock than just about any other garden vegetable. Come planting time, slit a hole in the plastic at each emitter, gently set the plants just a tiny bit deeper than they were in the pot, and then turn on the water to settle them in their holes. We like to spot in basil and gem marigold plants along the edge of the bed, in alternation with the eggplants.

Once the plants are in, we cover them immediately with a floating row cover to moderate the normal June temperature swings and keep flea beetles at bay. The covers can generally be removed within about three weeks. From then on the plants won't really require any attention beyond an occasional inspection for potato beetles, which consider eggplants their favorite food, even over potatoes. In fact, it is worth putting any extra eggplant seedlings you might have in the potato patch to attract them so they can be picked off and crushed.

The yellow-orange eggs of this beetle are laid in masses on the underside of leaves, and stretch in a cylindrical, bowling pin fashion down from the leaf as they mature. Crush them before they hatch and you'll save yourself a lot of trouble. Once the young grubs get going they can eat a lot of foliage before you even notice they're there; and eggplants need all the leaf surface they've got if they're going to ripen a decent crop. In Northern sections of the country, standard eggplants will bear four to six fruits per plant; warmer-climate gardeners can count on eight to ten, and in hot climates the plants may bear twelve to fifteen fruits. The smaller kinds bear proportionally more fruits, but the yield by weight is basically the same.

Eggplants can be harvested anytime after they are about one-third their final size, which varies from the size of a marble to the size of a softball, depending on cultivar. I have found that if conditions are not right, they will simply set fewer fruit, not smaller fruit. During a poor growing season we have had 8-inch-tall plants with a single 12-inch-long fruit jutting unceremoniously from underneath its paltry leaves.

In marginal areas, the best varieties will be the newer, disease-resistant hybrids like Dusky or Orient Express. If you'd like to play around, there are many other possibilities. Eggplants come in every color from green to pink to red to white, and all shapes from round to cigar-shaped, from half an inch in diameter to a foot long! Some catalogs even list heirloom varieties from around the world.

ENDIVE

See Chicory.

HERBS

Herbs are an essential part of a vegetable garden as they provide companionship in the kitchen as well as in the ground. The range of plants used as herbs is wide. Many are hardy perennials that, once established, will last for years. Of these, there are special, more flavorful or beautiful strains that cannot be grown from seed, but only reproduced by cuttings or division. For that reason, they should be purchased as plants. Be sure to taste what you buy, though, to make sure it's what you're after; not all nurserymen (or women) know their business.

The big four herbs that we grow from seed in our garden are parsley, basil, dill, and fennel. We put the dill in the first part of our rotation, with the cabbage family; parsley and basil go in the second part, with the tomato family; fennel is planted with the fall root crops.

There are many kinds of basil, a tender perennial shrub native to tropical Asia. Most gardeners are familiar with the common sweet basil that is such a good complement to tomato dishes, but there are also scented basils that hint of cinnamon, licorice, and lemon, as well as ornamental basils that add a special touch to vinegars. All are easy to grow as long as a few inflexible rules are followed.

Point number one is that basil is the single most frost-sensitive plant in the garden. While the plants should be started 8 to 10 weeks before the frost-free date, they shouldn't be set out in the garden until the weather is completely settled and there is absolutely no danger of frost. Once chilled, basil rarely recovers; you're better off waiting to plant until summer has definitely arrived than being forced to wait for the basil to recover from the inevitable—though we always call it a freak—frosty late spring night.

If grown in a bed by itself (as we do with the main crops of pesto basil and drying basil) we set the plants on 8-to-12-inch centers; this is a 3:2:3 pattern on a 30-inch bed. The scented basils are often just spotted in around the tomato, eggplant, and pepper beds, providing a nice bit of fragrance while making the most of what would otherwise be wasted space. Once the plants are in, basic cultivation is all that is required; we've never had any pest problems with our basil.

Basil should be kept from flowering to get the best flavor and the maximum yield. Once the plants have six sets of leaves, pinch the tip of the plant just above the top pair. That will cause the two uppermost sprouts to take over as the growing points of the plant; pinch both of them once they have six leaves each and you'll have a basil bush. Harvest basil in mid-morning, just after the dew has dried off the leaves, to get the best flavor. If you make sure to always cut just *above* a pair of leaves, the plant will branch at that point and produce another harvest two or three weeks later. Whenever you see flower buds, pinch them out to keep the plant in a vegetative state, producing new growth instead of flowers.

In my opinion, the best pesto basil is the Italian cultivar Genovese Profumistissima, or Sweet Genovese. For drying, we use Monstruoso, or Mammoth; this huge lettuce-leaved cultivar has consistently won taste tests all around the country, and doesn't get bitter after long cooking, as many cultivars do. The scented basils are known simply by their scents, and while there is some difference from strain to strain you will only find out which is which by experimentation. My favorite of the scented types is cinnamon basil, which is a beautiful ornamental plant as well as one of the hardiest and most vigorous of the basils. Purple-leaved basil is the one most frequently used for vinegar, because it imparts a nice color as well as classic basil flavor to a clear vinegar. There is a small-leaved purple basil, but it is rare; your best bet is to buy the cultivar Purple Ruffles; while it is slow to get started in spring it is by far the most vigorous purple basil, once it gets growing.

Parsley is grown in so many gardens it practically ranks as a vegetable rather than an herb. It is a hardy biennial, a member of the carrot family, and usually grown for its leaves, though there are several cultivars that produce usable roots. There are two basic leaf types: curly parsley, which is the kind seen most frequently in home gardens, and used as a garnish on all kinds of dishes; and flat leaf, or Italian parsley, which though it has more flavor, is not seen as often, because the simple, celerylike leaves don't have quite the visual appeal of the other, more common kind.

Big Sam was able to harvest parsley almost from the moment the snow was gone in spring until the hard frosts and short days of fall stopped short its production of tangy new leaves. He did this with two plantings. The first was sown mid-spring, after the danger of hard frost was gone; that planting provided a supply of fresh sprigs from the middle of July until almost November. The second planting, in late summer, yielded a supply of seedlings by first frost just the right age to be transplanted to the cold frame and held over for early spring cutting; the leftover plants would winter over in the garden most years and provide a crop soon after the early, cold-frame crop ran to seed. By the time the outdoor overwintered crop itself ran to seed the first of the spring planting was ready.

I do the same, except that I start the first planting indoors 8 to 10 weeks before the frost-free date, and set the plants out a month to six weeks later, eight inches apart each way. That way I've got the first new cuttings before the previous season's plants have begun to run to seed and their flavor has started to become bitter. The direct-seeded crop can be thinned to the same distance after it's had a good chance to get established, with the thinnings set in the cold frame. It's important to do this early on; or else take a large amount of soil with the plants, as parsley has a large taproot and doesn't appreciate transplanting if it damages that root.

The only problem we have had with our parsley is an occasional

SCHEDULE FOR YEAR-ROUND PARSLEY Set out seedlings in spring for summer harvest. Sow seed in mid to late summer, then transplant to cold frame; harvest early the next spring until it runs to seed. By then the next set of spring seedlings will be ready.

parsleyworm, which we have left alone, as it eventually becomes a beautiful butterfly. If faced with a horde of them you can spray with *Bacillus thuringiensis* as soon as the first caterpillars appear. Parsley can be harvested at any time. But if you restrain your harvest to the older outside leaves, the plants will continue to produce throughout the season.

After extensive taste tests, my favorite parsley is a Dutch cultivar named Krausa. Most flat-leafed parsleys are not named, so you'll need to experiment with different suppliers until you find one you like.

Dill is a tall, ephemeral plant whose ferny young foliage eventually turns to a winsome spray of delicate flower heads that are used for pickling, and whose seeds are themselves useful for breads, meats, and cheeses.

We sow dill on the edges of a bed that is growing broccoli, cabbage, or cauliflower. The seed should be sown at the same time the transplants are set, putting the seed ¼ inch deep, two or three seeds to the inch. It can be thinned once the covers are removed, and the young thinnings used for salads or seasoning. Dill should eventually be thinned to a foot per plant so that it has the room to produce a large crop of seed heads. To get a continuous crop of the greens simply re-sow periodically throughout the summer.

For pickles, harvest the immature seed heads with a few leaves attached. For seed, let the flowers mature fully. They, and the foliage, will turn from green to a rich tannish yellow; cut the heads in late morning, just as the dew is drying off, and dry on a clean cloth in the sun for a day, then shake loose the seed and winnow to remove the chaff.

My favorite dill is Dukat, also called tetra dill. This is a vigorous dwarf cultivar. For really large plants, try Mammoth.

Young fennel looks just like dill, but it has a different, licorice flavor. As it grows, the base of the plant swells, and it is the swollen leaf stalks that are the harvest.

Fennel grows best as a fall crop. It can withstand light frosts, but the lengthening days and rising temperatures of spring are likely to make it run to seed without producing an edible stalk. It should be direct-seeded ¼ inch deep, about 60 days before the beginning of cool fall weather. We sow a few short rows across the bed in any odd spot we can find among the fall root crops. Thin gradually until the plants stand 8–12 inches apart in the row, depending on the size bulb you want. The thinnings are nice in salad.

The best bulbing fennel by far is Zefa Fino. For extra interest there is also a red-leaved fennel called, simply, Bronze. It is used primarily for salads and is related to the wild roadside fennel common along the California coast.

KOHLRABI

Kohlrabi is one of the least grown members of the cabbage family, but nonetheless one of my personal favorites. Even if I didn't like to eat them, I'd put in a few for curiosity's sake, because they are one of the oddest looking vegetables in the garden. Just above the ground, the stem of kohlrabi swells into a round ball-shaped knob anywhere from an inch to a foot in diameter (depending on the variety and the growing conditions), and the leaves of the plant spring directly from the top and sides of this knob, giving it the appearance of some sort of satellite with leaves. When we had our farm stand we sold them as "sputniks." There are pale green and reddish purple cultivars.

Kohlrabi is a quick-growing plant, and the spring varieties should be direct-sown in the garden a month before the last frost, 1/4 to 1/2 inch deep in rows 12 to 18 inches apart. It should be thinned at the 4-leaf stage so the plants stand 4 to 6 inches apart. You can also sow it in beds, placing two or three seeds in spots 6 to 8 inches apart, in all directions, and thin out the weakest seedlings.

Pests and diseases are the same as the rest of the cabbage family, but kohlrabi is rarely bothered in our garden. The biggest problem we have is splitting, and many new hybrid kohlrabi are quite resistant. Regular watering will prevent the cycle of wet and dry conditions that cause it. We let the knobs reach two or three inches in diameter before harvest, then cut the plants off just above the ground. Some fall varieties will get quite large and should be left until the danger of hard frost threatens. If protected, and then stored in a high-humidity, low-temperature root cellar, they will keep for 3 to 4 weeks.

The heirloom non-hybrid cultivars Blue and White Vienna are still some of the best tasting kohlrabi available, but they are prone to cracking under unfavorable conditions. Some excellent European hybrids are available, though: some I've tried and liked are Blaro, Lanro, Express Forcer, Rasta, and Capri. If you'd like to try a huge fall kohlrabi, there is Superschmelz, an eastern European non-hybrid strain.

LEEKS

Leeks are a member of the onion family, and so essential to my notion of a vegetable garden that they are practically a member of my own family. We use them in salads, soups, pies, or braised on their own as a vegetable dish. My wife Ellen freezes bags of leeks, already chopped, to use for midwinter seasoning, and—during all but the depth of winter, when the ground is frozen solid—we can harvest them directly from the garden.

Leeks go in the third part of our rotation, among the root crops, with a little extra compost or well rotted manure as they, like onions, are actually as much a leaf crop as a root crop.

We start two plantings of leeks. The first, for late summer and early fall harvest, is sown in seedling trays 10–12 weeks before the last spring frost, to be set out two months later. For the largest leeks, use a cell tray or soil block, and sow two seeds per cell or block, and thin to the strongest seedling after emergence. At planting time the seedlings should be 6–8 inches tall. Prepare the bed, and then, using a dibble or broom handle, poke holes 4–6 inches deep, six inches on center, or every 6 inches, in rows a foot apart. Drop a plant into each hole, then water them in with a mixture made of one tablespoon each of fish fertilizer and liquid seaweed to settle soil around their roots. Don't fill in the holes; that will happen naturally over the course of the season. The plants should just be showing their growing tip at the surface of the soil; if they are not tall enough, fertilize the seedlings and delay planting, or make the holes shallower. The bigger the seedling, though, the bigger the leek and the more usable stem you'll have at harvest time. If the seedlings are grown in open trays and have to be broken apart to transplant, be sure to trim the tops to bring the root and leaf masses back into balance.

We direct-seed the second crop—our overwintering leeks—outdoors about a month before the last frost, sowing the seed 1/4 to 1/2 inch deep in rows only 6 inches apart, in a spare corner of the root crop bed. We let them grow along there, weeded but not thinned (since we want them to stretch out) until the early peas are harvested. Once the pea trellises have been dismantled, we renew the bed and dig a 4-to-6-inch furrow right where the peas were, using the Warren or the Ogden hoe, and sprinkle a light layer of compost in the bottom. Into this we set the plants, which have been gently dug from their nursery rows, had their roots and tops trimmed back one-third, and been sorted so that the biggest, healthiest plants are used first. Then we lay the plants in the furrow, upright, every six inches. Working back down along the row, we set them into the compost and firm them in a vertical position. As soon as all the plants are in we irrigate, but we do not fill in the trench.

After the leeks are actively growing we gradually fill in the trench, always keeping the level of the soil just below the first leaves, in effect challenging the stem to outgrow our cultivation. Once the trench has been completely filled, so that the ground is again level, we take the excess soil from the edges of the bed (where, in spring, the spinach had grown) and use it to hill the leeks further. By the arrival of hard frost the stems should be fully banked up and ready to endure the winter without further protection.

We have had no insect or disease problems with our leeks, but we are quite scrupulous about rotating them from plot to plot each year and making sure that they have everything they might need to grow as quickly as they can. All in all, they are trouble-free, even if slow to mature.

Leeks can be harvested at any stage, and in fact baby leeks—the thinnings from the row—are considered a delicacy and bring such a high price in the markets that many commercial growers plant them solely for the restaurant trade. Overwintered leeks must be harvested in the spring before they begin to produce a seed stalk, as the shafts become quite fibrous at that time and are worthless for the table, though the flowering plants are quite beautiful.

To blanch leeks, set seedlings in holes formed with a hoe handle or along the bottom of a six-inch-deep trench. Fill the trench gradually as the leeks grow.

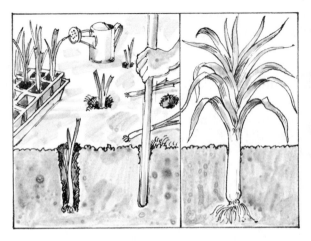

Some early leek varieties we have had good luck with are King Richard, Tivi, Pancho, and Titan. For overwintering we grow the old heirloom French cultivar Blue Solaise, though we have also had good harvests with newer strains like Nebraska, Alaska, Blizzard, and Furor. King Richard is the standard for baby leeks.

LETTUCE

Lettuce is my favorite crop, and in fact we've always called our hillside Looseleaf Farm, both for the hundreds of lettuce cultivars we grow and the notebooks that are almost as much a part of our gardens as the spading forks, cloches, and seedling trays. It is a beautiful crop, and well adapted to our Northern climate. Lettuce goes in the first section of our rotation, ready to benefit from all the fertility we can give it. It is best grown fast, and we don't want anything to hold it back.

There are literally thousands of cultivars, ranging in color, shape, and leaf type from tiny, smooth-leaved Bibbs to large, savoyed red romaines. They fall into roughly five types. The largest class of lettuces is the butterheads. They have soft, tender leaves and relatively loose heads. Colors range from a rich burgundy and gold to light green flecked with pink and beautiful rich grassy greens. Within the butterhead group are some of the most heat- and cold-tolerant lettuces known, and they can be grown nearly year round almost anywhere in the country with proper choice of cultivar and a little extra attention.

Crisphead lettuce has firmer, tighter heads. Here in America we call this kind of lettuce Iceberg, but in Europe it is known as Batavian lettuce. Crispheads do, indeed, have crispy, juicy leaves, though with less flavor than other types, due to the blanching of the inner leaves. Here, too, there are cultivars in just about every color from scarlet to shamrock green.

The third type is looseleaf lettuces, which for the most part do not form heads. In general these are the earliest to mature, and are probably the most common kinds in home gardens. The leaves can be smooth or savoyed, pointed, lobed, curled, or ruffled. Colors cross the rainbow from deep ruby red to pale greenish yellow, with just about every combination in between.

Romaine, or Cos, lettuces are tall, upright, and thick-leaved; their thick midribs and juicy texture have made them especially prized for certain salads. They range in size and color from tiny eight-inch-tall green mini-Romaines to large, smooth-leaved red heads that can reach almost two feet tall.

The last type is really a catch-all category for those that don't seem to fit into any one group, but share something from a couple: almost-butterheads that are just a bit too tall and whose leaves are more substantial than they should be; looseleaf lettuces that, if left to mature, form a small head surrounded by their normal complement of widely splayed foliage; or the reverse—crispheads that can be cut when young as a looseleaf.

We grow almost all our lettuce from transplant. The first batch of seedlings is sown in flats or blocks 8–10 weeks before the frost-free date, to be ready for transplanting as soon as the beds can be prepared. From that point on we start enough plants every week to last a week at harvest time. Depending on the size at which you harvest, that might be anywhere from six to twelve plants per family per week.

When the bed is ready we set the plants out on 12-inch centers, which is a 3:2:3 pattern on our three-foot beds. If you like really big heads (and are using a cultivar like Red Sails that is capable of producing them), you can set them on 18-inch centers, which is a 2:1:2 pattern. If the weather is particularly cold a given spring, we might cover the first planting with a floating row cover, but other than that they will require no more attention (beyond regular, shallow cultivation) until harvest. This cycle of seeding, transplant, cultivation, and harvest is kept up right through the growing season, with a change of cultivar as the weather, season, and our own needs dictate. During the hottest part of the summer we make sure to shade the beds after transplanting, and water more frequently to keep the lettuce from succumbing to heat stress, which leads to bolting and bitterness.

If you prefer to direct-seed lettuce you can begin as soon as the soil can be worked in spring. You'll probably have an easier time managing the planting if you sow the seed in short rows across the bed. That way you can simply plant a row or two a week. The process, however, is essentially the same, except that you'll have to thin the rows—actually a bonus since the thinnings are some of the best salads there are. The seed should be set only ¼ inch or so deep, in rows 12 inches apart, and thinned as soon as it reaches a few inches high, first to a couple of inches between plants, and later to the full 8 to 12 inches you'd have with transplants.

Thinning isn't actually necessary unless you want to harvest mature heads. You can simply keep sowing and harvesting young plants. Some gardeners sow the seed as thinly as possible, let the plants grow up to, say, 4-to-6-inches tall, cut all they want with scissors—direct into the salad bowl—and then either replant or let the plants regrow for another harvest. For the ultimate in this kind of culture, mix the seed of a range of salad plants—lettuce is best, but you don't need to limit yourself to it—then broadcast the seed on a section of the bed, rake it in, and water. Three weeks later you'll have a ready-made mixed salad just for the trouble of cutting!

When the weather turns hot you'll have to trick the lettuce into germinating; it has a built-in dormancy trigger that won't allow it to sprout if the soil temperature is above 80°F. Newly sown rows can simply be watered thoroughly and then covered with a 2 × 6 piece of lumber to insulate them from the heat of the sun. Broadcast sowings can be shaded with a piece of plywood, supported above the bed on cinderblocks or pieces of firewood. Either way, be sure to check underneath daily. Once the lettuce sprouts it needs light immediately.

If you want to try overwintering lettuce in a cold frame or simply out in the garden with a floating row cover for protection, start the seedlings a month before the first fall frost or in late September, whichever is earlier. Particularly in the North, where day lengths shorten rapidly in late summer, the lettuces need time to grow to a size where they can withstand lower winter temperatures and re-

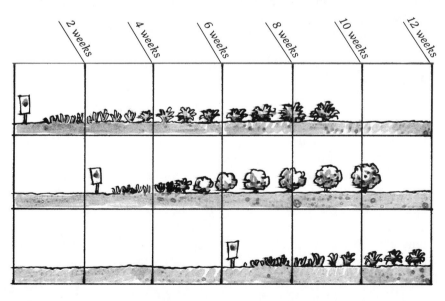

For continuous lettuce harvest, sow just a bit every week or so. The thinnings make great salad!

2 weeks · 4 weeks · 6 weeks · 8 weeks · 10 weeks · 12 weeks

1st crop

2nd crop

3rd crop

grow in spring. The ideal size is about four inches in diameter with only a half-dozen leaves or so. Don't cover them until the ground is frozen; otherwise you won't be able to keep the bed cultivated to kill late-growing, cold-tolerant weeds.

There are so many good lettuces it is hard to recommend just a few, but if I had to choose I would probably grow one or two from each group. Space-conscious gardeners should consider buying a packet of each and mixing them together; that way they'll get the most variety from the least space. For butterheads, I'd choose Four Seasons or Red Riding Hood for their beautiful color, and Orfeo or one of the other Kagran Sommer descendants for their heat tolerance. My favorite crispheads are Red Grenoble, which has beautifully savoyed wine-red leaves, and Ice Queen, also known as Reine des Glaces, a startlingly beautiful lettuce that could equally go by the name Crown of Thorns. For looseleaf lettuce I like Royal Oakleaf, Tango, Red Salad Bowl, Green Salad Bowl—all of which will make very large, beautiful plants if spaced widely—but also work as cutting lettuces; and a tiny heat-tolerant Italian cutting lettuce called Lollo Rossa that is a godsend for small gardens. My favorite romaines are the large green Winter Density (which does well in both heat and cold), Little Gem (a sweet and juicy miniature romaine), and Red Leprechaun (which has wonderfully intense burgundy-colored leaves and good heat tolerance). The European butterhead Winter Marvel is probably the most winter-hardy lettuce I've grown to date; and for heat tolerance, nothing beats the French semi-crisphead cultivar Sierra.

MELONS

While there are many types of melons, most American gardeners are really familiar with only a few of them. The most common is the muskmelon, called a cantaloupe by most people, though that name properly applies to the French Charentais types, with smooth gray skins and more or less prominent radial stripes. Muskmelons have "netted" skin. Honeydew melons (at least some varieties) can also be grown throughout most of the country. They have a smooth grayish-green rind that whitens as they mature. Then there is a whole range of exotic types like Crenshaws, Casabas, and Persian melons, that are suitable only for the really warm, long-season parts of the country.

Like their relative the cucumber, we put melons in the second part of our rotation, but give them an extra dose of compost or well-rotted manure to make sure they have the nutrients for quick vine growth in early summer. It is important, in a short season area like ours, to bring them into bearing early so that the fruits will have time to ripen. Ideally, you should lay a drip irrigation line down the center of the bed, put a shovelful of compost at each emitter, then cover the bed with a black plastic mulch. That will warm the soil considerably, stop the weeds, and give you control over the water supply.

You can direct-seed melons, but you *must* wait until after the last spring frost. The seed should be sown three seeds to the foot, ½ to ¾ inch deep, in a single row down the center of the bed; or in rows three to six feet apart. Because of the need to get a jump on the season, we start the plants indoors in large soil blocks or cell trays a couple of weeks before planting time. Don't push it—rootbound seedlings will never amount to much and the plants will grow fast under cover. They can then be set out one foot apart after the soil is fully warmed. When transplanting, make a small depression in the soil, fill it with a mixture of fish fertilizer and liquid seaweed—a tablespoon of each per gallon of water—then quickly set the plant's root ball right down in it and pull a bit of dry soil back over the spot. The roots resent handling, so let the liquid settle them instead of packing the soil by hand.

Cover the bed immediately after planting with a floating row cover, to keep off cucumber beetles. If they find the seedlings at this stage—and they always seem to come out of hibernation within a few days of melon planting time—they can kill the plants in a matter of days. Keep the cover on until their first reproductive cycle is over, and you'll lessen the damage quite a bit.

With cucumbers it's a snap to trellis the plants, but if you want to get melons up off the ground you'll have to make provision for supporting the fruits. Most of the common varieties "slip," or detach themselves, from the vines at maturity and would be damaged when they fell to the ground. The most common method is to use nets made of old stockings or onion bags. With the true cantaloupes this is not a problem as they stay attached to the vine until cut loose.

Melons need plenty of water when they're young. But once the fruits have reached the size of a baseball you should stop watering. Too much water at ripening time ruins the flavor, and they don't really need it by then. Melons develop a deep root system soon after they begin to flower, and so are able to fend for themselves. One of the benefits of drip irrigation when growing melons is it allows you to get plenty of water to them when young without getting the foliage wet. That's a great help in avoiding foliage diseases like powdery mildew, which thrives on wet leaves.

Do not harvest your melons until they are fully ripe; melons do not improve in flavor once off the vine. It's easy to tell when a muskmelon is ripe: the background color of the netting flushes yellow, and the stem separates from the vine with only a slight tug. The other kinds do not "slip" like muskmelons, and you'll just have to learn to recognize the signs of maturity. Honeydews and some of the Oriental melons turn white; most of the others develop a yellow or tan cast to the rind. All become soft to the touch on the blossom end, and most will smell ripe to an experienced sniffer. Become one! When ready they will need to be *cut* from the vine.

Making melon recommendations is difficult; a cultivar that is well adapted to one region may not do well in another. For muskmelons I advise asking knowledgeable local gardeners what they grow and then experimenting. Nonetheless, here are a few of the more unusual types you might like to try, and that I know will do well in short-season areas. Charentais is the classic French melon. You may wish to try the original, but there are now many improved hybrid Charentais cultivars on the market. A very early one is Prior; if you have a longer season try Savor. Green-fleshed Middle Eastern melons can also do well, even in what would normally be considered marginal areas; try Galia or Passport. Some smooth-skinned Oriental melons we've had good luck with are Snow Crown and Sun; both of these are real kid pleasers and productive even here in our cool Northern climate.

ONIONS

Onions are one of the most frequently grown garden vegetables, yet most gardeners know little more about them than how to push a handful of sets into the ground and wait for the tops to fall over. That's a shame, because there are a lot of different kinds of onions that you can't grow from sets: ribbon-winning state fair bulbs the size of softballs, special "sweet" onions, flat- or bottle-shaped Italian heirloom strains, even storage onions that last much longer than those grown from sets—well into the following summer!

Growing onions is easy if you keep a few things in mind. Most people think of onions as a root vegetable, but don't you believe it! Onion bulbs are actually swollen leaves attached to a small, disk-shaped stem. If you want good yields you need much higher fertility than you'll normally provide for root crops. Onions are one of a group of vegetables needing abundant nitrogen early on, so they can grow a big plant, but less once they start to mature and prepare to go dormant. So, although we include them in the third part of our rotation, we make sure that section of the bed gets a bushel or so of compost or well rotted manure per one hundred square feet to bring nutrient levels up early in the season. If you can't get the plants up to size before the average daily temperature and the number of daylight hours trigger the bulbing reflex, you simply won't get a big onion.

This day length—actually night length, but it means the same thing to us as gardeners—distinction is very important in deciding what onions to grow, as bulb onions can be generally grouped in three categories: short day onions, long day onions, and day neutral onions. While every cultivar has specific adaptations, and there is a fairly large gray area in the middle of the country, the standard rule-of-thumb is that south of a line running from between North and South Carolina out to San Francisco, you should stay away from long day onions; north of that line you should avoid planting short day onions. Southern gardeners who ignore this advice will likely end up with huge scallions as the long day types will keep growing without the bulbing reflex ever being triggered; Northern gardeners who plant short-day types will end up with tiny onions as the plants will bulb while still seedling size. If your seed source doesn't know the adaptation of the cultivars they list, buy elsewhere.

This bulbing reflex is also affected by a combination of other factors as well. High nitrogen levels at what should be the normal bulbing time will delay it or cause the bulbs to form two centers, which ruins their storage ability. Phosphorus deficiences in the soil will also delay maturity. In addition, the temperature must also be above a certain level—about 60°F for most cultivars—or your onions simply won't start to bulb. To complicate matters further, once bulbing has begun the speed at which it proceeds is also temperature-related. Hot weather right after bulbing has started will reduce yields, and cool weather will increase yields, because the onions will have longer to grow before going dormant. Though high nitrogen and/or rainy weather at harvest time can reduce the storage life of onions, all other factors being equal there seems to be no connection between the size of the bulb and its keeping quality and flavor.

The keeping quality and flavor of onions are related, though. Storage onions keep well for the same reason they make you cry when you slice them: sulfur. Sulfur is a potent fungicide, bactericide, and eye irritant. Well grown, thoroughly cured storage onions have a high sulfur content. Many onion cultivars are also quite sweet, containing up to 8 percent sugar by weight, but if they are high in sulfur it's hard for their natural sweetness to shine through the tears. The sweetest onions are grown on soils naturally low in sulfur. So if, like us, you work a soil that is naturally acid and high in sulfur compounds, you'll never grow an onion as sweet as they do in places like Vidalia, Georgia, or Walla Walla, Washington, where the soil conditions, climate, and cultivar all work together to produce an onion you can eat almost like an apple. But you can come close if you go about it right.

We start our bulb onions—sweet and storage—indoors in flats as much as three months before the frost-free date, so that by the time the garden is ready to plant we already have vigorously-growing plants. That way we can be sure that the plants will reach a decent size before they bulb. Using a twenty-row tray, we sow the seed ¼ inch deep, water, and then cover with a humidity dome until the seed germinates; at 72°F it should take no more than three or four days. The first leaf to break ground will be doubled over like a hairpin. This is called the "flag" leaf, and once it unfolds, you can thin the seedlings to ¼ inch apart in the rows. If you want to grow really big onions—blue ribbon bulbs for the state fair—and you've chosen a cultivar that is appropriate for that, transplant the thinnings to individual cell packs. Plants kept in the twenty-row trays should be given an occasional haircut, if necessary, to limit their height to only 3–4 inches tall, so they stay upright. Just clip the tops with scissors, being careful not to cut off the tip of the young leaf in the center of the plant, which is the growing point.

These transplants can be set out as soon as they have adjusted to the outside weather and the soil is dry enough to prepare thoroughly. We might put out the first of our transplants as early as April 15, only 6 weeks after seeding; but the main crop doesn't go in until almost a month later. For really big onions, set them out 6 inches apart on center or in rows. If you're more interested in continuous yields than in bulb size, set the seedlings only a couple of inches apart, and pull every other one for scallions once they have grown up a bit.

Some of the classic sweet onions like the Vidalia and Walla Walla sweets are grown on an overwintering schedule. Southern gardeners should sow the seed of a Granex hybrid (that's what a Vidalia really is) 1/4 inch deep in a nursery bed or flats in late September, then transplant to the garden 60 days later. Early plantings are more likely to run to seed without bulbing, according to the experts at the University of Georgia. Trim the plants to three or four inches tall and set them 1/4 inch or so deeper than they were in the flat, to help protect the bulbs from cold. Six-inch spacing is the normal recommendation for large bulbs which, in an average season, will be ready in May.

Northern gardeners who want to try overwintering should direct-seed one of the sweet varieties available to them (see below) in a nursery bed or (if in a very cold climate) in a cold frame. Sow the seed sparsely, say, four seeds to the inch, 1/4 inch deep, around mid-August. Cover them with a floating row cover. Don't fertilize; you want them to grow just to about 1/8 inch in stem diameter and two to three inches tall before winter. Smaller plants are more likely to winterkill; larger ones are likely to run to seed without bulbing. As soon as the ground can be worked in spring, gently lift the plants, trim the roots and tops, and set them in the growing bed on 6-inch spacing. Care from that point on is the same as for spring-sown plants. NOTE: we have done extensive testing in our garden (minus 35°F annual low) and found that spring transplants, if started very early and grown rapidly, work just as well.

Most onion diseases are best prevented by crop rotation. The two major pests are root maggots in the North and thrips in the South. The onion root maggot is very closely related to the cabbage root maggot and controlled the same way. If you have a history of infestation, place a floating row cover over the bed immediately after seeding or transplanting. Big Sam used wood ash as a control on onions as well as cabbage family plants. Thrips can be controlled in a number of ways. They can simply be washed from the plants by a strong stream of water, or sprayed with an insecticidal soap; they migrate into the garden from drying field grasses, so keeping the area around the garden mowed will help some. Vigorous plants can outgrow thrip damage, so be sure to keep your onions well-fed and well-watered.

To produce the best bulbs, make sure your onions don't lack for water. During their first few months in the garden they need an inch or more of water a week. Irrigation should be cut back at bulbing time, though, so they can cure properly.

The biggest problem with growing onions is weeds. Because of their limited foliage, onions don't compete well for space with most of the common garden weed species. To make sure the weeds never get established, we go over the bed every few weeks, using a narrower hoe each time. Once the onions begin to bulb, stop cultivating and just keep an eye out for any weeds that grow up and threaten to set seed; it's rarely more than a few and they are easy to pull up and discard.

Once half of the tops have fallen over, bulb onions are ready to harvest. If you can, wait for the beginning of a dry spell, then bend over the remaining plants, and a few days later pull the plants and lay them beside the row to cure for two or three days. If wet weather threatens they can be removed to a dry, airy shed to finish curing. Once the outer layers of onion skin become dry and opaque, and the necks are shriveled and dry, either braid them or put them in mesh bags and store in a cool, dry place. Discard or use right away those bulbs with thick necks, double hearts or any imperfection; they won't store well.

This curing process is very important. The storage life of an onion is closely related to curing conditions, because the resistance of the bulbs to rot organisms depends partly on how well the scales, or outer skin layers, of the onion have dried. Also, the internal color of red onions will not be consistent unless they are allowed to mature fully, and then cured properly.

Onion cultivars are classified by shape and color. There are flat, top-shaped, globular, and bottle-shaped onions. The range of colors is red, yellow to golden-brown, and white, though not every combination of shape and color is represented by a cultivar currently available as seed.

Most onion sets are yellow, though you'll sometimes see red and white sets, too. While the sets themselves are usually globular, the bulbs at maturity are likely to be flattish, as it is the nature of onions to be flatter at maturity than as sets. When buying sets, choose those that are ½ to ¾ inch in diameter; smaller than that they may not be sufficiently vigorous, and larger sets are more likely to run to seed without forming a bulb. If you have to buy them pre-bagged, simply plant the off-sized sets in a different spot where they can be pulled for green onions, and fill your main planting with properly sized ones.

In the North, the standard for long-day sweet onions is Walla Walla, an open-pollinated heirloom cultivar first brought to this country by a Corsican immigrant almost a hundred years ago. It takes its name from the town in Washington State that has become famous for growing it. For many years the seed stocks were jealously guarded; but it is now available. It produces a very large, mild bulb anywhere it can be overwintered, and is reliably hardy to about 0°F, unprotected, if there is decent snow cover. We have had good luck with early-sown, transplanted spring crops as well. There are other sweet onions of this type, including one called the Willamette Sweet, which many consider a Walla Walla strain particularly well adapted to the Willamette Valley of Oregon. A new high-yielding, hybrid, overwintering sweet onion that is even hardier is Sweet Winter.

In the South, the standard short-day sweet onion is the Granex hybrid. There are a number of strains, each adapted to different conditions or growing schedules. The actual cultivar used to grow Vidalia onions is Granex 33. This hybrid is a cross between two venerable Southern cultivars, Bermuda and Texas Grano 502. If you are a seed saver you might like to try these parents instead of the hybrid.

A red sweet very popular where it can be grown—it is from an area on the line between long-day and short-day—is Stockton Red; some sources list it as Fresno Sweet Red. I know I'm going to try it.

I especially like bottle onions. They don't store well, but they are quite beautiful, not too pungent, and their shape makes them easy to slice. They are also relatively daylength-insensitive, and due to their shape, tolerant of closer planting than other varieties. At maturity they are about the size of a standard pickling cucumber: 1 to 1½ inches in diameter and 4 to 6 inches long. The only two cultivars I know are currently available are Owa, a golden yellow cultivar from Denmark, and Red Florence, which is also known as Rouge de Florence or Red Lucca, a non-hybrid heirloom from the region around Florence, Italy. This is the cultivar that many mass market seed sources list as Italian Red Torpedo, or even just plain Red Torpedo.

To grow exhibition size onions, try the cultivars Lancastrian or Kelsae Sweet Giant; these two can get as big as a soccer ball if pampered, and average five pounds or more each. In the extreme North Ailsa Craig may work better. All three of these are English cultivars, and are adapted to very long days, due to England's latitude. For the best results, make sure to start them early, provide plenty of fertility, and water early on, with at least eight-inch spacing. None is a good keeper.

Most of the good storage onions are yellow, globe-shaped long-day cultivars. In fact, the traditional onion of this type is called Yellow Globe. There are, however, white and red strains as well, and a whole plethora of names, some of which, like Southport Red Globe, for example, include a place name to indicate their region of adaptation. One short-day onion that is a good keeper is Creole or Red Creole, a flat, pungent onion that is resistant to thrips but prone to bolt if planted too soon in the fall. Any of these is likely to be a good bet for the kitchen gardener. But keep two things in mind: first, the red and white cultivars rarely keep as well as the yellow; and second, many of the traditional cultivars are not as well maintained, now that most seed companies have shifted their attention to hybrids. So you should be certain to buy only from reliable, well known companies, not just from a seed rack at the hardware store.

For storage, try the newer hybrid types. They change fairly frequently in the seed catalog trade, so if the cultivars I note aren't listed, look for a reference to them in the catalog description to find one with similar characteristics. For an early storage onion, try Buffalo; it is milder than many others, hardy enough to overwinter, and relatively insensitive to daylength, so it can be grown a bit farther south than many others. It stores moderately well, lasting until around the first of the year. For a longer storage onion, try Copra hybrid. It matures a full month later than Buffalo, but will keep until the following spring with little loss. It is also high in sugar, so once cooked—which reduces pungency—it is quite sweet. For a storage onion that gets sweet on its own during storage, try Sweet Sandwich. This excellent-keeping, super-high-yielding variety matures at the same time as Copra; but after three months of storage becomes sweet enough for fresh use in salads. It does not hold up well when cooked, though, so should be used fresh. For a red storage onion you can try the hybrid Tango, or the open-pollinated Bennie's Red, which will store at least until Christmas.

PARSNIPS, SALSIFY, AND SCORZONERA

These three slow-growing root crops are grouped together because they require the same attention. All three belong in the third part of the rotation, and as long as the soil is deeply prepared there is likely to be little problem growing them. Plant as soon as the ground can be worked in spring, setting the seed ¼ to ½ inch deep in rows

8–12 inches apart, and thinning the plants to stand 4–6 inches apart once the second set of true leaves appears.

Since all are slow to germinate, a little radish seed sprinkled in the row will help them break ground and provide a free harvest of radishes. The leaves of parsnips look a bit like those of celery, but young salsify and scorzonera shoots are grasslike, and might easily be yanked out by mistake without young radish seedlings to mark the row. The roots will not be ready for harvest until late fall, and many gardeners leave them in the ground through the winter, as the cold weather sweetens them considerably.

The standard parsnip cultivars are Harris Model and Hollow Crown. We have also had good results from the English cultivar Cobham Improved Marrow. The only commonly available salsify cultivar is Mammoth Sandwich Island; for scorzonera we have done well with Duplex and Gigantia.

PEAS

Of the three common garden vegetables that are grown for their edible seeds—peas, beans, and corn—peas are my favorite. They can be planted right off in the spring and thus provide a no-wait thrill for spring fever; they improve the soil wherever they grow; and they taste good, really good.

Until a decade or so ago there were two types of peas for fresh use: the traditional shelling pea, and the flat, edible-podded kind called, variously, snow peas, Chinese peas, or by the French, "pois mangetout," or "eat-all" peas. Now we have a third kind, a best-of-both edible-podded shelling pea, called the snap pea. The first snap pea, called Sugar Snap, was released in 1979 and was awarded an All America Selections Gold Medal; that is just about the highest award a vegetable can receive. Since then American gardeners have been treated to a steady stream of new snap pea introductions.

Peas go in the last part of our rotation, so that the nitrogen-hungry leaf crops which follow can benefit from the fertility that they help build in the soil. Like beans, peas are legumes, and their roots, under the proper conditions, will support a population of bacteria called *rhizobia,* that are capable of extracting nitrogen directly from the air—which makes up 25 percent of the soil by volume—and converting it to the plant-usable form of nitrates. In the process some of this nitrogen as well as significant amounts of phosphorus are made available to the host plant. That is good for the peas; and after harvest, when the plant residues are turned under or composted, the remaining nitrogen these bacteria have "fixed" becomes available to other plants as well. There are a lot of different *rhizobia* bacteria, and each leguminous plant creates its little nitrogen factory in concert with a specific strain to which it has become adapted over the eons of evolution.

They have learned to work together quite well, and the amount of nitrogen extracted, for free, from the atmosphere by this process is larger than you might imagine. Commercial nitrogen fertilizers require the energy equivalent of a third to half a gallon of gasoline to produce every pound of fertilizer. Using *rhizobia* to create the same fertility is considerably more energy-efficient. The *rhizobia* that work with peas can capture 60 to 80 pounds of nitrogen per acre, which is, entirely by itself, enough to grow root crops; clover—which in our rotation is cover-cropped on the pea bed immediately after the peas are harvested—can provide another 100–125 pounds of nitrogen, enough to grow a good crop of sweet corn. The two, together but with no additional fertilizer, provide almost enough to grow even the greediest garden crops.

This bit of garden magic is accomplished by an elaborate sort of mating dance between root and bacterium. Each legume species and its companion *rhizobium* share a kind of chemical polarity that causes them to attract each other, and the bacterium to adhere to the legume's root hair once they contact each other. At that point the bacterium secretes a hormone that causes the root hair to curl around and envelop it, and eventually it is absorbed into the tiny root, where it multiples and spreads, essentially as an infection (though in this case a beneficial one). As the bacteria multiply, a sort of wart, called a nodule, forms on the root and it is in this bacterial "colony" that the nitrates which are of interest to both pea plant and gardener are formed. When, at harvest, the plant is removed, the bacterial stores of this valuable nutrient are released.

The *rhizobia* bacteria that perform this unpaid service are present in most soils—at least those that have grown peas and beans before—but it makes good garden sense to be sure, and so most experienced gardeners "inoculate" their pea seed before planting. The process is simple. A dried, commercially propagated culture of the proper strain of *rhizobia* is dusted on the seed just before planting, and then, once in the soil, multiplies as the peas are sending out their first tentative roots. That guarantees an abundant supply of bacteria early on in the pea's growth. Legume inoculants are readily available through mail order seed catalogs and at farm and garden supply stores.

Plant your first peas as soon as the ground can be worked in spring. If the ground is reasonably fertile, no fertilizer is necessary; but we spread a couple of pounds of a 50/50 mix of wood ash and colloidal phosphate to provide a ready source of potassium and phosphorus, and to buffer the natural acidity of our boggy upland soil. A soil test will tell if this or some other minor treatment might be a help in your own particular situation.

We then sow the inoculated seed of all the climbing peas an inch deep, in double rows 2 inches apart, down the center of a three-foot-wide bed. After the seed is in place we put up a trellis for the vines to climb. All peas—except the so-called leafless bush types—do better if given something to climb on. Not only does trellising make harvest easier, allowing more air to circulate among the vines—a great help in preventing disease—but it also helps them grow more quickly and vigorously, by exposing the pods to sunlight. A pea pod is actually a modified kind of leaf, and a significant amount of photosynthesis takes place right in the pod if it is exposed to sunlight, instead of being lost in a tangle of vines snaking along the ground.

The tallest types, like Sugar Snap, Telephone, or Alderman, and their modern descendants, will need a sturdy trellis at least 6 feet tall. We use the same design as for pole beans. Shorter cultivars can get by with posts 4 feet tall. Untreated twine shouldn't touch the ground, or it will rot before the crop is harvested, but it is essential that the first horizontal line be only an inch or so above the soil surface. That way the plants can find the trellis early on. And they do actually find it—as pea tendrils grow they rotate slowly in a widening arc through the air until bumping into an obstruction, and then try to wrap their tendrils around it. Something thin like a string, wire, or small, brushy branches is just right. But peas will not climb a pole or a picket-type fence, as the tendrils are not long enough to wrap around and grab hold of anything larger than about an inch in diameter. At the end of the season just cut the twine from the trellis, and compost the whole mass of plants and twine.

Bush, or leafless, peas are even easier to manage, because they don't need a trellis at all if you plant them in such a way that they can support themselves. This can be done either by sowing three (or more) rows 10–12 inches apart, or by broadcasting the seed evenly across the surface of the bed and then tilling or raking it in to the proper depth of one inch. The final density of broadcast peas should be one plant every four square inches or so. Either way as the plants grow, their abundant tendrils—which like the pods are just modified leaves—intertwine, and the plants, with their stiff, dwarf stems, hold each other erect. Overall, we have found that three rows per three-foot-bed produces better peas than simply broadcasting the seed, at least for a spring crop.

There are two traditional ways to lengthen the pea harvest: either plant a range of cultivars that mature at different rates, or plant the same cultivar more than once, say every two weeks, so the plantings mature over a longer period come summer. Personally, I prefer the first method, partly because it saves having to remember to replant, and partly because it gets all the peas in early. I like to interplant peas with spinach, and the spinach only does well if planted right off in the spring. We plant a row of early spinach 6 inches or so in from each edge of the bed (a foot out from the trellis on either side) at the same time we seed the peas; by the time the peas have flowered six weeks later, the spinach is ready to harvest.

Our final planting of peas every season comes in mid-summer, during the first cool spell after the Fourth of July. Then we inoculate and broadcast-plant bush pea seed for a fall harvest 60 to 80 days later, shortly after the first fall frosts. To time a planting like this in your own garden, simply count back 60 days from the first frost, and seed during the first available cool spell. Peas are hardy down to the teens until they flower, but the blossoms (and later the pods) are not. Even a light frost during flowering is enough to cause a failure of pod set. That's not a problem with bush peas, though, because the absence of a fence jutting up in the middle of the row makes them a snap to cover. We use a piece of floating row cover left over from our spring plantings of brassicas. We have found that it will protect our peas down to at least 25°F. If frost is predicted (or even seems likely) we lay the floating row cover over the pea row and pin it down with #9 wire pins.

Powdery mildew, mosaic, wilt, and enation virus (spread by aphids) are the primary pea diseases; there is not a whole lot to be done about them. Crops planted early, grown on trellises—and in wet soils, on raised beds—will be trouble-free most seasons. We've found that even during a cloudy, wet, still season, when disease pressure is highest, we will still get a decent crop before the vines give out. A worse problem is not planting on time; if the weather turns unusually hot before the vines have gotten up to size they may never make it. Good garden sanitation and proper rotation are a big help.

The difference in pea types shows up at harvest time. Snow peas can be harvested anytime after the pod begins to emerge from the flower. Most gardeners harvest snow peas just as the seeds begin to swell—known as the "slab pod" stage. Depending on the use we have in mind, we harvest at whatever size is appropriate: snow peas are actually sweeter once the peas have swollen and the pods begun to curl around, but the texture of the pod becomes tough and stringy. Regardless of your needs, be sure to keep all peas thoroughly picked off, because if the vines are allowed to mature any pods at all they will stop producing new ones!

Shelling peas, whether bush or vine, should be harvested after the pods have completely filled out, but before they have lost the sheen of youth. That may sound a bit vague, but the pods really do have a luster that they lose once the peas have matured and are beginning to ripen as seed. Just as with sweet corn, once this happens all the sugars that have concentrated in the seeds-to-be start converting to starch, and the peas, instead of being sweet and tender, get increasingly bland and pasty. There is one other way to recognize when this moment has arrived: check the seam on the pod; when immature it looks like the seam on a pillow turned inside out; at harvest time it will look like the same seam, turned right side out and fluffed up. Start checking about three weeks after the plants begin to flower.

Snap peas can be treated either way: harvested anytime after they emerge from the flower until they fill out completely, and then eaten whole—pod and all—or shucked out and eaten alone. They make a fantastic garden snack food to munch while you are leaning on your hoe contemplating the fate of the universe.

Most of the climbing shell pea varieties grown in America are of English descent. The traditional tall cultivars like Telephone, Alderman, and Thomas Laxton—all favorites when Big Sam was a boy—are still popular today, though recent breeding has increased the pod set on these as well as dwarf varieties. Multistar is a recent release of this type that, after a short period of single pod set, starts producing two pods at every flowering node. Its disease resistance and production are unparalleled, but be sure to provide a strong trellis.

This same double-set characteristic has been bred into dwarf varieties, and a wide range of disease-resistant, highly productive cultivars are available. Knight, Maestro, Green Arrow, and Patriot are some of the top choices, but I must confess that I have, for the most part, stuck with the old New England favorite that Big Sam grew and which is, to me, still the best tasting—Lincoln. The vines are manageable, production adequate, and though it is not as disease-resistant as some of the new releases, boy, does it taste good. If you like dwarf vines, you might find it interesting to try the old heirloom variety American Wonder. This eight-to-ten-inch plant is still available from a few seed houses, and was a very popular variety during the first quarter of this century, known for its earliness and sweet taste. Most of the earliest cultivars are smooth seeded and, as in sweet corn, this translates to less sugar and more starch, which I don't consider a worthwhile tradeoff for earliness.

Probably the sweetest peas are those of the European "petit pois" types, which bear tiny pods full of tiny peas. You'll spend a lot of time shelling, but they are very tasty. If you've ever wanted to grow the kind of peas you see in the little cans in the gourmet section of the supermarket, try the varieties Giroy or Waverex. They are grown and harvested like any other shell pea.

Bush peas represent the conscious combination of three genetic traits: dwarf stems, production of tendril-leaves (since tendrils are actually leaves), and relatively stiff, erect stems. Their benefits have already been discussed, but I want to touch on them again because pea breeders have found that these genetic traits do not seem linked with any negative characteristics, and so it is likely that this low-labor habit will be bred into more and more of the cultivars currently available. Sometimes called "leafless" peas, these kinds actually do have leaves—one at the base of each tendril branch, called a stipule leaf, instead of the normal two or three per branch. The first cultivar with this trait released to the home garden trade in this country was Novella, which has since been upgraded to Novella II, with increased disease resistance. Some other recent releases are Bikini, Twiggy, Lacy Lady, and Curly. The key element to growing these bush peas is to realize that they were originally bred for the freezer trade, and so they have been selected to mature all at once. That is good for the home gardener who freezes peas, too. But it also means that you need to pay close attention to the plot once they near maturity, because when they are ready to be picked there can be no delay. Ninety percent of the problems I have heard of with bush peas are related to improper, delayed harvesting.

Sugar Snap, the first of the new snap peas, was bred by crossing the old snow pea variety Mammoth Melting Sugar with an "off-type"—that means no good—processing shell pea found in the trial fields of an Idaho freezer-pea breeder. It is a modern story of serendipity if there ever was one, and one Big Sam never got to enjoy as it was first released in 1979, the year after he retired from gardening.

There are two key differences between a regular shelling pea and a snap pea: the pod is much thicker and clings more tightly to the peas (which is the characteristic that made Sugar Snap's shell pea parent an off-type); and the pods lack the parchment, or papery inner lining (which is what makes regular shelling peas tough and chewy), the trait drawn from the edible-podded snow pea part of the family. The original Sugar Snap also inherited its snow pea parent's incredible vigor, and that is the source of most complaints about it: given fertile conditions the vines can grow up to ten feet tall, making trellising something of a problem.

Since the introduction of the original Sugar Snap, the breeder, Dr. Calvin Lamborn, has been working to both decrease the vine size and to get rid of the last vestige of toughness: the stringy seam, which needs to be removed from mature pods before cooking. He has been quite successful in the first of these attempts, and has released a steady stream of new snap peas: Sugar Mel, Sugar Ann, and Sugar Bon are three of the best. The second goal has been more elusive, though, and for good reason. As we noted above, pea pods are modified leaves, and the string of the seam is actually the midrib of the leaf, responsible for transport of nutrients to and from the leaf, and therefore, by extension, to and from the peas themselves. If the string is bred out completely, how will the peas be able to grow and how will the plant store the sugars in them that make them so sweet? Nonetheless, he has been able to make the string unnoticeable, and release two varieties, Sugar Daddy and Sugar Pop, which are, to all appearances, stringless.

The true edible pod peas, however, are the Chinese or snow peas. Two of our favorite varieties, both for their flavor and for the beauty of the plants, even if you never harvested a pod, are Oregon Giant, and an old French variety, Carouby de Maussane, available in this country through some specialty seed catalogs.

PEPPERS

Peppers are the most trouble-free member of the tomato family. While they are very sensitive to frost, and even cool weather, peppers are much less bothered by pests and disease than their close cousins, eggplant and tomato. All three of these tropical perennials are grown as annuals here in the temperate North. Peppers belong in the second part of our rotation, so the soil will be fertile but not overly rich. High levels of nitrogen cause members of the tomato family to produce luxuriant foliage but little fruit.

Peppers are grown just like eggplants, and unless you want to grow some of the interesting and unusual types it might make sense to simply buy started plants, as the seedlings need both high temperatures and plenty of light to thrive. To start your own, though, seed 8 to 10 weeks before the frost-free date. Germination temperature should be above the normal 72°F that is our compromise temperature for most plants. Each time the leaves of adjacent seedlings touch they should be transplanted to a larger container, finishing in a 4-to-6-inch pot.

Two weeks before transplanting, prepare the bed by covering with black plastic to help raise soil temperatures; if you have 18-inch OC drip irrigation tubing, lay it along the center of the bed first, and dump a shovelful of compost on each emitter. That way, once the plastic is in place you can find the emitters by looking for lumps in the mulch, and then set a plant right next to each one. The plants should be hardened off gradually, because they are quite sensitive to transplant shock. Once the plants are in, we cover them immediately with a floating row cover to moderate the normal June temperature swings, and keep flea beetles at bay.

Unfortunately, flea beetles are not the only pest that might go after your pepper plants. They are sometimes affected by leaf miners, a pest more fully discussed under beets and spinach. The best control is to remove any damaged leaves and burn them, so that the reproductive cycle of the pest is broken. Row covers will keep out the fly whose maggot offspring does the damage, at least for as long as they are left over the plants.

The other occasional pest that bothers our pepper plants is a burrowing maggot that hatches from eggs laid within the ridges of the immature fruit. The offending adult is a small yellowish fly with three brown bands across each wing. You may be able to discourage it by dusting the fruit with talc during the midsummer active season of the fly. The burrowing of this pest will eventually lead to rotting of the fruit. I have heard of tomato hornworms bothering peppers, but have never seen one in our gardens; they, like other caterpillars, can be easily controlled with a *Bacillus thuringiensis* spray applied every 7–10 days during the egg-laying period of the adult moth.

Peppers share a number of disease and physiological problems with tomatoes, but since peppers are generally less susceptible than tomatoes, please see that section for a discussion of them. Many of these problems are made more severe by cool wet weather, and it makes sense, as with beans, to stay out of the pepper patch when the plants are wet. There is very little work you can do at that time and a lot of damage you can cause.

The most frequent problem we have with peppers is a lack of fruit set. This can be caused by three different situations, all of which you should try to avoid. Over-fertilization is discussed above, but cool temperatures and hot temperatures can also lead to poor fruit set. Temperatures above 85°F or below 60°F can cause a failure of pollination and subsequent fruit drop. There is nothing you can do about it except wait, but don't despair: the plants will continue to flower and set fruit as soon as the weather turns right. Remember—peppers are perennials; they are used to waiting around, and are in no real hurry to set fruit.

Pepper plants may also set a few fruit during the good weather in early summer, then apparently forget what they are supposed to be doing; if you wait for those first few to ripen fully, it may be too late for a second set to ripen where seasons are short. You can solve this problem by sacrificing those first few fruit. To be practical about it, I'd recommend taking half your plants and pinching out the first setting of fruit once they are the size of a marble; they will flower with renewed vigor and give you a bumper crop late in the season. The other half of the plants can be allowed to set a few fruit early and mature them for the first harvest.

As days shorten and the end of the season approaches, the same trick will have a different effect. To hasten the ripening of what fruit is on the plants and beat the fall frost, give the plants a little yank to loosen the roots just a bit, or cultivate deeper and closer than usual. Then pinch off all the remaining flowers and fruits smaller than the size of a marble. This will focus the plant clearly on your aim, which is to mature the fruits you've got!

From a gardener's perspective there are two kinds of peppers: hot and sweet; almost all belong to the species *Capsicum annuum*. Many people seem to think that the multicolored peppers at the supermarket come from entirely different plants than green peppers; but really these are just fully mature fruits from the same plants. In general, immature peppers range in color from pale (sometimes so pale they are almost white) to deep, rich green, or they may be a deep purple color. Green peppers will ripen to yellow, gold, orange, or red at maturity, generally depending on how pale they were at the start; purple sweet peppers ripen dark red to brown. All sweet peppers are much sweeter at maturity, and also much more nutritious. Unfortunately, as I mentioned above, leaving the first few fruits on the plant to ripen fully may mean a severely reduced harvest, at least in short-season areas. Hot peppers also increase in flavor as they mature; while they can be used at any point after the fruits begin to form, the active ingredients—called capscinoids—in the cell walls of hot peppers don't really reach the levels most gardeners are looking for until about three weeks after the plants flower.

Peppers also differ widely in their shape, from squat, almost flat, deeply lobed cultivars called "cheese box" types like Culinar Paprika, to the the standard, blocky, four lobed "bell" peppers like Staddon's Select, Gold Crest, Yolo Wonder, and the exotic orange hybrid Ariane, as well as long, pointed cultivars like the three-lobed, twisted red-and-yellow fruits of the Italian Corno di Toro and Marconi cultivars. Hot peppers are usually smaller, but reflect the same diversity of shapes. Flavor intensity ranges from the merely tangy-sweet of Anaheim Chili to the burning intensity of Serrano, Thai Hot, and Habanero.

To increase pepper yields in short season areas, remove the first few fruits just as they appear. To hasten late season ripening, disturb the roots and remove all fruits smaller than a marble.

POTATOES

Oddly enough, though one of his favorite tools was a potato hook, Big Sam didn't grow potatoes. In his estimation they took too much space for what they produced, and besides, they were cheaply available throughout the winter at the market. This is still true, but we do grow them (in fact, last season we grew twenty-five different kinds!) because, for one thing, the kinds you can get at the market are too limited for our kitchen tastes, and the growing methods used today create a potato I don't trust to be free of pesticide residues.

When I lived down in the Connecticut River valley of Massachusetts during college I was surrounded by potato fields, and I was alarmed to discover that at harvest time, rather than wait for the vines to die off naturally before digging, the local farmers routinely sprayed the tops with herbicide, waited just a few days to a week, then sent in the harvesters. Since then, I've grown my own.

We put potatoes in the fourth part of our rotation, with the other large-space crop: sweet corn. One reason is that potatoes work well as a companion to peas, if grown in alternate beds with them. As the peas grow, so do the potatoes, and hilling the potatoes creates additional room down the rows for pea harvesting. It also puts them two years away from their close cousins, the tomatoes, eggplants, and peppers.

The first step, unless you've purchased ready-to-plant cut eyes, is to prepare the seed potatoes for planting. The ideal size piece is two or three ounces; large potatoes can be cut into two or three sections, as long as each piece contains at least two eyes—the small depressions on the surface with buds in them—from which sprouts will grow. Cut the "sets" a day before planting, so that the cut inner surfaces have a chance to callus over; that will help prevent rot from setting in while they are underground starting to sprout. Some gardeners like to let the potato pieces sprout before planting, but I've found it slows down the planting process too much, as you've got to be overly careful not to harm the sprout during planting.

It's essential that potatoes be planted in well drained soil, as the crop is borne underground. To give our spuds plenty of fertile, friable soil to grow in, we plant a single row down the center of a three-foot bed. Remove a single shovelful of soil every foot; there's no need to measure—just put the holes right next to each other and the spacing will be right. Then take prepared sets and place them

PLANTING POTATOES

Cut seed potatoes into
one-ounce pieces with at
least one eye each. Allow
a day for the cut pieces
to dry.

Remove one shovelful of
soil each foot along the
row and replace with a
half shovel of compost.

Set pieces cut-side down
on top of compost and
cover with 4 to 6 inches
of soil.

in the bottom of the hole. If you're in a hurry or have a lot of planting to do you can just toss the sets in the hole, and they'll survive; but by putting them carefully in the bottom, with the eyes pointing up, you just make their job easier.

After placing the sets, we put a shovelful of compost on top of each—enough to cover it—and then fill the holes back in with the soil we removed. That's it, until the sprouts break ground. Once they do, there are two ways to proceed: hilling or mulching. The potato is actually a tuber, or stem offset of the plant, and to prevent the formation of mildly poisonous alkaloids in its skin, it must be kept completely dark. As the stem grows, more and more tubers form, so more soil or mulch needs to be heaped around the base of the plant over the course of the season. If you start by hilling, you can switch to mulching later; however, the reverse is not true, as once you begin to mulch you cover the soil that would be used for hilling.

The other problem with mulching is that straw, the ideal material, is expensive in most parts of the country, and hay—unless you cut it yourself before the grasses from which it is made mature—will spread weed seeds all over the garden and lead to a cultivation nightmare the following season. On the positive side, though, is the fact that a deep straw or hay mulch will help keep the soil cool, which potatoes really like. We are fortunate to have a quarter-acre in clover each season from which we can cut mulch, but if you don't have the room to grow mulch I'd recommend hilling instead of using purchased hay.

The first hilling (or mulching) should be done when the plants are 6–8 inches tall. The idea is to force the plant to grow taller, so that there is as much room along the underground part of the stem as possible for potatoes to form. Soil should be brought as far up the stem as possible without actually covering any leaves—they provide the fuel for further growth! Over the course of the season we hill three times: first, we run a stirrup hoe down both sides of the bed, outside the potatoes and including the slopes of their hills; then, using the loosened soil produced by this cultivation, we raise the hills. The simplest method we've found for doing so is to stand in the path on one side of the row and, reaching across with a broad hoe, pull the soil from the other side toward us (and the potatoes). That way we can work quickly along the row, stepping sideways after each plant is hilled. After the third hilling you might want to spread a quick-growing cover crop like annual ryegrass in the loose soil—or spread a light mulch, if you haven't already—to shade the soil and prevent further weed encroachment.

The most serious pest of potatoes is the Colorado Potato Beetle (CPB to the initiated), a ½-inch-long, bulge-backed little devil that is yellow-orange with a series of black stripes running from front to back, and a mass of black spots on the head. The adults, which overwinter underground, emerge shortly after planting time and seek out the plants. Adult CPBs don't eat all that much, but they breed like crazy, and in worst case situations their offspring can almost completely defoliate the plants and thus prevent a worthwhile harvest. Fortunately, they can be controlled by means that

To hill potatoes, pull soil from the surrounding bed with a hoe. The potatoes are borne on the underground stems—a buried treasure for kids like Sam!

are not difficult. Use any and all appropriate, as noted below.

The first, and most effective defense—a treatment that no pest has ever developed resistance to—is simply to search out the adults when they first appear and crush them. I use my fingers or my feet, but the squeamish can use a couple of blocks of wood or two small stones. If you have some extra eggplant seedlings, set them (in pots or in the ground) at the edges of the potato patch; the beetles will show up there first as they seem to like eggplants even more than potatoes. That will make them easy to find.

The second line of defense is to destroy the eggs laid by the adults before they hatch. If you have kids who like treasure hunts, this shouldn't be a problem: the bright orange egg masses are laid on the underside of leaves. While you are showing the kids how to crush them you can explain all about how (in a garden that is grown without chemical sprays) lady beetles are constantly roaming the foliage of potato plants, looking to find some eggs for breakfast; offer bonus points to the first child who finds one. I can tell you that our kids jump right in (to the depth of their attention span) and before you know it they are asking why the potatoes grow underground, where the first potato came from, and can they help dig the tubers when harvest time comes? Kids are great students of both the social and the natural worlds, though they are also a little anxious about things that are too new, too far from home. A family garden is the perfect combination of the known and unknown, a familiar kind of wilderness, where new discoveries take place only barely off well-worn paths. This not only beats Saturday morning television, but it makes dinner time a lot more pleasant, as kids are much more likely to eat a vegetable they helped grow.

The third and final line of defense is to spray or dust the plants. The traditional organic dust for potato beetles is rotenone. Only the plants with serious infestations of young CPB grubs should be dusted, and even then you should wear a cloth face mask, since rotenone dust is almost as harmful to humans as it is to the insects, though it breaks down quickly in sunlight. Avoid dusting any more than necessary, because rotenone also kills the beneficial insects that help keep pests in check. Most seasons we find—with 400-500 feet of potatoes—that we need to dust maybe a dozen plants once or twice. Basically these are the plants that had a cluster or two of eggs we didn't find before they hatched. A new strain of *Bacillus thuringiensis* is just coming on the market that is effective against CPB larvae, as well as completely non-toxic to humans; that will make control of this pest even simpler. A full discussion of its use is in the broccoli section.

The major diseases of potatoes are blight and scab. The scab fungus exists in most garden soils, but can be counteracted by crop rotation and adjusting the level of soil acidity (as fungus growth is promoted by a high pH, that is, low acidity). In areas of the country with naturally acidic soil, pH can be kept low by not liming the section of the garden where potatoes will grow. A fall cover crop of annual ryegrass also discourages scab and adds fresh organic matter to the soil, thus increasing the activity of competing soil microorganisms. Scab is worse in dry soil, so make sure that your potatoes receive regular irrigation if rainfall is less than an inch a week.

Late blight is also a soil-borne fungus, though it can also be carried over on tubers saved for future planting. It is brought on by moist conditions, and can spread rapidly once established, killing a whole planting of potatoes outright. The symptoms are sunken, blackish areas at the margin of older leaves, which then wither and fall; eventually the whole plant is affected. An outbreak often follows a hot and humid spell of weather which breaks to a cool, clear night below 60°F with heavy dew, and then warms up again. This is a common weather scenario where I garden and our potato plantings are quite likely to develop late blight. It can be prevented by spraying the plants with a copper solution during susceptible periods, though I don't like putting all that copper on my garden. Blight usually kills the plants only after they have already set a good crop of potatoes. Rotation also helps with control of late blight, by keeping new crops away from a source of infection. Mulch, by preventing soil splash during rainy spells, may also slow its growth.

Harvest of potatoes is usually left until the end of the season. But with most varieties you can start digging a few small, "new" potatoes as soon as the plants flower—if they flower. Many varieties never do. My recommendation is to plant a few hills of an extra early, moist-fleshed variety like Early Norland, and use those for fresh harvest; then the higher-yielding, better-storing types can be left undisturbed.

The proper curing and harvest of potatoes is an imprecise art. At maturity the skins of potatoes are thin and tender, easily hurt during harvest, which shortens their storage life considerably. The trick is to let the tops wither and die, then let the tubers cure for a week to ten days before gently unearthing them. During this time the skins will thicken.

If the tops die from disease rather than old age, though, you should remove and burn them; then—if the weather stays dry and reasonably cool—wait until frost threatens to dig the potatoes themselves. If rain or hot weather is in the forecast, the waiting period can be trimmed to two weeks, just long enough for the disease spores (left on the soil surface by removal of the tops) to die. That way the spores won't infect the potatoes themselves during digging.

Once you've got the potatoes out of the ground they will benefit from an additional week spread on the floor of a garage or shed—a cool but frost-free, totally dark location. During this period the skins will firm up further, and the sugars within the tubers will change to starch, which completes their ripening process. Also, any soil left on them will dry and at the end of the period they can be lightly brushed off before being put into storage. Don't wash them or let them get wet after harvest.

The range of potato cultivars is enormous—at least 10,000. Those that are easily obtained is much smaller, though with some new specialty seed potato companies now selling by mail order, there are at least one hundred kinds available in the United States. Many cultivars are more or less well adapted to a particular area, so search out those that will do well in your region for your main crop. Ask at your local nursery or farm and garden store, to find out which is best for you. Though, under good conditions, much higher yields are possible, you'll likely harvest up to 50-pound-bag's worth of potatoes from each 5 pounds or so that you plant. To help figure how many pounds you'll want, consider that the annual consumption of potatoes in America is 120 pounds per person.

Beyond the main crop kinds, though, there are some general classes of potatoes you might want to try. For each of these kinds, 2–5 pounds of seed potatoes should be plenty: you'll be able to plant 4–5 hills per pound, and harvest a pound or two from each hill planted. For potato salad, look for a European yellow-fleshed variety; their waxy meat holds together much better than the standard baking and fry types. These small, elongated potatoes go under names like Ladyfinger, Fingerling, Russian Banana, Bintje, or Yellow Finn. All are good keepers.

For early harvest and immediate use consider Norland, Cobbler, Early Rose, or other names that are variants of these. Though they may be red- or white-skinned, these cultivars are often small and roundish, rather than elongated, at the proper harvest time. Most are not good keepers and will grow large if left in the ground.

For a really unusual treat, try some blue potatoes. There are many kinds, in many shapes and flesh consistencies, but our favorite is Purple Peruvian. It is quite late, but plenty high-yielding, and the fingerling type tubers keep very well. The best thing about them, though, is that the flesh is purple right through, and great tasting. If that isn't reason enough to grow a few, consider the ease of getting your kids to eat their purple mashed potatoes!

SCALLIONS, SHALLOTS, AND GARLIC

Though many gardeners harvest young onions for fresh use and call them scallions, a true scallion belongs to the related species, *Allium fistulosum,* commonly known as Japanese bunching onions. They can be grown like regular bulb onions on either a spring or fall planting schedule, sown ¼ inch deep in rows 8 to 12 inches apart. We have had good results with Summer Bunching, White Spear, and Red Beard, an unusual red-skinned cultivar. Japanese gardeners blanch these types by hilling, just as we do with leeks, to produce the special "nebuka" onions sometimes seen in Oriental markets in this country. The hardiest varieties, like Evergreen Hardy White, White Welsh, and Red Welsh, will form perennial non-bulbing clumps, like an oversized chives plant, in all but the coldest climates. To maintain a clump of perennial scallions, pull the clump at harvest time, separate the stalks, and replant a few; they will regrow into a clump by the following season.

Shallots resemble oversized onion sets. While they are closely related to onions, they have a much more delicate flavor. They are part of a group of perennial onion relatives, called the aggregatum group, that form clumps of perennial bulbs. Shallots are as simple to grow as onion sets: just push the small bulbs into the ground, root end down, until the tip is just below the surface. They should be planted on 8-inch centers, as each shallot planted will grow into a clump of up to a dozen bulbs. Harvest and storage are also the same as for onions, though most kinds store much better.

You can get your start in shallot growing simply by going to the market in early spring or fall, buying a pound or two of shallots, and planting them. More unusual kinds can be ordered by mail or traded through a seed exchange. Some of the interesting kinds of aggregating onions we've tried over the years are Frog's Leg, or Brittany shallots, French Red, French Gray, and Giant Red shallots (though some knowledgeable growers consider this last type to actually be a so-called "potato onion"). If you ask around, you might find a neighbor who has a special heirloom strain of his or her own that they've kept in the family. Maybe you'd like Odetta's White, or Granma Featherston, or maybe one that I saw in the Seed Saver's Yearbook called Sleeping Beauty—a good keeper, I hope!

Everyone knows what garlic is, but how many of us grow it? I know my father tried for years before giving up in despair. Every spring he'd select a particularly nice bulb from those he'd bought, divide it into cloves, and carefully plant them in beautifully prepared soil; only to be disappointed come harvest time, when he would discover that the clove had barely grown to be a single, slightly larger bulb. After some study, and a few attempts myself, I found out he had two problems: first and most serious was that he was planting in the spring; second was that he used a commercial bulb from California adapted to a far different climate and growing schedule, and it simply didn't respond to the Vermont season. Fall-planted at the same time as tulips, garlic is easily grown; for the very best results, try to find a cultivar adapted to your region. They are available. Spacing is the same as for shallots, as is harvest and storage.

SPINACH

Spinach is an easy, quick-growing crop, relatively free of problems as long as you keep to its favorite season: early spring. It should go in the first part of your normal rotation (leaves, fruits, roots, and soil builders). Big Sam always planted his spinach in between the pea rows, and I learned it from him. That way it picks up a little extra nitrogen from the symbiotic relationship that peas enjoy with nitrogen-fixing bacteria in the soil, while enjoying the shade provided by the pea trellises. Since our spinach stays with the peas throughout the rotational sequence, it still doesn't grow in the same place more than once every four years.

Spinach should be sown as early in spring as the soil can be worked, so we plant at the same time we put in our peas. The seed should be set two seeds to the inch, ¼ to ½ inch deep in rows 6 inches apart, or a foot out from the pea rows if you want to interplant as we do. Spinach sprouts and grows quickly in fertile soil; within a few weeks the first thinnings will be ready for harvest. Thin the plants to 3–4 inches apart as soon as they are large enough for the salad bowl. The remaining plants will fill in the row, and in another few weeks you can harvest them for the freezer.

Spinach can also be grown in the fall, but the timing is tricky, because if the seed is planted while the soil is still too warm it will not germinate well, and the plants may run to seed almost immediately. Planted too late, they will not mature before the onset of the cool wet weather and short days of late fall, which bring on mildew. Your best hope is to plant at the beginning of a cool, wet spell about a month before the first fall frost. If you're lucky, though, you won't get a weather pattern like that because it plays hell with the harvest of everything else. Southern gardeners can plant a fall crop as soon as the weather cools down for good.

As long as the soil is well drained, fertile, and not too acid (pH 6.5 or above), spinach has few problems, largely because it is in the ground for such a short time. The only problem we've had is leaf miners, and even this is rare. In an interplant with peas they are hard to control, but spinach in beds by itself can be covered with a floating cover as soon as the seed is sown; this will keep out all kinds of flying insects.

We harvest spinach with a field knife—running the blade horizontally along the row just below the soil surface. This cuts the plants off just below the crown, so they stay in one piece for their trip to the kitchen. Scissors or clippers will work just as well. You'll get about a bushel of spinach (20 to 30 pounds) for every hundred feet of row.

To harvest spinach (and other fast-growing greens) hold the plants with one hand while cutting just below the point where the leaves meet the roots.

Our favorite spinach is a Dutch hybrid called Sputnik. But it pays to keep an eye on new releases, because the development of hybrids proceeds much faster than that of gardening books; by the time you read this, Sputnik may no longer be available. The reason we like it is that it has some tolerance to the long days and high temperatures that make late crops of spring spinach so risky. But it is also resistant to mildew, making it a good choice for fall crops as well. Another good, current hybrid with these qualities is Tyee. In perusing seed catalogs you should look for the qualities you want more than the names themselves. Our choice for an open-pollinated spinach cultivar is Estivato.

SQUASH AND PUMPKINS

The needs of squash and pumpkins are similar. If your garden is small you might not want to bother with winter squash or pumpkins as the vines take a lot of room and cannot be easily trellised, due to the weight of the fruits. The lightest of the winter squashes may weigh only about as much as a melon, and can be supported with nets in the same fashion; but some of the larger winter squashes and pumpkins can weigh 20 or 30 pounds. The largest pumpkins, like the cultivar Atlantic Giant, have reached over 600 pounds!

Because of this, we will concentrate here on bush summer squash. We put squash in the second part of our rotation. The planting method is essentially the same as for cucumbers: we plant a single row of squashes down the center of a three-foot bed, spacing the plants every 18 inches, because that is the distance between the emitters on our drip irrigation; the plants can be spaced only a foot apart if need be. As with other heat-loving vegetables, we lay the drip tubing along the center of the bed, put a shovelful of compost on top of each emitter, then cover the bed with black plastic mulch.

Once the frost-free date has arrived, we make a small crosslike incision at each lump in the plastic, and two or three seeds are pressed into the compost heaped there. If we have started plants— you can sow the seed two weeks earlier in a large soil block or a 50-cell plug tray—we set one in each spot. Immediately after planting we cover the bed with a floating row cover to keep out flying insect pests, and then turn on the drip irrigation for an hour or so to thoroughly wet the soil around the seed (or plant).

Once the plants flower we remove the covers. From that point on, a few cucumber beetles may find the plants and take up residence, but by then the plants are growing so fast that not even a cuke beetle can hold them back. We used to spray them with a mixture of rotenone and pyrethrum, but eventually decided it was not only too much trouble for the amount of control we got, but basically unecessary.

Summer squash, unlike winter squash and pumpkins, can be harvested at any time. While most American gardeners wait until the fruits are, say, 8 inches long before harvest, we believe in harvesting much sooner, at the 4-to-6-inch stage. At that size the fruits are much more tender. The French call them *courgettes (courge* is the word for mature squash) but we just call them delicious. I guarantee that if you start picking and eating your summer squash early, as we do, you will never have to complain about a "zucchini glut" in your garden.

Don't despair if the first few flowers don't produce fruit; the first few to appear may fail to grow. But if you look closely, later on, you'll notice that there are two kinds of flowers. Those borne on long, slender stalks are the male flowers; the ones borne on the ends of small, nascent fruits are the females. Until the first male flowers appear the females can't be fertilized, and so they fall off rather than growing to harvestable size. Later on, once both types are flowering together, things will go fine. Hold on—soon enough you'll have more squash than you know what to do with.

There are an enormous number of summer squash cultivars available, all falling into a few basic categories. Cylindrical to bulbous yellow types, some with thin curved necks, are the ones usually called summer squash; dark green cylindrical to round types are called zucchini; cultivars with bulbous light green fruits are called Lebanese squash; flattened, disk-shaped cultivars are called patty pan squash. Within each type there will be an old-time variety which gave its name to the category, and then dozens of recent hybrids, each with some special adaptation and use. As they change fairly rapidly, no specific recommendation will make a lot of sense; simply read the catalogs carefully for the characteristics which are important to you.

There are a few new cultivars of winter squash and pumpkin that grow on compact bush plants, but with most cultivars the vines will run 10, 20, even 30 feet or more. Winter squash and pumpkins should be left on the vine until frost threatens, or the vines die off. Each cultivar has its own particular signs of ripening based on the color of the fruit, though all must be allowed to firm up their skins so that they will store well. If you have a hard time nicking the skin with your fingernail, the fruit is ready.

After harvest most should receive a few extra days of sun curing before being put in storage. Some gardeners wipe the outside of the fruits with a very mild dilute bleach solution (10:1) to kill any bacteria that might lead to rot while in storage. Though there is wide variation among cultivars, if kept at 40–50°F in a dry, airy place, the fruits of most winter squash and pumpkin cultivars will keep four to six months.

One of Big Sam's favorite winter squashes, and ours as well, is Gold Nugget. The space-saving bush plants bear small, globular, golden-orange fruits weighing up to a pound apiece, that keep well and taste great. There are also bush forms of acorn and butternut squashes; you'll find them in mail order seed catalogs under a number of different names. Bush pumpkins are also available, but yields and fruits are smaller than with the free-running types. Our favorite pumpkin is an old French variety called Rouge vif d'Etampes. This vigorous heirloom plant bears flattened, deeply ribbed, cheesebox-style fruits that start out a creamy yellow color and turn a deep burnt-orange-to-red at maturity. They are beautiful fruits, store well, and make a great pumpkin pie. But for the very best pumpkin pies, grow the special pie cultivars like Small Sugar, which have been specifically bred for that use and have smooth-textured flesh as well as high sugar content.

Actually there are a number of special varieties: Lady Godiva fruits are full of edible, hull-less seeds; Naked Seeded has small fruits whose seeds are pressed for a salad oil; Spooky is bred for making jack o'lanterns, and Atlantic Giant was bred to grow monster pumpkins for state fair weight contests.

TOMATOES

Tomatoes are far and away the most popular vegetable grown in American gardens. Nearly unheard of only a hundred years ago, tomatoes are grown now by eight out of ten American gardeners. Though all are tender perennials grown as annuals, there is, nonetheless, a very wide range of plant and fruit types.

The most basic distinction among tomatoes is between the bush and vine types. Bush tomatoes are called determinate, because their genetic programming causes them to grow a certain number of branches and flower clusters and then stop, much the way that peppers and eggplants grow. Because of their fixed habit they are considerably less trouble to grow than vining tomatoes; they are generally earlier as well. But they are usually less disease-resistant, and the flavor of a bush tomato will rarely match that of fruit from the larger plants; there just isn't enough plant to produce as good a fruit.

Indeterminate tomatoes are true vines. Being perennial they will continue to grow, sprouting new leafy and fruiting branches, until the plant is killed by disease or frost, or the growing tip is damaged or removed. I have seen eighteen-month-old greenhouse tomato plants fifty feet long! In long-season areas, outdoor plants trellised against the wall of a house may well climb to the roof. Trellising the plants can be a fair amount of trouble but—particularly if you have a small garden—it's worth it. With a bit of attention to training the plants, you can get them to bear almost as soon as a bush type. Actually, both bush and vining tomatoes should be supported, but each requires a different kind of support. When buying either tomato seed or plants, make sure you know which you are getting!

Tomatoes go in the second part of our crop rotation, while the soil is still rich but not too high in nitrogen. As with peppers and eggplants, too much nitrogen in relation to the available phosphorus and potassium will cause the plants to grow large, but bear few

Determinate, or bush, tomato vines *(left)* end in a flower cluster while indeterminate tomato vines *(right)* don't end at all; they just keep growing until killed by frost.

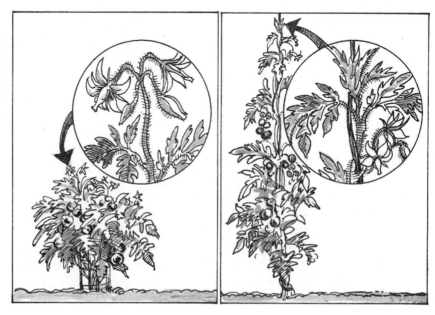

fruit. Some gardeners think that tomatoes, perhaps because they are perennials, don't need to be rotated, that they do better grown in the same spot continuously, fertilized with compost made from their own previous seasons' foliage. Big Sam didn't buy that reasoning, and neither do I; we change the tomato plot yearly and keep four years between successive crops in the same plot.

In all but the warmest areas, tomatoes should be started indoors 6–8 weeks before the last frost. Sow the seed ¼-inch deep and germinate at 75–80°F. Transplant to successively larger cells or containers as soon as the leaves of adjacent plants touch.

Many writers suggest an earlier start, but I feel that a younger plant (started later) will do better once out in the garden and quickly surpass one held too long in the inferior conditions of the average south-facing window. A common mistake made by home gardeners who buy their plants is to purchase huge, spindly transplants complete with little fruits already forming. *Nothing* could be worse in terms of the plant's adjustment to outdoor conditions; once it has begun to set fruit its most vigorous vegetative growth period has already passed. In terms of productivity, you'd do better to hold off flowering a little while to give the plants time to put on plenty of foliage, before they begin to bear. Research has shown conclusively that the best tasting tomatoes are the ones borne on plants with the most foliage per fruit.

Even if those first few flowers produce early fruits, they won't taste like much, and you are sacrificing the later productivity of the plants to get it. If you must, put in a couple of plants for early harvests; but don't start your main crop of tomatoes too early. And if you buy, buy young, stocky plants, without flowers or fruit. A good tomato transplant should be at least as wide as it is high.

Tomato seedlings are grown just like other heat-loving plants, with one exception. Long study has confirmed that you can increase the number of flowers (and therefore fruit) on the first few clusters borne by your tomato plants if you lower the temperature they grow at (in the indoor flats) for the first three weeks after they have their true leaves. As soon as the seedlings have a first pair of serrated leaves, let the growing area cool down to 55°F at night, but keep it at 65°F or above during the daytime; continue this for three weeks, then go back to keeping the temperature at 65°F or above at night as well. If this causes too many problems—eggplants and peppers won't like it, so it means segregating the plants—don't bother, but it is a little trick we bedding plant growers all use, and you can, too.

While the plants are hardening off (see the section on growing and hardening off transplants for details), prepare the bed as for other heat-loving crops: that is, lay drip irrigation with emitters spaced at 18 inches along the center of the bed, and dump a shovelful of compost on top of each one, then cover the bed with a black plastic mulch to conserve moisture, exclude weeds, and prevent soil splash (which is one of the major sources of tomato disease). Unlike peppers and eggplants, though, the transplants should be set considerably deeper than they were in the pot. In fact, after carefully stripping off the lower leaves, you should bury the vines up to within three or four branches of the top, or the first flower cluster, if one is visible. The buried part of the stem will then send out extra roots, which later in the season will help the plant supply the nutrients necessary for a bumper crop of tasty tomatoes. We like to set small basil, parsley, or gem marigold plants along the edges of the bed, alternating with the tomatoes, both because it makes more efficient use of the space, and because it looks nice. Some gardeners also feel this kind of interplanting makes for healthier, better-tasting tomatoes, and if so, so much the better.

Immediately after setting out the plants, I recommend covering them with a floating row cover. This will protect them from wind, sun, and temperature variation, plus keep out flying insects until they have established themselves. After a couple of weeks, remove the covers, store them neatly in a dark place for later, and set up the tomato supports.

As mentioned above, the two different kinds of tomato plants require different kinds of support. Bush, or determinate tomatoes, can be grown in cages, simple wire or wooden enclosures two or three feet high and about eighteen inches across, which are simply stuck into the ground over the newly uncovered plants. They should be securely anchored against the wind, however. If a whole row is to be planted, a "quonset cage" (described in Chapter 4) makes more sense. The plants grow up through the support, eventually all but hiding it, and—with its help—hold their fruit up off the ground, a great help in preventing fruit rots and the depredations of field mice, moles, and other crawling tomato eaters. That's all there is to it.

For vining tomatoes, set up a trellis like that used for pole beans and tall peas, but string it differently. Instead of creating a meshwork of string, run a single line from each plant up to the top bar. First, tie a non-slip knot about four inches in diameter around the base of the plant; then, before cutting it off the spool, run the other

Four good ways to support tomatoes *(from left):* string trellising, "quonsets" and cages (both suitable for determinate types), and teepees (best for windy areas).

Tomato vines grown on a string trellis are "braided" around a vertical line as they grow. Each branch should have its own string, wrapped once for each flower cluster.

end of the line up and over the top bar. Cut it off about two feet beyond the top bar. Tie the loose end to the bar with a granny knot that will come out easily later, leaving a fair amount of slack between the top and the plant.

Once all the plants have been attached in this fashion, their training begins. If you look closely at how a tomato vine grows, you'll see that it starts out as a single stem with leafy branches and flowering branches. But soon sprouts appear at the stem joint (called an axil) of each leafy branch, and begin to grow; left on the plant they too will produce both leafy and flowering branches—first, three leafy ones, then a flower cluster, then three more leafy branches, and so on.

This is important to the training of the plants. We can control how the plant grows, how many fruits it sets, and when, by our judicious pruning. After each of these axial stems reaches three branches, pinch off its growing tip to stop further development. That way, except for the axial foliage, which we want, we can keep the plant growing as a single stem. This makes it easier to trellis; keeps the number of fruits low in relation to amount of foliage, which makes for better tasting fruit; and assures that each plant will get plenty of air—another factor that will help fight disease.

Some gardeners like to let the first sprout arising from the base branch of the plant grow out as well, giving them a two-stem plant. One benefit they see is that the extra foliage will help protect the fruit from sun scald. That's hardly a problem in the North; the extra growth allowed on the axial stems can provide the same protection. I'd rather set more plants—the 18-inch spacing is as close as you'll want to go—and keep each to just one stem; this way you get just as many stems in the same space, but each has its own root system to supply nutrients.

The actual training of the vine is simple. You just take the slack vertical string (which is loosely attached to the base of the plant) and wrap or braid it around the growing vine, a minimum of one wrap for each fruit cluster. As the plants get taller, the slack hanging from the top bar will be taken up, and the knot can be periodically released to make more twine available. This, as well as the pinching out of the axial stems, need only be done every week or so, and takes just a few moments per plant. Once the plants reach the top of the trellis, pinch out the growing point of the plant. That will cause it to stop growing and start ripening the fruit it has. If you want super-early fruit, simply pinch out the end sooner; yields will be sooner though smaller.

The major pests of tomatoes are flea beetles (when the plants are young) and a large green caterpillar called the tomato hornworm. Flea beetles are easily outwitted by putting a floating row cover over newly set plants until they have a chance to get well established. Hornworms, if left unchecked, can make a real mess of your tomatoes, but are also easily controlled. Because hornworms are so large, they are not hard to find and pick off the plants by hand. If there are too many, *Bacillus thuringiensis* is quite effective against them. If you find one that has a small white egg case "hitchhiking" on its back, though, leave it alone, as it has been parasitized by the tiny, predatory Trichogamma wasp; soon there will be many more of these beneficial insects. Fortunately, there are some excellent reference books on organic pest and disease control: it would be

To control the number of branches, pinch off the growing point of those you don't want just before the first fruit cluster.

wise to add a few to your library. A full list of those that I recommend can be found in the Bibliography.

Newer varieties of tomatoes are resistant to common tomato diseases, and this resistance is almost always noted in the catalog description. Look for the following capital letters following the name or description: V means resistance to Verticillium; F means resistance to Fusarium; N means resistance to Nematodes; and T means resistance to Tobacco Mosaic Virus.

Verticillium and fusarium are long-lived soil fungi. Fusarium is favored by warm soil and verticillium by cold soil; both are best controlled by crop rotation and, if necessary, planting resistant varieties. Nematodes are small worms that live in the soil; some feed on plant roots, including tomatoes. Tobacco mosaic virus (TMV) is a mostly preventable disease of tomatoes that nonetheless claims a lot of casualties. A scourge of the whole nightshade family—which includes not only peppers, eggplants, and tomatoes, but also potatoes and tobacco—it causes deformed or mottled leaves, but is not always easy to recognize. Affected plants do not yield as well as healthy ones, and the fruits may be bitter.

The reason this virus is such a problem is that it is transmitted on the hands of tobacco smokers, and once established in your garden takes up residence in the soil, where it can persist for two years or more. Tobacco is a field crop; in the process of manufacturing, many, many plants are shredded and mixed together before being rolled into cigarettes. What this means is that each cigarette may have shreds of tobacco from many plants in it. These shreds will have come in contact with an even larger number. When you consider that a smoker is likely to have smoked many cigarettes over the course of two years, it is easy to see that the virus may well be in residence on his or her fingers.

If, at the greenhouse where you bought your tomato plants, they were handled by a smoker, there is a chance they will have become infected. Most greenhouses are very careful about this, but it is also possible that the customer before you was a smoker and handled the plants before you bought them. And if you, or someone in your family is a smoker. . . . The simplest prevention—which is used by many greenhouses—is to make sure that smokers who will be handling any of the plants in the nightshade family dip their fingers in a weak bleach solution (ten parts water to one part bleach) before first touching them. That will kill the virus. *Important:* Once it has infected your plants, you should not use them for compost; and do not plant any member of the nightshade family in the same plot for at least two years (a good idea anyway).

Many new cultivars are resistant to TMV. But weather may make more problems for your tomato patch, amplifying the effect of disease or deficiency present in the soil. The most common disease of tomatoes, perhaps, is early blight, or alternaria. It is recognizable by brownish-gray spots, with concentric circles within, that develop first on the older leaves, and then move up the plant. Infected leaves will eventually yellow, wither, turn brown, and fall off. Early blight is basically a foliage disease, and only in severe cases does it affect the fruit; but then, in severe cases, there may be little fruit to worry about. Early blight spreads when rain or irrigation splashes spores of the fungus from ground to leaf, and then from leaf to leaf. We have been able to control it almost completely, through crop rotation and mulching to prevent rain splash; with drip irrigation there is no reason for irrigation splash.

Septoria leaf spot is another foliage disease favored by rainy weather. Its habit is somewhat similar to alternaria, but the spots are much smaller; its progress, results, and control are much the same. A somewhat similar problem, subject to a similar cure, and which occurs primarily in the South, is gray leaf spot. Another fungus, known as anthracnose, can cause serious fruit rots, but only following foliage disease, or if the fruit is in contact with the ground. Mulch helps prevent this.

There are also several fruit problems that can develop due to variations in moisture availability. Fruit cracking occurs when there are alternating periods of dry and wet weather. During a dry spell the skin of the fruits gets too rigid, and once good growing conditions return it can't expand fast enough to accommodate the swelling fruit tissue, and ruptures. These cracks then offer an ideal site for bacterial or fungal infection.

Blossom end rot occurs during dry periods when the lack of water creates a deficiency in calcium uptake. First the end of the tomato gets soft, then turns hard and leathery. Once this occurs, you might as well remove the fruit from the plant as it will never recover. Blossom end rot is more prevalent among trellised tomatoes, because their upright, airy posture draws more water from the soil; but both this problem and cracking can be avoided by consistent watering with a drip irrigation line beneath the mulch.

Two final problems we have seen with tomatoes—and that may well concern you if they happen in your garden—are the premature abortion of the flowers, which fall to the ground without forming tomatoes, and grotesquely misshapen fruits. I'm afraid there isn't much you can do about either except wait for the weather to improve. Flowers abort mostly because the temperature was either too high or too low—during the critical two-day period after they open—for pollination to take place, and unpollinated flowers are simply discarded by the plant. Catfacing (a malformation suggesting a cat's face) is caused by a disturbance of pollination that doesn't halt it completely, resulting in fruits that develop unevenly.

In tomato cultivars (in terms of the fruit) there are at least three types, and within each, a number of colors. All three types are available as either determinate or indeterminate plants. Cherry tomatoes have tiny fruits from half to an inch-and-a-half in diameter and weigh only an ounce or so; they are juicy, often quite sweet, and great for out-of-hand munching. Salad, or slicing tomatoes are larger, from two to as much as six inches in diameter, and can weigh up to two pounds apiece; these larger ones are called beefsteak tomatoes. The third major class of tomato is the processing kinds, which are much meatier than either cherries or beefsteaks; this lack of juice makes them much better for drying or boiling down for sauce.

The sheer number of cultivars available makes it unreasonable to list them all with their attributes. Let it suffice for me to mention those that I have tried, and recommend a few that have done especially well for us. Among cherry tomatoes my favorite is the vigorous indeterminate Sweet 100 hybrid. Vigorous is almost an understatement, as this plant will grow to enormous size and bear literally hundreds of fruit if not kept properly pruned. The first year we grew it in our market garden I had two rows, four feet apart, under a large walk-in plastic tunnel, and didn't train them to a single stem. Instead, I put a new string for every branch that appeared. By the middle of August I was no longer able to get into this tunnel for harvest, and had to take a machete to the plants to hack out a path. The sole weakness of Sweet 100 is cracking, and the breeders have now improved it in this respect, and renamed it Sweet 100 Plus. For an open-pollinated cherry tomato, there is the indeterminate Gardener's Delight. Our favorite bush, or determinate, cherry is the yellow-fruited Golden Nugget. It has the singular advantage of being parthenocarpic, which means simply that the fruit will set without pollination, a great boon to those of us in cool, short-season areas.

For paste tomatoes we grow an old Italian heirloom called San Marzano. It is an indeterminate, and the fruits, when fully ripe, are nearly all meat. They can be easily dried after harvest by splitting

the fruit lengthwise, scooping out the seeds, which will have re-
tracted from the wall, and laying the fruit face up on a cookie sheet.
Twenty-four hours in the oven, using just the heat from the gas pilot
light, or if your oven is electric, a setting of 150°F or less, and you'll
have an easy-to-store, easy-to-use, flavorful tomato for winter. Just
layer the slices in a jar, alternating with basil leaves, and then fill
the jar with good quality olive oil to exclude air. Add a clove of
garlic to the top if you like. Bush varieties like Roma and Yellow
Roma will give you plenty of fruit from smaller plants, but we use
a Dutch hybrid variety called Artela, which is very high yielding.

Slicing tomatoes are the largest group, and they are also the most
diverse. This is an area where there are two distinct trends apparent: on the one hand, there are a number of modern hybrids (mostly
determinate, since that trait makes them easier to manage) that are
quite productive, reliable, and disease-resistant; and then there are
a whole bunch of heirloom types (almost all indeterminate) that are
sometimes ugly, often susceptible to disease, but almost always
tasty, and invariably interesting. In the middle are a number of
popular varieties of twenty to forty years ago that taste good, but
have fairly distinct regional adaptations.

Representative of the modern hybrids are Big Boy, Better Boy,
Early Girl, Big Girl, Ultra Boy, Ultra Girl . . . the list goes on but I
hope you get the picture. Here's a taste of some interesting heirloom
tomatoes: Dad's Mug, Oxheart, Dinner Plate, and Mortgage Lifter;
two of our favorites are Brandywine, a three-lobed purplish-red
fruit; and Big Rainbow, an incredibly beautiful golden-yellow beefsteak with red marbling in the flesh. These last two are large-fruited
indeterminate plants, fairly disease-resistant, and totally unlike anything you'll see at the supermarket. The middle category includes
many long-term favorite garden tomatoes: Rutgers, Ponderosa, the
original Big Boy, New Yorker, and two of our old favorites, Jet Star
and Moreton hybrids. All of these are standard-sized, red-fruited
tomatoes. Some yellows of the same type are Jubilee, Sunray, and
Early Sunrise.

I should also mention two kinds of interesting novelty tomatoes
we've tried. The first of these is the stuffing tomato. It grows very
much like a pepper rather than a tomato, as it is almost completely
hollow. At harvest you cut off the top, scoop out the insides, stuff,
and bake. Very easy. The cultivar we've grown is called Yellow
Stuffer. The other novelty is a "keeper" tomato. It is red on the
inside, but yellow on the outside. If harvested at the proper stage

and stored under good conditions, keeper tomatoes will keep four to six months. Since you don't want these tomatoes ready for harvest until the end of the season it makes sense to start them a couple of weeks after the main crop. After harvest they should be stored in single layers, not touching each other, in a 55°–60°F room until use. The two we've had good luck with are an old heirloom called Garden Peach and Burpee's Long Keeper.

TURNIPS AND RADISHES

Turnips and radishes are not always considered together, but as they fall into the same group and are grown the same way, we will do so here. They can both be grown spring and fall, and there are cultivars appropriate to each season. We put them in the third section of our rotation, though they are brassica relatives; this way they get the fertility appropriate to their status as root crops, and still are not planted in a bed that has had or will have brassicas in a successive year.

Spring turnips and radishes should be planted in succession from the moment the ground can be worked in spring until a month or so before the onset of hot, dry, summer weather. Sow the seed ¼-inch deep in rows only 6 inches apart in the bed, as the plants will never have a chance to get very large. As soon as they have their first true leaves thin them to two inches apart in the rows. Harvest when the roots are one to two inches in diameter.

As mentioned in the carrot section, it is not really necessary to make separate plantings of spring radishes, as the harvest from the carrot, parsnip, salsify, and scorzonera rows (whichever of these you plant) will likely be enough for your needs.

Fall radishes and turnips are much larger and later, and should be planted ninety days before the first fall frost, ¼-to-½-inch-deep in rows 8 to 12 inches apart. As soon as they have their first leaves, thin to 3 inches apart in the row. For fresh use they can be harvested at any time, and many Southern gardeners relish turnip leaves for boiling greens. Radish greens are a well known herbalist's purgative, and thought to strengthen the kidneys. For storage, the roots should be left until the tops have been nipped by frost, but be sure to harvest before frost is strong enough to damage the crown of the plant, or else they will rot in storage—usually about 25°F is the critical temperature to avoid. The roots can be protected from an early frost if necessary by hilling soil over the crowns. Both should be stored in damp sand or leaves in a cold basement or root cellar, where the temperature will stay between 35° and 40°F.

Aside from the soil diseases avoidable by consistent crop rotation, the major pests of both turnips and radishes are the same root maggots that bother other brassica crops, and the control is the same: cover the rows immediately after planting with a floating row cover, and don't remove it during the active laying season of the fly. Remember the principle of trap crops: it is often worthwhile to set out a few leftover, susceptible plants in an out-of-the-way part of the garden to attract particular pests, that can then be easily found and destroyed.

The best turnips for spring use are the Milan turnip and its relatives, plus the various Japanese hybrids whose names change frequently (you'll be able to tell which ones they are by the Japanese names). For fall we have used two traditional varieties: De Vertus Marteau, a great old French storage variety with white one-pound roots shaped like a spool of thread; and Golden Ball, another old variety with golden-orange roots, also known by a number of variant names.

Our favorite, though, is the Gilfeather turnip, a round-to-top-shaped white cultivar grown here in southern Vermont for generations (and thought by some to actually be a rutabaga, due to the appearance of its leaves and the large size of the roots). It is probably the cultivar grown by Big Sam and recommended in the original *Step by Step* as a rutabaga, though by the time I took over the garden he didn't grow any fall storage crops—his root cellar was no longer in use.

There are hundreds of spring radish cultivars in a multitude of shapes and colors, but we limit ourselves to just one: Easter Egg hybrid. The reason is that this multi-line hybrid contains four colors of round-to-top-shaped Champion type radishes and gives us the most variety for the space we devote to it. In addition, the old Champion strain is more heat-tolerant than earlier types, and resistant to pithiness. If you want to grow single-color, round radishes, try Cherry Belle, the best of the standard red type; or Plum Purple, a beautiful lavender-to-royal-purple cultivar; or Sparkler, for white roots. One particularly unusual cultivar is Valentine, which has white skin but red flesh! The best fall radish in my opinion is China Rose, a large, bulbous, pink-rose root with white flesh.

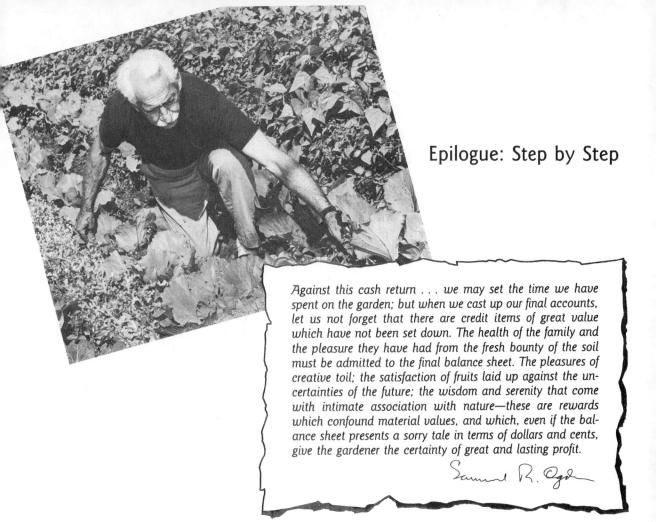

Epilogue: Step by Step

Against this cash return . . . we may set the time we have spent on the garden; but when we cast up our final accounts, let us not forget that there are credit items of great value which have not been set down. The health of the family and the pleasure they have had from the fresh bounty of the soil must be admitted to the final balance sheet. The pleasures of creative toil; the satisfaction of fruits laid up against the uncertainties of the future; the wisdom and serenity that come with intimate association with nature—these are rewards which confound material values, and which, even if the balance sheet presents a sorry tale in terms of dollars and cents, give the gardener the certainty of great and lasting profit.

Samuel R. Ogden

This book was written for those in the middle, who want to garden without danger to themselves and without damage to the environment. We've tried to chart a reasonable middle course between the fanatics of techno-boosterism and the misty-eyed practitioners of ritual. The gardening methods we've discussed are based on a firm connection between ends and means, and an equally firm commitment to the long term.

Converting your garden to the safe, sane, sustainable methods we've outlined in this book is just a matter of putting them into practice bit by bit, step by step. Though you could start right in next spring with all the parts of this method, leaving behind the sprays, the dusts, the caustic fertilizers, there is no absolute need to go ''cold turkey.''

So if the threat of weeds and pests seems too great, after a long period of gardening by current conventional methods, begin slowly and convert over the course of a few seasons. You can start making your own compost this year, grow a cover crop, or manure the garden this coming fall, and spend next winter planning a long-term rotation. Then put it into place the following spring. Once you begin to think about how these methods apply to your garden you'll see that, given their integrated nature, you can't really put them all into place immediately anyway, because these are not "off the shelf" solutions, pre-packaged in a four-color bag and marked up to retail.

Two processes should go on simultaneously in a garden in the process of conversion to organic methods: cleansing of the garden and repairing its infrastructure. The first of these happens naturally over time, though there has been some work done on the specifics of de-toxifying soils. The second, on which we gardeners will spend most of our time, involves rebuilding the foundation of the garden—its soil—and reestablishing the various plant and animal communities and their life cycles on which a garden's permanence depends.

The first step to both goals is to stop using general purpose chemical pesticides. That is something you can do right away, right now, that will, in the long run, benefit both your garden and the world at large. The more problems one product is claimed by its manufacturer to solve, the more it is likely to cause, because the less discriminate it is in what it kills, and the more toxic ingredients it is likely to contain. If you have partial containers of pesticides, store them safely until your town or county has its next household hazardous waste collection day. Don't simply throw them away; what that does is worsen the pollution problem at your landfill. Don't just "use them up" either—an alcoholic who vows to give up the bottle as soon as the current one is gone rarely gives up the bottle at all. The sooner you stop using these "broad spectrum" pesticides, the sooner natural plant, animal, and micro-organism populations will return to your garden, and the sooner pollution problems related to the manufacture of these products will subside. Without this first step the chemical spiral will never be broken.

The second step, mentioned earlier, is to begin a compost pile, even a small one. One of the most basic principles of organic gardening is that all garden "waste"—that is, anything not consumed by the gardener—should be returned to the soil. Soil improvement by composting is one of the simplest, most effective things you can do to: (1) help your garden and (2) cut down on the solid-waste and air-pollution problems created by conventional lawn and garden practices. Brush and trimmings that might otherwise overwhelm the local landfill, and leaves that would have to be burned, can be simply and easily converted to a rich, mellow compost that will spur your vegetables to thrive.

In addition, a compost pile breeds innumerable diverse micro-organisms that, when added to the soil, fuel the release of the earth's mineral fertility. The chemical hucksters like to say that, because the dictionary defines "organic" as any compound (including their poisons) containing carbon, we organic gardeners are confused. But they are trying to sell us something that nature, if we let it, will provide us for free. We are not confused or mistaken, we just have a wider, wiser view. The "organic" in "organic gardening" really refers to that living 5 percent of the soil called the organic matter (in scientific jargon). The heart of our method is that we work with (and within) that living community—rather than fighting it. It is simplicity itself: all we do is facilitate the natural, ecological processes of nutrient cycling and pest control that have been going on, and evolving, since life began on earth—long before the first human took stick in hand to scratch the ground. Composting brings this eternal cycle into your garden and starts it turning in concert with the rest of life.

These two steps are immediate actions you can take—the first a one-time decision, the second an ongoing activity; both, however, affect the whole garden at once. A second group of actions can be instituted on just a portion of your existing garden each season, and over time will improve it. In order to do this, though, you should have a plan. Take some time this winter to figure out a garden rotation that fits your situation, based on the general principles found in Chapter 5. Then put the complete organic method into place in a single part of the rotation every season and maintain it; by the end of the first cycle you'll have improved your whole garden, and gotten things off to a good start. From then on incremental improvements are all that will be necessary; as your appreciation of the subtleties increases, ways to do this will be found at every turn!

Concentrate your efforts on one part, one plot out of your rotation each year, if time and energy for the project are scarce. Start the previous fall if possible—establish a weed-choking, organic-matter-building cover crop. Then make sure that section is thoroughly prepared the following spring, and the soil is brought into a high state of friability by liberal use of compost and other amendments, and that drainage problems are resolved. Start with the legume stage of your rotation; fertility will be less of an issue since peas and beans are both easy to grow and relatively tolerant of nutrient-poor soils. If fertilizer is needed (according to the soil test) buy long-term, slow-release organic mixtures. Look closely at what you buy, though; as interest in organic methods has grown, so have the attempts of the chemical fertilizer manufacturers at masking their bagged products to seem more benign.

In that one part of the garden at least, make sure that weeds are scrupulously removed, and that diseased and stressed plants are banished as soon as they begin to show symptoms. Dispose of them in a way that prevents the problems from spreading, either by composting them in a well-made "hot" pile, or by burning. Both will kill the spores and bacteria responsible for disease. Cover crops during the off-season, and the cultivation tips in Chapter 8, will help stop weeds in their tracks and make maintenance mostly a matter of pulling the occasional overlooked escapee from the hoe.

Use that area as a study center: get down on your hands and knees every now and then, and watch closely how the inhabitants of your garden go about their business; before long you'll know which of those insects are working *for* you, not against you. You'll also learn to spot the pest insects and their effects early, before they can do much damage, and destroy them. I usually walk through the garden as I drink my coffee in the morning. There is no more beautiful time, and insects are sluggish in the cool of dawn (no pun intended) and thus easier to see. I often take a twilight stroll after work as well, and so problems don't have much time to develop before I see them and make a mental note to take remedial action. Often it is just a matter of pulling a stray weed or crushing a cluster of recently laid eggs. If, after years of neglect or abuse, the plot you hope to make over lacks the *natural* enemies of resident insect pests, you can import them: companies have begun breeding and selling beneficial insects by mail order. If released in your garden-to-be at the right time of year they will quickly establish themselves and go to work.

In extreme cases perhaps one part of the garden should be taken out of crops for a year. Combined with a four-year rotation of the type outlined in Chapter 5, this will break the cycle of pest-and-weed infestations over time, while at most only lowering the production of your garden 25 percent. If cucumber or squash beetles are firmly entrenched, forgo planting members of the squash family for a season; you can always plant extra of something else, and then trade with neighbors. The same will work for soil-borne diseases. Take the crop out of that area for a year, and then don't put it back in the same place more than once in four years; your problems will be drastically reduced. Even rampant perennial grasses can be licked this way, as we have done here in our gardens. A single season of intensive cover-cropping can choke out any pest plant, and some cover crops—like rye and marigold—will even discourage particular diseases and insects as well. After that year, the soil will also be greatly improved so that all subsequent crops in your rotation will benefit.

You can put this simple transition into place throughout your garden immediately. But don't despair if you feel time is too short. As you can see, you can convert bit by bit, step by step, a season at a time. The positive effects your choice has for the greater environment on which we all depend will be immediate; the benefits will build in your own garden over time as you reestablish the natural cycle of abundance on which the growth and civilization of humanity was built.

ONCE YOU ARE up and running with your garden rotation, maintaining it is a simple matter of keeping the basic principles of organic gardening in mind. We have alluded to them throughout the book, but before closing I want to summarize them as a sort of green-thumb-manifesto:

First, remember to *feed the soil, not the plants.* If you take care of the soil, and constantly enrich it, the plants will thrive and provide plenty of harvest for you. Don't let the plants suffer for lack of nutrients; but, even if you give them an occasional shot of fish emulsion or compost tea, remember the long term. Do whatever you can to enrich the soil by concentrating nutrients, whether by composting, growing green manures and cover crops, or simply mulching and then turning under the mulch.

Second, *take only what you need.* Harvest the part of the plant that you want, and then compost the rest; return as much as possible of the biological yield from the earth to the earth, just as is done in nature, and the amount of additional material you'll need to provide will be minimized.

Third, *embrace diversity.* One of the greatest problems in conventional farming and gardening is that large groups of identical plants are not only attractive to, but also susceptible to, massive pest and disease outbreaks. The farmer grows corn, corn, and more corn, until the corn won't grow anymore. Grow a wide range of plants, and even a wide range of varieties of each plant; that way you hedge your bets and increase the resiliency of your garden.

Fourth, *work with the natural, seasonal cycles in your garden* and nature will do much of the work for you. Plant to miss the peaks of insect reproduction; schedule your harvest at the best time for flavor and ripening. To do so takes attention on our part to the daily details of life in the garden, to observing the subtleties of the interaction among the plants, the animals, the weather, the natural cycles of earth, air, water, and sun. It takes thought to find the "touch points" at which the gardener can tweak the system to create a surplus—a harvest—without disturbing its equilibrium.

Fifth, since robust plants are less subject to insect and disease problems (and thus require less control), *intervene as little as possible* in the predator-and-prey relationships that exist in the garden. Let the natural systems of control operate. If you must act to control an insect, do so as precisely as possible, so you don't upset other relationships and create new problems.

Sixth and finally, *live and learn*. One of the things I like most about being a gardener is that there is always something new to learn. It is a puzzle, a challenge, a game that never ends. Each season the combination of soil, plant, and weather is different, and the garden that results is unique. By paying attention and keeping track of the changes over time, we come to know all three better. We learn, with a sniff and a squeeze, to know what the soil needs and when it is ready to plant; a quick glance at the peas tells us that it is time to harvest; the sound of the wind, the quality of the light, and the antics of the swallows let us know that rain is near.

Thought and attention over time are, as we mentioned in the introduction, the attributes of cultivation, not control, and not "production," in the industrial sense. But then, these two are also precisely the things that give meaning to life, strength to our families, and security to our way of life. It should come as no surprise that cultivation is characteristic of an evolving society, and control characteristic of a declining one—that while "standard of living" may continue to rise, "quality of life" suffers. If we stop paying attention to our gardens and learning from them, even though their apparent yields may increase, undeniably the quality of our time spent there suffers. May your garden be both a living, learning place, and a model for a better future.

SOURCES

SEEDS

Abundant Life Seed Foundation
PO Box 772
Port Townsend, WA 98368
(206) 385-7192
A non-profit organization devoted to growing, collecting, and distributing open-pollinated seeds suited to the Pacific Northwest. Catalog $1.00

Becker's Seed Potatoes
RR 1
Trout Creek, Ontario
Canada POH 2Lo
Wide range of interesting potato cultivars. Catalog $1.00

Bountiful Gardens
5798 Ridgewood Rd.
Willitts, CA 95490
A non-profit organization offering open-pollinated vegetable, herb, grain, and green manure seed.

W. Atlee Burpee & Co.
300 Park Ave.
Warminster, PA 18974
(800) 888-1447
One of the oldest American seed companies, and probably the best known. Full line of vegetable and flower seed, mostly untreated.

Companion Plants
7247 North Coolville Ridge Rd.
Athens, OH 45701
(614) 592-4643
Very wide selection of herb plants and seeds. Catalog $2.00

The Cook's Garden
PO Box 535
Londonderry, VT 05148
(802) 824-3400
Our own seed company. Full line of vegetables, herbs, and flowers. Catalog $1.00

Farmer Seed and Nursery
PO Box 129
Faribault, MN 55021
(507) 334-1623
Good source for cold-climate gardeners.

Filaree Farm
Rt. 1, Box 162
Okanogan, WA 98840
(509) 422-6940
Over fifty strains of garlic from around the world! Catalog and Research Journal $3.00

Fox Hill Farm
444 W. Michigan Ave.
Parma, MI 49269
(517) 531-3179
Herb plants and seeds. Catalog $2.00

Garden City Seeds
1324 Red Crow Rd.
Victor, MT 59875
(406) 961-4837
Non-profit organization specializing in open-pollinated varieties suited to the Northern Plains and Rocky Mountains. Catalog $2.00

The Good Earth Seed Co.
PO Box 5644
Redwood City, CA 94063
(415) 595-2270
Formerly called Tsang & Ma. First-rate selection of oriental and specialty vegetables.

Harris Seeds
60 Saginaw Dr.
Rochester, NY 14623
(716) 442-0410
An old-line northeastern company. Unfortunately, most of its seed is treated.

Hastings
PO Box 115535
Atlanta, GA 30310
(404) 755-6580
An old-line southeastern company. Many varieties suited for southern climates.

Heirloom Seeds
PO Box 245
W. Elizabeth, PA 15088
(412) 384-7816
Selection of very old varieties, some dating back over one hundred years. Catalog $1.00

High Altitude Gardens
PO Box 4619
Ketchum, ID 83340
(800) 874-7333
Vegetable, herb, and flower seed for cold climates. Lots of Russian tomato varieties. Catalog $3.00

Horticultural Enterprises
PO Box 810082
Dallas, TX 75381
Specialists in chili pepper seeds.

J. L. Hudson Seedsman
PO Box 1058
Redwood City, CA 94064
Very wide selection of unusual items. Catalog $1.00

Johnny's Selected Seeds
Foss Hill Rd.
Albion, ME 04910
(207) 437-9294
Full line of vegetable, herb, and flower seed adapted to New England conditions.

Kalmia Farms
PO Box 3881
Charlottesville, VA 22903
Specializes in multiplier onions, shallots, topset onions, and garlic.

Landreth Seed Co.
PO Box 407
Baltimore, MD 21230
(301) 727-3922
The oldest seed house in the country, established 1784. Catalog $2.00

Native Seeds/Search
2509 N. Campbell Ave
Tucscon, AZ 85719
(602) 327-9123
Non-profit organization dedicated to food plants adapted to the southwestern United States.

Nichols Garden Nursery
1190 North Pacific Hwy.
Albany, OR 97321
(503) 928-9280
Wide range of specialty crops, especially varieties adapted to the Pacific Northwest.

Nourse Farms
RFD Box 485
S. Deerfield, MA 01373
(413) 665-2658
Asparagus, rhubarb, horseradish, and other perennial food crops.

Park Seed Company
Cokesbury Rd.
Greenwood, SC 29647
(803) 223-7333
Large, old-line seed company. Carries a wide selection of vegetables, herbs, and flowers.

The Pepper Gal
10536 119th Ave. N.
Largo, FL 34643
Lists over 200 cultivars of peppers!

Pinetree Garden Seeds
RR 1, Box 397
New Gloucester, ME 04260
(207) 926-3400
Wide range of seeds and supplies. Specializes in small, inexpensive packets.

Plants of the Southwest
930 Baca St.
Santa Fe, NM 87501
(505) 983-1548
Specializes in seeds adapted to the southwestern United States. Catalog $1.00

Redwood City Seed Co.
PO Box 361
Redwood City, CA 94064
(415) 325-7333
Wide range of unusual food plant seeds (as well as others). Catalog $1.00

Richter's
PO Box 26
Goodwood, Ontario
Canada L0C 1A0
(416) 640-6677
One of the broadest listings of herb seed anywhere. Catalog $2.50

Roninger's Seed Potatoes
Star Route
Moyie Springs, ID 83845
(208) 267-7938
Organic seed potatoes; an incredibly wide range of types! Catalog $1.00

S&H Organic Acres
PO Box 1531
Watsonville, CA 95077
(408) 983-7226
Specializes in garlic, shallots, multiplier, and Egyptian onions.

Seed Saver's Exchange
PO Box 70
Decorah, IA 52101
Not a seed company, but an organization of gardeners who trade home-grown seed and maintain heirloom varieties of vegetables. Write for membership information.

Seeds Blum
Idaho City Stage
Boise, ID 83706
(208) 343-2202
Over 1,000 varieties of heirloom, open-pollinated seeds. Catalog $3.00

Seeds of Change
621 Old Santa Fe Trail
Santa Fe, NM 87501
(505) 983-8956
Organically grown seed of heirloom, open-pollinated varieties.

Seeds West
PO Box 2817
Taos, NM 87571
(505) 758-7268
Heirloom and specialty seed for high elevation, short-season areas. Catalog $1.00

Shepherd's Garden Seeds
6116 Highway 9
Felton, CA 95018
(408) 335-5400
Select list of gourmet and specialty vegetables, plus herbs and flowers. Catalog $1.50

Southern Exposure Seed Exchange
PO Box 158
North Garden, VA 22959
Heirloom and open-pollinated varieties adapted to the Mid-Atlantic and the South. Catalog $3.00

Stokes Seeds Inc.
PO Box 548
Buffalo, NY 14240
(416) 688-4300
One of the most extensive listings anywhere—be sure to specify untreated seed.

Sunrise Enterprises
PO Box 10058
Elmwood, CT 06110
(203) 666-8071
Very wide selection of oriental vegetables. Catalog $1.00

Territorial Seed Co.
PO Box 27
Lorane, OR 97451
(503) 942-9547
Vegetable, herb, and flower seed adapted to the Pacific Northwest.

Thompson & Morgan
PO Box 1308
Jackson, NJ 08527
(201) 363-2225
Unique selection of vegetable, herb, and flower seed.

Tomato Growers Supply Co.
PO Box 2237
Fort Meyers, FL 33902
More than 150 varieties of tomatoes, plus peppers, too!

Vesey's Seeds, Ltd.
PO Box 9000
Calais, ME 04619
(902) 566-1620
American branch of Canadian company specializing in short-season, maritime climate–adapted varieties.

TOOLS AND SUPPLIES

Gardener's Supply
128 Intervale Rd.
Burlington, VT 05401
(802) 863-1700
Wide selection of tools and supplies, especially for season extension.

A. M. Leonard
6665 Spiker Rd.
Piqua, OH 45356
(800) 543-8955
Tools and supplies for the professional nurseryman and gardener. Catalog $1.00

Mellinger's
2310 W. South Range Rd.
North Lima, OH 44452
(216) 549-9861
Incredible selection of garden gadgets, tools, supplies—even seeds and nursery stock.

Necessary Trading Company
PO Box 305
New Castle, VA 24127
(703) 864-5103
Wide selection of pest controls, plus raw materials for soil building. Catalog $2.00

Ringer Research
9959 Valley View Rd.
Eden Prairie, MN 55344
(800) 654-1047
Natural lawn and garden products: fertilizer, pest controls, and machinery.

Smith & Hawken
25 Corte Madera
Mill Valley, CA 94941
(415) 383-2000
Beautiful and responsible catalog of tools, some supplies, and garden gifts.

NOTES

1 Michael Pollan, *Second Nature* (New York: Atlantic Monthly Press, 1991).

2 Philip Shabecoff, "New Safeguards for Home Pesticides are Debated," *New York Times*, May 11, 1986.

3 *Climates of the States* (Detroit: Gale Research, 1978).

4 D. Webb, "Eating Well," *New York Times*, November 28, 1990.

5 Peter Tompkins and Christopher Bird, *Secrets of the Soil* (New York: Harper & Row, 1989), p. 44.

6 David A. Perry and Michael P. Amaranthus, "The Plant-Soil Bootstrap: Microorganisms and Reclamation of Degraded Ecosystems" in *Environmental Restoration*, ed. J. Berger (Washington D.C.: Island Press, 1990), p. 98.

7 Environmental Protection Agency, *Suspended, Cancelled, and Restricted Pesticides*, Document #2ot-1002, February 1990.

8 L. Mott and K. Snyder (NRDC), *Pesticide Alert* (San Francisco: Sierra Club Books, 1987) p. 19.

9 J. W. Biggar & J. N. Seiber, eds., *Fate of Pesticides in the Environment* Pub. #3320 (Berkeley: University of California, 1987), p. 6.

10 T. Gipps, *Breaking the Pesticide Habit*, IASA #1987-1, (Minneapolis: City International Alliance for Sustainable Agriculture, 1987), p. 23.

11 W. D. Guenzi, ed. *Pesticides in Soil and Water*, (Madison, Wisc.: Soil Science Society of America, 1974), pp. 268, 294.

12 See *Fate of Pesticides* (pp. 8–9) for a discussion of the metabolic activation of organophosphates. In its original form Diazinon is a weak nerve enzyme inhibitor, but partial conversion of the type discussed on page 144 of *Pesticides in Soil and Water* apparently activates it.

13 L. Fishbein, in *Insecticide Biochemistry and Physiology*, ed. C. F. Wilkinson (New York: Plenum Press, 1976), pp. 579–603.

14 Guenzi, *Pesticides in Soil and Water*, p. 207.

15 Ibid., pp. 143, 336–37.

16 Ibid., p. 91

BIBLIOGRAPHY

Note: The books listed do not represent any kind of comprehensive bibliography, nor are they ranked in order of importance. Simply stated, they are some of the titles I own that I feel the reader might find either useful or enlightening, or both. Unfortunately, some are out of print. Editions listed are those in my own library, not necessarily the first or the latest.

GENERAL

Bubel, Nancy. *The New Seed Starter's Handbook.* Emmaus, Pa.: Rodale Press, 1988.

Coleman, Eliot. *The New Organic Grower.* Chelsea, Vt.: Chelsea Green Publishing, 1989.

Damrosch, Barbara. *The Garden Primer.* New York: Workman Publishing, 1988.

Foster, Catherine Osgood. *The Organic Gardener.* New York: Alfred A. Knopf, 1972. (Out of print—since revised and re-issued as *Building Healthy Gardens.*)

Hunt, Marjorie B., and Brenda Bortz. *High Yield Gardening.* Emmaus, Pa.: Rodale Press, 1986. (Out of print)

Hunter, Beatrice Trum. *Gardening Without Poisons.* Boston: Houghton Mifflin, 1964. (Out of print)

Jeavons, John. *How to Grow More Vegetables. . . .* Berkeley: Ten Speed Press, 1991.

Ogden, Shepherd, and Ellen Ogden. *The Cook's Garden.* Emmaus, Pa.: Rodale Press, 1989. (Out of print)

Patent, Dorothy Hinshaw, and Diane E. Bilderback. *Garden Secrets.* Emmaus, Pa.: Rodale Press, 1982. (Out of print—since revised and re-issued as *The Harrowsmith Country Life Book of Garden Secrets.*)

Seymour, John. *The Self Sufficient Gardener.* New York: Doubleday, 1980. (A British title, possibly out of print.)

Wickenden, Leonard. *Gardening with Nature.* New York: Devin-Adair, 1954. (Out of print)

REFERENCE

Carr, Anna. *The Color Handbook of Garden Insects.* Emmaus, Pa.: Rodale Press.

Denckla, Tanya. *Gardening at a Glance.* Franklin, W.V.: Wooden Angel Publishing, 1991.

MacNab, A. A., A. F. Sherf, and J. K. Springer. *Identifying Diseases of Vegetables.* University Park, Pa.: Pennsylvania State University Press, 1989.

Olkowski, William, Helga Olkowski, and Sheila Daar. *Common Sense Pest Control.* Newtown, Conn.: Taunton Press, 1991.

Staff of *Organic Gardening* magazine. *The Encyclopedia of Organic Gardening.* Emmaus, Pa.: Rodale Press, 1978. (There are newer editions.)

Yepsen, Roger B., ed. *The Encyclopedia of Natural Insect and Disease Control.* Emmaus, Pa.: Rodale Press, 1984. (There are newer editions.)

BACKGROUND

Balfour, E. B. (Lady). *The Living Soil.* New York: Devon-Adair, 1948. (Not dated except in Preface.) (Out of print)

Berry, Wendell. *The Unsettling of America.* San Francisco: Sierra Club, 1977.

Carson, Rachel. *Silent Spring.* Boston: Houghton Mifflin, 1962.

Conford, Philip, ed. *The Organic Tradition.* Hartland, Bideford, Devon (UK): Green Books, 1988. (Out of print)

Fowler, Cary, and Pat Mooney. *Shattering (Food, Politics, and the Loss of Diversity).* Tucson, Ariz.: University of Arizona Press, 1990.

Howard, Sir Albert. *An Agricultural Testament.* New York: Oxford University Press, 1940. (Out of print)

Jensen, Dr. Bernard, and Mark Anderson. *Empty Harvest.* Garden City Park, N.Y.: Avery Publishing, 1990.

Pfeiffer, Ehrenfried. *Bio-Dynamic Farming and Gardening.* New York: Anthroposophic Press, 1940. (Out of print)

Tompkins, Peter, and Christopher Bird. *Secrets of the Soil.* New York: Harper & Row, 1989.